THE ASTONISHING JOAN GRANT

became aware as a child of her uncanny gift of "far memory"—the ability to recall in detail previous incarnations, both male and female, in other centuries and other lands. Her books, published and reviewed as historical novels, have been highly praised for their extraordinary vividness and richly diverting detail, and are in fact the author's memories of her earlier lives.

Such a book is SO MOSES WAS BORN, the exciting life of a member of the royal family of ancient Egypt during the time of its greatest power and most tempestuous upheaval.

"Joan Grant is a writer with unique qualities . . . Her conceptions have originality and novelty; her style is simple and beautiful."

Times Literary Supplement

Also by JOAN GRANT

EYES OF HORUS
LORD OF THE HORIZON
SCARLET FEATHER†
LIFE AS CAROLA†
RETURN TO ELYSIUM†

published by CORGI BOOKS
† to be published by CORGI BOOKS

So Moses Was Born
Joan Grant

CORGI BOOKS
A DIVISION OF TRANSWORLD PUBLISHERS LTD

FOR
M.S.

SO MOSES WAS BORN
A CORGI BOOK 0 552 09813 2

Originally published in Great Britain
by Eyre Methuen & Co., Ltd.

PRINTING HISTORY
Eyre Methuen edition published 1952
Corgi edition published 1975

Corgi Books are published by
Transworld Publishers Ltd.,
Cavendish House,
57-59 Uxbridge Road,
Ealing, London, W.5
Made and printed in the United States of America
by Arcata Graphics
Buffalo, New York

CONTENTS

I

TESTAMENT TO MOSES

*By the hand of Nebunefer, in the twenty-fourth year
of Ramoses II*

WHEN I awoke this morning, so vivid had been my dream that
I was surprised to find myself not only alive but in my usual
excellent health. A dream which occurs three nights in
succession, and is identical in every detail, cannot be ignored.
I find it annoying that the dream provides me with so little
exact information, and yet indicates that I, Nebunefer, am
unlikely to be able to fulfill my promise to play a lively part
in the education of my nephew, Moses.

Pharaoh already has more than sixty sons, so why do I,
with such a plethora of nephews, select Moses as the target
of my reminiscence? I believe that he is born to a destiny
which will vitally affect the future of Egypt. Ramoses, although Moses is only a year old, is already determined that
the boy shall surpass him in magnificence. He is convinced,
as I am, that Moses is not only the chosen son of Pharaoh
but a true Son of Horus.

It had been my intention to persuade Ramoses to allow the
boy frequently to visit me, and I had hoped that in the seclusion of my estate, the Living Water, he would acquire a faith
in the basic simplicities of human relationships, a lack of
which can turn a beneficent power into an agent of destruc-
tion.

I know only too well, having in my time been the Royal
Heir, how difficult it is for a boy to value truth when he is
offered adulation and flattery instead of honest criticism. Will
anyone, even his father, tell him the real circumstances of
his birth? Will anyone have the courage to warn him of the
unique conflict which he will feel within himself, the conflict
which stems from the opposing forces of his physical hered-
ity? I doubt it: I doubt it so much that I impose upon myself
the task of covering a large quantity of papyrus with writing-signs.

I am unskilled in the use of words which have no voice to
warm them; so I pray that Moses will read with the insight
that I will strive to bring into this record of events which
must so intimately concern us.

7

To return for a moment to my dream. I see a chariot to which are harnessed two stallions. The chariot is richly decorated; even the bosses of the wheels being ornamented with gold. The trappings are of red leather studded with turquoise, but it is the color of the horses which is remarkable. They are both black and white, the variation occurring in irregular patches. They appear docile, and stand quietly mouthing their silver bits in the shade of some date palms.

I now see a man standing in the chariot, which moves smoothly along a track that I recognize for the one leading eastwards across the desert. The man increases the pace to a gallop, and leans back with his hair streaming in the wind. Far from being alarmed at the speed, which is surely excessive considering the increasing roughness of the ground, he appears exultant.

A hare, pursued by a jackal, dashes almost under the horses' hooves. They swerve, and the man is flung from the chariot like a stone from a sling. From the way he is lying it is certain that his neck is broken. It is only at this stage of the dream that I realize the dead man is myself.

The only additional information I could gather from the repetitions of the dream is that the dates on the palm trees which occur in the first scene are ready for picking. This is sound evidence that I shall have several months to complete this record. If the chariot should arrive before my task is finished, then the horses will have to be exercised by my charioteer until I have made arrangements for my final journey.

Why do I not take this dream as a warning of an accident which could be easily avoided? Naturally I could refuse the gift, or the loan if such it proves to be, of such a conspicuous vehicle. I could take the further precaution of refusing to travel except on foot or in a carrying-litter, tedious as this would soon become. Am I then the victim of the illusion that predestination encases us in the future as though we were helpless as flies mummified in amber? Do I accept as inescapable the fact that I shall die before I am forty-four, and therefore prefer the swift death to some slower but equally certain one that would pursue me even though I dared not leave my bed?

To answer these questions I ask another. Would any reasonable man be ungrateful if a friend sent a message informing him that it had been decided to send him abroad within a few months? Surely he would be glad of the foreknowledge which gave ample opportunity to leave his affairs in such good order that he could enjoy the vistas of a new horizon without a backward glance.

How can I rely on information which comes from an anonymous source? Were I a more competent wearer of the Golden Sandals, a priest of such authority that he has no need of symbols, then I would be in a position to say, "My wife, Sensen, has sent me a message to tell me that at the time of the date harvest I shall have the felicity of joining her on the other side of the River."

Why do I consider Sensen to be the source of my dream? Because during the last twenty years she has constantly advised me, using dreams to convey news to my waking mind which is not sufficiently burnished to reflect her intentions more clearly.

I frankly admit that when she died I became so absorbed in grief that every one on my estate became affected by my apathy. To kill myself was impractical, for that would have been more likely to turn me into an uneasy ghost than to re-unite me with Sensen. I fell into the common heresy of believing that my soul would be more perceptive if my body were subdued. I fasted: I indulged in prodigies of physical endurance. When this failed to produce anything except fantasies which did not convince even myself during my more rational moments, I went to the other extreme, bemusing my senses with concoctions of poppy juice until I ignored even the rhythm of the sun's rising and setting.

Only the implacable sanity of Meena, who was Sensen's foster mother and is still the benign ruler of my household, saved me from a permanent retreat into futility. She treated me as a child, a child who in spite of its efforts to be hated remains beloved. She was my only link with reality, for it is impossible to be pompous in the presence of a woman who insists on feeding you with broth and raw eggs when you are too weak with hunger to protest.

However, until I had a true dream even Meena could do no more than keep my body in a state from which, with due care, it would again become decently habitable. This dream had all the essential qualities of Sensen: a directness and simplicity, a refusal to be led into side roads either flowery or beset with thorns.

I found myself in the room where I conduct the stewardship of my estate. I heard her calling to me and hastened to the garden whose green shade I had created for her pleasure. It was deserted, but the door in the wall was open and I saw Sensen sitting in the white dust of an unfamiliar road. Across her lap lay a child whose eyes were bright with hunger, whose ribs under the dry skin were harsh as a withered palm leaf. "He is hungry," she said. "Neb, help me to carry him to the granary so that I can show him that no one here need ever be hungry or afraid."

I took the child in my arms, and Sensen walked beside me, confident that I would protect them both. The door of the granary swung idly on its hinges, creaking in a gray wind that scurried sand into water-channels which were sluggish with the refuse of neglect. The granary was empty.

I woke to find Meena moistening my cracked lips with wine. "You wouldn't want her to see you like this," she said briskly. "Ill as you are, you can stop being a disgrace to her memory if you will remember that she wouldn't have loved you if you weren't worth loving."

From that day onwards I think I can claim, without falling into the pit of pride or the more subtle slough of humility, that I have not neglected the vineyards whose wine jars bear my cartouche. I am neither High Priest of Amen, nor Pharaoh of the Two Lands. I believe that Moses has the innate authority to fulfill both roles and yet that the stelae of the future will record his destiny as being greater than either.

II

ROYAL TOMB

HAVING explained why I write, I shall now endeavor to do so with less formality. As, my dear Moses, the history of our family will be an early part of your education it may seem redundant to remind you that your illustrious grandfather, Seti I, had only two wives and four children.

To the first Great Royal Wife were born two sons: Karaden, whose fame as Vizier of the Two Lands will have made him well known to you even should he die during your infancy; then, two years later, myself, Nebunefer, who at the age of fourteen was declared the Royal Heir.

Why was I chosen instead of Karaden? The reason is simple, and implies no superior merit in myself. Karaden suffered an affliction of the eyes which made it impossible for him even to drive a chariot, and Seti, who had led the armies of Egypt to subdue the kings of Syria, considered it vital for any future Pharaoh to wear the Warrior Helmet as well as the Red and White Crowns.

My childhood was happy and uneventful. Even the death of my mother, when I was three years old, did not greatly disturb me, for she and my father were so deeply devoted to each other that they grudged sharing even with their sons the little privacy which their royal duties allowed. Sensen, the orphan daughter of my mother's sister, was brought up with us, and that she and I would marry on her fourteenth birthday always seemed inevitable as the rising of the Nile. My virtues, such as they may be, are a plant which never lacked the water of her compassion or the sun of her laughter, and in her company even Karaden forgot his solemnity.

When Seti, no doubt influenced by advise from ambitious courtiers and certain factions of the priesthood, took Tuaa for his Queen, we noticed very little change, for we continued to have our own household and Tuaa seldom accompanied our father when he came to visit us.

To Tuaa was born Ramoses, followed two years later by a daughter, a plain child who remained a nonentity until she died in her nineteenth year. I shall not bother to describe her,

11

but if she arouses your interest her history is preserved in the Nome of the Tortoise, whose Nomarch she married.

Nor shall I describe my three years in the House of the Captains, for by the time you read this you will probably be only too familiar with the routine of a young warrior's training. I found it dull but not arduous, for having been born with an aptitude in the use of destructive weapons I became the Leader of a Hundred at fifteen and a Captain the following year. Because I could use a throwing-stick with precision, and split a papyrus reed with an arrow five times out of six at fifty paces, I was able to conceal the fact that I have always disliked the needless slaughter of animals. However this did not disturb me unduly, and I frankly admit to a certain pleasurable excitement when hunting lion.

I had been married to Sensen for three years when we accompanied Seti on a Royal Progress. He decided to prolong his stay at Thebes, even though he usually preferred the Delta in high summer, for he was interested in the great hypostyle hall which was being added to the complex temples of Karnak. Neither Sensen nor I expected this to be more than a pleasant interlude, for since I had been declared the Royal Heir we had a house of our own adjoining the palace garden and so, to a limited extent, could be free of the extreme formality on which Tuaa always insisted.

Ramoses took every opportunity to visit us there, and for the first time we came to know him well, and to see the many excellent qualities which had previously been concealed under the boastful and domineering manner which he had copied from his mother.

The more I liked him the more I resented Tuaa, and realized how frequently Father must have regretted marrying her. She was too clever to show her jealousy openly, but her tongue could be more irritating than the bite of a hundred gnats and she never failed to use it against Sensen. With the intelligence of a gad-fly that chooses the thin skin of wrist or elbow for its attack, she used to pretend to sympathize with her because we had no child, insisting that Sensen see foreign physicians, all of whom, doubtless on Tuaa's instructions, declared that my wife was barren. She had the audacity to urge me to take a concubine, saying that my refusal to demonstrate the efficacy of my seed might seriously jeopardize the future of Egypt. She even made Sensen try to persuade me to do this, and I had to promise that if the Gods had not answered our prayers when I came to the throne then I would take a secondary wife to secure the succession. But it never occurred to me that this problem was urgent, for

I was only twenty and my father was still in vigorous middle age.

We were due to leave Thebes in three days when there was an official announcement from the Palace, saying that Pharaoh had postponed his visit to the Royal Tomb owing to a slight recurrence of fever. I thought this a most sensible decision, for he had already been several times to see the new rooms which had been added during the previous year and I had urged him to abandon the custom of holding there what was in fact a travesty of a light-hearted picnic. Tuaa had been annoyed at my suggestion, and said that even though I was afraid of my wife catching a chill I should have sufficient recognition of my duties to tell her to remain at home rather than allow her ill health to interfere with my obligations as the Royal Heir.

Like most of Tuaa's threats, this was barbed with the hearer's particular fear. Sensen's first serious illness *had* started after her going to Father's tomb . . . I shall describe the incident, for it may encourage you to use your influence to prevent children taking part in a similar performance.

Sensen was eight and I eleven at the time. Father had allowed the custom of having a ritual meal in his tomb to fall into disuse, but Tuaa, who never failed to grasp an opportunity of stressing her importance, persuaded him to do it on a larger scale than usual.

Meena protested vehemently when he said that Sensen was to come with us, saying that it was most unsuitable for a highly imaginative child and would be sure to give her nightmares. This was tactless of Meena, for the purpose of the custom was to demonstrate that the wise Egyptian has no need to fear the prospect of death. If she had been sensible enough to say that her real anxiety was that Sensen would be harmed by the sudden contrast between the torrid heat of the Valley of the Dead and the cold of the rooms in the deep rock, he would probably have listened to her. Meena fussed over Sensen as though she were cosseting a lamb chosen for sacrifice on an alien altar. This made Sensen determined not to miss what was obviously an exciting adventure suitable only to grown-ups; so determined that she never even told me that she had a sore throat quite bad enough for Father as well as Meena to insist that she stay in bed. Had I known that she was feeling ill I certainly would not have helped her to hide the woolen lion-cloth that Meena had made her wear under her dress . . . we hid it in a hollow fig tree on our way to join the ceremonial procession.

It was fairly cool while we were in the shade of the ave-

13

nues which radiated from the temple built by Queen Hatshepsut, but when we entered the narrow defile leading to the tomb I noticed that Sensen's face was flushed, though I thought it was only because she was feeling as ordinarily hot as I was.

Following Father and Tuaa down the entrance passage felt like walking very slowly down the steps of a swimming pool, for the air was colder than water. Only four of the offering chambers were completed at that time, though in two others the walls had been smoothed by the stoneworkers, ready for the drawing-scribes to make their first black outlines which would then be corrected in red by priest scribes before the stone-carvers in their turn gave place to the men who would add the final colors.

There was very little furniture, for this would not be put in the tomb until Father was dead. What there was seemed incongruous and reminded me of the time we had unexpectedly had to spend the night in the house of a village headman who had hastily borrowed what he thought was suitable to the Royal guests.

The inner room, where Father's body would be put when he had finished using it, did not yet contain the sarcophagus that I had seen, as a drawing, only a few days earlier. Instead there were two ivory stools that I recognized as those Father and Tuaa usually sat on when receiving tribute in the smaller towns where we paused for a few hours on a Progress. The room was crowded, for Tuaa had insisted on many officials being allowed to come with us; most of whom were either her relations or else in her favor.

Meena, once she had accepted the fact that she could not prevent Sensen coming with us, had carefully instructed us how to behave. "You must pretend to feel *gay*," she said. "Though why anybody should be expected to feel gay in the place where the body of their father will lie alone for eternity is no business of mine; far better to be born a linen-weaver, like my father, and have children that laugh when you play with them and cry when you are dead, than all this training in how *not* to show what you really feel. . . ."

I was interested to see that the officials who had not previously been present at this ritual found it equally difficult to assume the correct expression: they smiled with their lips tight against their teeth, and when they spoke their voices were either too loud or unnaturally husky.

Father and Tuaa also seemed a little unsure of themselves. First they sat staring straight in front of them over the heads of the audience, then I could see them deliberately relaxing

14

the muscles of their forearms, although they did not actually shift their position. Sensen nudged me, because she too was amused that the grown-ups found it difficult to be formal and companionable at the same time. Then Father made a speech, to which I forgot to listen because one of the lamps began to smoke and I knew Sensen was desperately trying not to cough.

The Keeper of the Royal Vintage, a nice old man who had often brought grapes crystallized in honey to Sensen, lifted a wine-jar from a gold stand which had both Father's and Tuaa's cartouche on it, and declaimed, "The wine of the Two Lands, which will be offered by the cup-bearer of the Gods in the name of the illustrious Pharaoh, Seti the First, throughout the future."

Father took the wine-jar, and every one stood aside so that he could lead them into a smaller room, the third on the left of the entrance passage, where a picture of a Royal Vineyard was painted on the wall. There was also a wine-jar in the painting. Father held up the one he carried, broke the seal and poured the yellow wine into a row of gold cups that had been neatly set out on a table with a white linen cloth. He spilled a few drops, and I thought how delighted his cup-bearer would have been to see that Pharaoh at last understood how difficult it is to pour tidily from a heavy jar.

With the wine we were each given one of the small loaves which had been arranged in a pyramid on an alabaster dish like the one Seti was offering to Ptah on the opposite wall. The bread was very dry, and Sensen whispered to me that it was a pity that the drawing-scribe had not thought of adding a jar of honey.

In another room we were given fruit, including mulberries, which were rather nasty because although the artist was good at painting mulberry trees, he could not have been expected to know that Pharaoh would decide to eat their reflection when no one could find any that were properly ripe. The figs were better and so were the pomegranates, but the dates were very withered.

Even the grown-ups were ill at ease. They tried to make polite conversation, pretending that this was an ordinary party which Pharaoh was sharing with a few intimate friends, so Sensen and I slipped away into one of the unfinished rooms where I tried to amuse her by seeing which of us could spit date-stones the farthest.

She pretended to enjoy herself until Usermentu, the High Priest of Thebes, found us and was so disapproving that he made Sensen cry, which was a very unusual way for her to behave just because she had been scolded by some one she disliked. Usermentu hurried away, but when I tried to comfort Sensen she went on crying and said it was because her throat was sore through having swallowed the date-stone she had hidden in her cheek when she heard some one coming.

She was sick on the way home, which annoyed the Keeper of the Royal Chariots, who was driving the one I shared with Sensen, for he had to lose his proper place in the procession through waiting while I held her head behind a convenient tree.

Meena was not particularly worried about Sensen being sick, for she thought, as I did, that it was due to the mulberries being not only unripe but moldy. Even when Sensen had a very bad nightmare and woke screaming that she was lost in the dark Meena only said it was no more than could be expected from a child who had been forced to spend the day in an empty grave. But Sensen was very ill. Her throat swelled until she thought she was going to choke and at times she could not even recognize me. When I held her hands to stop her trying to get out of bed I could feel the pulse in her wrist fluttering like a bird trying to escape from a net. I tried not to think that it might be her soul trying to fly out of her body.

That was the beginning of the years when only her determination not to leave me alone made her believe that one day she would no longer have to pretend that her body was as strong as her spirit . . . sometimes she even made me believe that the Gods would let her live with me until together we could cross the River.

III

SONS OF SETI

As I have already told you, I was not alarmed by Seti's illness even when our departure from Thebes was again postponed. Tuaa told me that she had persuaded him to take a well-earned rest before continuing the Progress, so when he sent for me, on the eve of his thirty-ninth birthday, I thought it was only so that I could hear what arrangements he wished to be made for the journey North.

His bed had been moved to the window, but his face was in the shadow of the half-open shutters which protected him from the direct rays of the sun that beat into the quiet room.

He smiled at me and said, "To grow up in an environment where every reasonable desire is immediately granted, and one has been taught not to demand the unreasonable, is not a perfect defense against the heavy mace of circumstance."

I thought he wished to discourse on some aspect of rulership, a pleasure he often gave me when we were alone together, so I selected a comfortable chair and settled myself to listen.

"Prepare yourself for the mace, my son . . . the mace being the news that I am dying."

He said it so calmly that I thought he meant it only in the sense that with each day's sunset and sunrise all men die and are born again. He lifted the linen napkin that covered a dish on the table beside him. "If you need proof that I speak in all seriousness, it is here. A mouse boned and seethed in honey. So pathetic it looks, curled in its nest of jasmine, but it is a sign, certain as the seal of Pharaoh, that the Royal Physician shares his master's recognition of the inevitable."

His voice was so level that I still thought he was indulging in paradox . . . a form of words which amused him as lesser men test their skill with ivory pegs set in a gaming board.

"I shall not trouble you with the squalid details that have caused me to lift the siege which my soul has held in the citadel of my body. I find that even during one's last hours one must still consider the usages of courtesy: should I refuse to attempt this remedy which only as a last resort would have

17

been offered to Pharoah, or is it my duty to die with a mouse in my gullet, as so many village children have done?"

He picked the mouse up by its tail, that had been wrapped in a whisp of linen to protect the Royal Fingers. Only when he dropped it through the window did I realize how much it cost him to make even so small a physical effort. I felt a surge of grief press against my breast-bone and the back of my eyes; but his quiet voice served as the dyke which holds back floodwater.

"How gracious are the Gods," he said. "Knowing that I would feel remorse if one of my last actions seemed ungrateful, they have arranged for Haha, my favorite hunting-cat, to seize what is to him a delectable morsel and swallow it in the shade of an oleander."

He knew that I could not discipline my voice to answer him without betraying the grief and despair which held my body rigid. "Let me talk, Neb . . . it is good to be able to speak freely instead of having to clench my teeth against unseemly sounds which would have showed that I suffered great pain."

"Are you still in pain? Father, there must be something we can do! You can't die . . . I won't let you die!"

"I am not running away from responsibility, Neb. Everything has been done which should be done; no one need reproach himself that Pharaoh could have been kept alive—I need not even reproach myself. I no longer feel pain, but already my body seems less substantial than mist-linen. I am in the Boat of Millions of Years . . . I belong to neither side of the River."

I tried to hold back my tears. "Weep if you wish, my son. It is natural for us both to grieve a little that soon we shall not be able to talk to each other. But do not weep for me when I am dead, for who need weep for the dead unless the dead must weep because they dared not live?"

He gently stroked my hand. "There is a pleasing aptness in dying at Thebes. Your grandfather died at Memphis, so I had to stand at the steering-oar of his funerary barge for seventeen days—I always hoped that my son would not have to repeat such an arduous performance. I have given instructions that my funeral shall be as simple as tradition permits, but Tuaa may insist on a public demonstration that her husband was not inconspicuous."

I could not contain my hatred of Tuaa. "If she had made you happier you would not be dying."

"Can you blame her for insisting on the full measure of the bargain we made in our marriage? She knew, though of

18

course I was not so cruel as to tell her so, that I have never loved any woman except your mother. Can you blame me for being glad that I am so soon to be reunited with my heart?"

"Couldn't you live just two or three years, until Sensen is quite strong again?" I was horrified at my selfishness but could not hold back the spate of words. "When I am Pharaoh I shan't be able to look after Sensen if she is ill. I might even have to go out of Egypt with the army. Surely you could stay a little longer. You *must* understand, Father. You came home from Syria when Mother was ill, but . . ."

"But I arrived too late. Neb, do you love Sensen more than you love Egypt?"

I thought that truth would be the last bitter arrow, but I dared not hold it back. "I love Sensen more than anything . . . anything!"

He smiled. "I am well content. Perhaps it is the most cherished wish of any father to know his dreams will be fulfilled in the lives of his children. I have been in turn the lover, the warrior, the administrator. The last two without the benison of the first have proved too difficult for me . . . that is why my body, which is wiser than I, has refused to support the role any longer."

"Yet you expect me to be strong enough!" I thought that if I made him angry he might stop drifting away from me. But he was not angry.

"Only during the last few days have I come to realize that Egypt will not demand the same sacrifice from you. I have three sons. Neb, who loves Sensen with his whole heart: in him I shall renew my youth. Karaden, who as Vizier of the Two Lands will find full expression of his special talents. Even as a small child he enjoyed playing with tallies . . . all the wearisome details of administration will be of supreme interest to him. Egypt will never lack strong granaries or well-fitted treasure-rooms, and only dishonest officials will have cause to fear him." He sighed. "Poor Karaden, I hope that he never knew how dull I found his conversation."

"And what of Ramoses?"

"You must not dislike him because he is Tuaa's son . . . he is also mine. He has a certain ruthlessness which you and Karaden lack, as I do. He will never allow Egypt to suffer because he wishes to believe that men are better than they are. . . ."

Was he telling me that Ramoses was to be Pharaoh instead of me? Before I could ask him this urgent question, a blow-fly came through the window and began to sip honey that had seeped from the mouse. Father spoke to it as though he had forgotten I was in the room.

"Blow-fly, should I have refused the mouse and so saved others from the ineptitude of physicians? But I pleased Haha —surely that is something in my favor, for one seldom manages to please even oneself. Am I becoming garrulous at the imminence of bodily decay, or wise because I find it curiously unimportant?"

The blow-fly buzzed against the ceiling and then returned to settle on the Royal Forehead. "How odd it is that I can still feel the delicate tread of your feet, yet I shall shortly be oblivious to the diligent excavations of embalmers. Instead of talking to you I ought to summon my family and such scribes, priests, and officials as are needful, and make an utterance suitable to the final audience of Seti the First. It is odd that I already think of myself as the *first* Seti, thereby flattering myself that some future Pharaoh will take the same name."

His eyes closed and for a few moments he slept. The door opened and the Royal Physician came softly into the room. He stood looking down at the slow rise and fall of the linen sheet that covered my father's chest. Then he noticed the mouse had gone and nodded to himself. "The old remedies are best . . . I should have used them before." He spoke in a whisper, but I knew by the pressure of Father's hand that he had heard.

"We must not wake him," I said in a low voice.

The Royal Physician patted me on the shoulder. "I have insisted on perfect quiet for him . . . but how long I shall be obeyed I do not know. The Queen is becoming annoyed that you have been with him so long."

Tears glistened in his eyes. "I still believe that he will recover." But his old voice sounded like a child trying to pretend it is not afraid of nightmares.

When he had left the room, I whispered, "We are alone now, Father."

A bead of sweat trickled slowly down his forehead and I leaned forward to wipe it away. He opened his eyes and smiled.

"You, and Karaden, and Ramoses . . . I think I have done all I could for the three of you. I have even tried to make some compensation to Tuaa . . . she was always resentful that I so seldom took her advice. My final gift to her is that she will think that giving Sensen to you and the Crook and Flail to Ramoses was her wish instead of mine. Poor Tuaa . . . I must remember to say something kind to her before I die . . . really kind, not just courteous words which hide sparse affection."

I heard Tuaa's voice in the ante-room. "You must go now, my dear son," he said. "Tell her that I am asleep."

Tuaa was standing by the window of the ante-room. She swung round to face me, and even if I had not known what she planned to do I think the expression in her eyes would have warned me that she would no longer trouble to conceal her hostility.

"How is he?" she demanded. "You stayed with him far too long. You must have tired him." She seized hold of my arm, her thin fingers cold as a vulture's talon. "You had no right to stay with him so long!"

"I had the right of a son, to obey his father's wishes. He is asleep, and does not wish to be disturbed by *any one*."

"What did he talk about? I insist that you tell me . . . it is *my* privilege to protect him from anxiety."

"He spoke very little, and only of trivial matters. I did no more than watch beside him."

She tried to conceal her relief by becoming conciliatory. "You must forgive me for appearing angry, Neb. I am distraught. When he recovers he will scold me for not being better able to conceal my fear that the Gods will take him from me."

Did she really believe there was still a chance he would recover? "Is there anything I can do to help you?" I said. I nearly added, "to help you steal my throne for your son," and wondered how she would have reacted to my challenge.

"Behave as though he were not dangerously ill. In spite of all my orders a rumor must have reached the people, for there were crowds outside the Palace this morning, waiting for news. If he sees them from the window he might feel it his duty to send them a personal message of reassurance . . . but he is far too weak to waste his strength on such trivialities."

Why could she not be honest enough to say that she guarded his failing vitality hoping that he would use it to declare her son as his successor?

"Does Ramoses know the truth?"

She looked at me intently before answering, but seemed reassured. "Ramoses has not seen his father for several days. He is too young to conceal the emotion he would feel at knowing that not only he but Egypt may soon weep for the death of Pharaoh. I told him to spend the day in his sailing boat, I said it would reassure the people . . . I was right, for the crowds began to disperse soon after he left the landing steps."

She paused, and then said, rather too casually, "Neb, there *is* a way you could help. When Ramoses comes back, I told him not to stay out later than sunset, could you and Sensen take his boat and sail down-river?"

"Why down-river? If the wind drops we could not get home against the current."

"There are more villages down-river . . . you must be seen by as many people as possible. If the wind drops, and I am sure it will not do so, then you can spend the night with Bakur and I will send a chariot to fetch you in the morning."

"Would Bakur, whoever she may be, welcome unexpected guests?"

"Neb, do not be silly . . . of course she would be most honored. Surely you remember her . . . the wife of the new Captain of the Bodyguard."

"And your cousin; how discourteous of me to forget her name."

"I am sure Sensen will find her most congenial . . . I will send her a message to expect you."

"To expect us only if the wind drops."

"Of course," she said, as though she were doing no more than make arrangements for the entertainment of a guest she wished to flatter. "You must forgive me if I leave you now . . . there is so much which needs my attention."

"You are sure that you would not prefer me to stay here? I might be able to take some of the burden from your already over-taxed shoulders."

"No," she said hastily. "You go with Sensen . . . keeping the people happy has always been the first consideration of your father."

It was easy enough to understand why Tuaa wanted us out of the way: only those who preferred Ramoses to me would be allowed to approach Pharaoh. But what did she intend to do if he died without naming his successor? Would she take the risk of inventing his final words? Yes: but she would not be believed if I could have been present, formally to relinquish the title of Royal Heir in front of my younger brother. I thought I could see her plan: when Pharaoh was beyond the power of speech she would send for me, but Sensen and I would arrive too late to hear his death-bed declaration.

If I agreed to her suggestion of spending the night in the house of Bakur it would lull any suspicions she still held. So why not agree? For Sensen's sake I should have to learn how to give Tuaa cause to despise me.

"Shall we wait at the landing steps for Ramoses?" I said. "Or would you prefer to send a message when his boat is available?"

"I will send a message," she said quickly. "If you see Ramoses he will question you about his father. I shall know better how to break the news to him."

Was Ramoses already aware that he was to take my place? If I asked him he might tell me the truth; almost certainly he would not lie to Sensen.

Tuaa was tapping the floor with her foot, the only sign she gave of her impatience for my departure.

"You will send for me if there is any change in his condition?"

"Of course," she said. "The Royal Physician expects to have no definite news for several days. Even if you spend the night at Bakur's, you could be here within an hour or two hours at most."

As I passed through the Room of the Sixty Pillars I saw the Captain of the Bodyguard talking to Usermentu. The priest's shaven skull gleamed in the light that streamed down from the roof. His eyes under the wrinkled lids were hidden in the shadows of his jutting brow but I knew he had seen me, though he turned away.

Did they already know I had been deposed? Did Karaden know?

I was in no mood to spare even belated sympathy for Karaden. Every one knew his eyes were weak, but what excuse could I give for this terrible humiliation? I could never let Sensen know I had relinquished the Crook and Flail for her sake, so I should have to pretend I was unaware of the malicious gossip which would torment me like a swarm of sandflies until no one could be bothered to wonder why Nebunefer had been denied his right to the throne.

IV

ROYAL HEIR

I PACED up and down a secluded walk of the Palace garden in a torment of indecision. Should I tell Sensen as soon as I got home, or wait until we were alone on the river? Would she still love me, thinking, as she must, that Father, with the insight of the dying, had judged me unworthy? Yes, of course she would always love me . . . but would she be disappointed not to be queen? We had often talked of what we would do when we wore the Red and the White Crowns. When Tuaa was more than usually annoying, Sensen would stop me being angry by saying, "Poor Tuaa, think how much more difficult it will be for her to be informal in our Court than it is for us to behave pompously in hers." We drew plans for the new towns we would build, Sensen insisting that there should be gardens "even for the people who are very useful." We had expected to be quite old by then, so had arranged imaginary estates for our grandchildren as well as for our sons and daughters. I think until that evening I had always believed we would have children.

To avoid being seen I went to the door in the boundary wall which led into the small garden on which our private apartments opened. I expected to find her by the pool, but there were only scattered cushions in the shade of the mulberry trees. She usually rested during the afternoon, so I looked through the window of our bedroom in case she was asleep. I was startled to see everything in disorder: clothes trailing out of open chests, cloaks and sandals lying on the floor. A reed pannier, such as is carried by pack animals, lay on its side, and another was half full of neatly folded dresses.

The door into the room beyond was open, and I heard Sensen's voice raised in protest. "Neena, I *can't* leave my alabaster monkey behind. I know he has only one ear and he's heavy, but Neb gave him to me when I was five."

"You have already made the same excuse about your faience hippopotamus and your wooden hunting-cat," said Meena. "Now stop fretting and I will pack them together so they can be company for each other."

24

They came into the bedroom but did not see me. I stepped back so that I could watch through the slats of the shutter, deliberately listening so as to learn the best way of breaking the news to Sensen. My unease increased. Why was she packing? Surely she would not decide to leave home even for a few days without telling me. Meena looked as though she had been crying, she *was* crying while she folded a dress that was embroidered with moon daisies. Where had I seen that dress before? It was the one Sensen wore on the first day of our wedding journey.

Sensen suddenly put down the ointment jar she was holding and flung her arms round Meena. "You mustn't be unhappy! Meena, if you don't try to believe this is an exciting adventure I shall think you are cross because you will only have a very unimportant person to look after instead of being the chief of the queen's attendants."

"As though any one with sense would want to live in a palace," said Meena. "I'm upset because I never thought Prince Nebunefer would run away."

"He is *not* running away," Sensen exclaimed indignantly. "I am going to make him leave Thebes because otherwise he will be in terrible danger. I shall be his sweet, pretty toy which will make him forget all the things he has lost. I won't let him be unhappy, I *won't!*"

"Only a fool would be unhappy with you, and he's no fool."

"Neb has so often been unhappy, and nearly always it was because I was ill. But I am not going to be ill any more. When I don't have to worry about Tuaa hating me, and about not having a baby, and about what might happen if I wasn't strong enough to be a real co-ruler with Neb, then I shall stop coughing . . . *I know* I shall, Meena."

"Of course you will," said Meena soothingly. "Would I have agreed to this wild plan of yours if I hadn't been sure that the air of the high desert is just what you need? But you mustn't get over-excited, or you'll get those too bright eyes which worry him . . . not that it isn't good for husbands to worry about their wives, it keeps them from getting into trouble with their other silly ideas. Now don't keep interrupting me or we shall never get finished in time. Which mirror do you want to take? You can't have more than one."

Sensen picked up a copper mirror with an ivory handle, then put it down and handed Meena another, a disk of silver supported by the wings of a lapis lazuli swan. While it was being wrapped in what I recognized as one of my kilts, Sensen said:

25

"Meena, I have quite often been your obedient child, but yesterday I was your brave and clever child. Aren't you proud of me?"

"I've always been proud of you, but I'm not at all sure you haven't been doing something which rates a thorough scolding."

"Well, I think I have been clever; even more clever than Neb, and much more subtle than Tuaa. Ramoses will make an excellent Pharaoh, not at all magical but just what Egypt needs at the moment."

"Prince Ramoses is far too conceited, even for a boy of his age, and much too like his mother for me to trust him."

"Conceit won't matter when he is Pharaoh. It will make him build lots of monuments and palaces and things, which will keep the people busy. And he will marry Nefertari; I have always liked her and she will make a better queen than I could have done."

"Have you told Ramoses that you have arranged for him to be Pharaoh?"

Sensen missed the sarcasm in Meena's voice. "Of course not. I couldn't rely on him not to betray the confidence, quite unintentionally, by being more than usually grand." She sighed. "Poor little Ramoses. I am afraid he will feel guilty when he thinks that Neb and I were murdered to make way for him."

"Murdered! What are you talking about?"

"Didn't I tell you? I suppose I was too busy packing and everything. When I went to see Pharaoh yesterday I knew something was wrong. Tuaa had the High Priest of Thebes, that horrid old man who has always hated Neb since he advised Karaden not to increase the temple tribute, and the new Captain of the Bodyguard, in her *bedroom*. If she had been discussing anything ordinary she would never have received them there, especially as I had been told that she was asleep and on no pretext must be disturbed."

Meena sniffed. "How do you know they were there? It sounds a very unlikely story."

"It happens to be true. I was suspicious because I know she pretends never to sleep in the afternoon even in the hot weather . . . it is one of her ways of showing how strong she is. So instead of going straight to Pharaoh, I hid behind a curtain in her ante-room and listened."

"Oh Sensen! If she had caught you I don't know what would have happened!"

"Something very unpleasant I expect. But she didn't catch me, so don't fuss."

26

"What did you hear?"

"I couldn't hear everything they said, but enough to learn the plot by which she intends to become the Royal Mother when Seti dies. She has arranged for Neb and I to be murdered; she hasn't yet decided whether we are to be strangled or poisoned. Then our bodies will be thrown into the river for the crocodiles and our sailing boat will be discovered overturned. It will happen when Seti has just died, but the people will be told that the shock of hearing of our tragic accident killed him, and that he only lived long enough to declare Ramoses his successor."

"Child, are you mad! Why haven't you told Pharaoh so that he can expose her wicked plot before she can carry it out?"

"Don't be silly, Meena. Seti is far too ill to be worried by knowing that his wife means to murder his son."

"Then you must tell some one else . . . Karaden . . . everybody."

"What chance would I have of being believed? My word against the Great Royal Wife, against the High Priest of Amen, against the Army."

Meena began to sob noisily. "Is there no honesty in Egypt? To think the Army could betray the Royal Heir. I can believe anything of those horrid priests, but I thought *soldiers* could be trusted!"

"You can't really blame the Captain," said Sensen briskly. "He knows Neb doesn't like killing things, not even birds, so he would obviously try to stop killing people . . . I think the Captain believes a war against Syria would be a good idea, unless he only presses for it because it would give him an excuse to get away from Bakur."

"Pharaoh must be in danger! Sensen, how could you be so wickedly selfish as to keep this terrible secret. You must tell Prince Nebunefer everything at once . . ."

Meena rose to her feet and was about to rush out of the room in search of me when Sensen caught her by the arm. "Pharaoh is *not* in danger. Tuaa is perfectly contented as the Royal Wife: she is only making sure that when she loses that title she will be the Royal Mother."

"Does Pharaoh know you are leaving Thebes?"

Sensen shook her head gently. "Meena, *do* try to be sensible! Of course Pharaoh knows, how else would I know where to go? I have told you fifty times already that he has given me the house which he built for Neb's mother, years ago when they were first married. It was the only place they could be alone together, where no one knew they were royal."

"You mean to tell me that Pharaoh announced quite calmly that he was taking Egypt from you and giving you instead a house in some outlandish place no one wants to live in! I suppose you remembered your manners and thanked him prettily!" Heavy tears rolled down her face. "To feel your heart like a dead child in your womb is nothing to losing faith in Pharaoh. How could he choose Ramoses instead of Nebunefer? Oh, that I should have lived to see this day!"

She became so hysterical that I nearly ran to Sensen's assistance. Instead I watched my wife calmly take the flowers out of a vase and pour the water over Meena's head. "Now be quiet," she said firmly. "If there was any need to make a scene, or to weep, I should be doing both. If you insist on behaving like a silly child I will unpack my hippo for you to play with."

"Don't unpack him! He's in three layers of linen and two of wool, padded with one of your winter cloaks in the bottom of the third pannier."

Meena took off her wig and shook the water from it. Then she sat on the edge of her bed, her lank hair falling over her eyes.

"Now you are being good I will tell you what really happened," said Sensen, in much the same way that I had so often heard Meena speak to her when she was a child. "Pharaoh asked me whether I thought Neb and I would be really happy together if he allowed Ramoses to have the Crook and Flail. It was rather a shock at first, and of course I said that Neb must make the decision for himself; but after we had discussed it for quite a long time I agreed that it seemed the most sensible thing for everyone. Then he gave me the seal, the one I am wearing on a cord round my neck so I shan't lose it, and he told me that when the steward of the place we are going to sees it he will recognize us for the new owners. The cartouche on the seal means, 'The Lord of the Place of the Living Water' . . . he said it meant much more than just an especially fertile oasis."

"A few paltry wells instead of all the valley of the Nile! How long will you stay there before you get restless?"

"Probably much longer than it takes you to learn not to be so pessimistic . . . which at the moment seems like eternity! Pharaoh said that for the next year or two it would be wiser for us not to let any one know that we belong to the royal family. By then Tuaa will have ceased to fear that we would have ousted Ramoses if we had had the chance, so we can let

Karaden know where we are and he will arrange for us to have everything we want . . . except the throne." She paused. "I felt so sorry for Seti, wanting to die quietly so that he would remember exactly what he wanted to say to Neb's mother the moment he saw her again, and still being pulled back into the body, which didn't want him to live in it any more, because he was worried by things he ought to have decided years ago."

"No one ought to listen to him when he's too ill to know what he's saying! When you had nightmares you used to think there were spiders in the bed, but at least you had the sense to know the difference between Tuaa and a spider!"

"Pharaoh is much wiser than you or I, Meena. He believes that Neb should not cause civil war in Egypt by staying to challenge Ramoses."

"If he had been wise there would have been no Ramoses! Sensen, how can you be so selfish as to let him steal the Two Lands from your husband?"

I saw a tear glisten on Sensen's cheek. "Meena, I am trying very hard not to be selfish. Of course I want to be free to go away with Neb, to have him all to myself instead of seeing less and less of him. But I am thinking of Neb more than myself, really I am."

"And is the Prince Nebunefer a weakling who must be protected by his wife?" The indignation in her voice was some small solace to my pride. "Do you think that Ramoses at fifteen is a stronger man than your husband?"

"Ramoses will never allow himself to be troubled by doubts which conflict with decisions of expediency. The Army will follow him because he will enjoy leading them . . . to him a war will be as exciting as a lion hunt. He will not be dominated by the Amen priests, because he does not believe in magic; but he will build many temples because he will like seeing his name on their walls. And he will have children . . . many children, Meena."

V

QUEEN TUAA

THERE are times when a man does not have to be an initiate to know how it feels to fight with the warriors of the Underworld. False pride and self-pity squeezed my heart so cruelly that I nearly cried out that I would shatter the peace of my father's dying and seethe Egypt in the dark broth of civil war rather than suffer the humiliation of accepting the placid future my wife considered suitable to my powers.

Anger flailed sweat from my body until I felt I should die of thirst unless I could plunge into cool, clear water. So strong did this longing for coolness become that I stripped off my sodden kilt and plunged into the shallow pool under the mulberry trees.

Sensen came into the garden and stood smiling down at me. I realized how foolish I must look, with the stalks of broken lotus clinging to my legs and bewildered fish darting in search of somewhere they could hide from this monster which had suddenly intruded on their quietness.

Before she could speak I said defiantly, "Am I also too young to be trusted not to drown even in such a small puddle unless you support me under the chin?"

I left the water with as much dignity as I could assemble. "Surely you brought a towel for me," I said. "Meena always insists that children should dry between their toes."

She sat down on a bench and looked at me in frank amazement. "Neb, what *are* you doing? If you want to wallow among the lilies as though you were a hippopotamus in a mud-hole, why shouldn't you? . . . but you needn't be cross about it."

"Why not? A child is allowed to be cross if some one deliberately breaks his favorite toy, so why shouldn't I be cross when my Crook and Flail are broken?"

"My love, of course you have every right to be angry, but you can't be angry with *me*. Neb, *dear* Neb, I thought you would understand. Perhaps I ought to have told you yesterday, but I was afraid if I did we should have talked and talked and I would never have been really sure that you had made your own decision."

"I congratulate you, my clever little wife . . . who is so clever that she knows her husband will always do as she wishes. If I may make a tentative suggestion, it would have been more tactful to postpone the packing so that I could have cherished the illusion of making up my own mind."

"Neb, you are being horribly unfair, and you know it."

Doubting Sensen was such an unfamiliar experience that I began to doubt myself. "Forgive me if I appear unappreciative of your efforts on my behalf. I feel sure that had I returned from the Palace with the news that tomorrow you would be Queen of the Two Lands, you would have told Meena to unpack discreetly."

"Neb, you've often told me, sometimes sounding nearly as pompous as Karaden, that it is unseemly to give judgment without full knowledge of the facts. If I have ever given you the right to suspect me of disloyalty, you can go on glowering; if not, you had better sit down and *listen*."

I sat down, but still refused to take the hand she tried to insert between my clenched fingers. "I am listening," I said coldly.

"If it wasn't so important I wouldn't bother to speak to you while you're being so horrid, but I haven't time to wait until you stop behaving like an ill-mannered child."

"Forgive me if I appear stupid, but being treated like a child is apt to limit the understanding to the narrow field of an infant . . . I might remind you, in all humility, that breast-milk does not lie easily in the stomachs of grown men."

I thought Sensen was going to slap me, but with an effort she controlled the impulse, an impulse which I secretly acknowledged was fully justified, and instead clasped her hands round her knees.

"I started to pack because although I did not know where we might be going I *did* know that we should have to leave Thebes."

"I suppose it did not occur to you that your husband might be interested to know why he was expected to make such a precipitate journey—or would "flight" be a more honest word?"

"Neb, *please* stop talking like Karaden! This is no moment to be clever with words—not that it is ever clever deliberately to misunderstand what some one is trying to say. You *must* listen."

"You have my ear. I nearly said 'You have the Royal Ear,' habit takes more killing than an eel."

"I happen to be fond of your ears, both of them; that's why you won't be able to make me lose my temper, however hard you try. How long were you listening outside the window? Oh, Neb, don't be so touchy! Of course I didn't mind you listening, but I want to know how much you heard so that I shan't waste time repeating myself."

"Everything from the moment when you were insisting on taking the monkey with you," I admitted reluctantly.

"Then you've even less right than I thought for being so obtuse," she said briskly. "The Captain of the Bodyguard and Usermentu are backing Ramoses, so our best chance of defeating them, if you *insist* on civil war, is to go North to try to get the Army of the Reed to follow you against the Army of the Bee. If you stay here you'll be murdered the moment Father is dead. Tuaa's already arranged it."

"It is not easy to murder Pharaoh," I said grandly, trying to hide in the shreds of my false pride.

"Oh yes, it is—when he doesn't know who, if any one, in the Palace can be trusted. You couldn't openly accuse Tuaa; no one would believe you. Poison in your wine, the wheel of your chariot breaking, a snake in your bed—don't you understand how easy it would be for her? Oh, Neb, *please* don't be so stubborn!"

"And she could kill you," I said slowly. "She could make me afraid to leave you even for an hour."

"Making me even more of a shackle than she's made me already! If only I'd liked her I might have been able to understand her wickedness sooner. Oh, Neb, I've been such a fool! I didn't mind being ill, because it meant you stayed with me instead of going away for months with Pharaoh or the Army. I thought Tuaa was *kind* to encourage you to stay, and when I tried to be unselfish she produced such reasonable excuses . . ."

"What excuses?"

"She said . . . she said that it was my duty to keep you with me so that we lost no opportunity of starting a baby. Realizing that Tuaa has used me against you hasn't been comfortable, Neb."

"Forgive me, Sensen. I didn't understand."

"Then you're not cross any more?"

"So very far from cross. Oh, my dear, I'm such a fool! No wonder Father chose Ramoses! Sensen, you say the Captain of the Bodyguard is in the plot?"

"I've told you that twice already."

32

The threads Tuaa was weaving suddenly began to show a meticulous pattern. "Now I understand why Bakur is so eager to offer us hospitality. I begin to see everything much more clearly."

"See what?" she asked quickly.

"Tuaa's plan of campaign . . . she would have made an admirable Captain of Captains, what a loss for Egypt that her command of strategy could not have been used against the Hittites! You and I were to have sailed down-river this evening. If the wind drops, as it almost certainly will when the moon rises, we were to spend the night at Bakur's house. She would have made some excuse to keep us there until she received word from Tuaa; and then . . ."

Sensen finished the sentence, "And then we would be murdered."

"One finds it difficult not to admire Tuaa's attention to detail. To arrange our death at Bakur's is so much easier than at the Palace."

"Crocodiles are another neat detail," said Sensen. "No extra bodies to deflect any of the glory from Seti's funeral." She shivered. "I would almost prefer the belly of a crocodile to a Royal tomb . . . especially if we were eaten by the same crocodile."

"We ought to leave Thebes tonight, but we shall have to risk waiting at least another day until I can think of somewhere for you to be safe while I arrange how we shall travel."

"Do you suppose I've done nothing but pack since yesterday? I forgot I hadn't told you about Hiboe. . . ."

"Father's body servant?"

"Yes. In the presence of Pharaoh he swore lifelong allegiance to you—he is the only Royal Attendant that Seti knew would always be loyal to us. You see, he knew your mother, and was the only person who had the courage to implore Seti not to marry Tuaa. He has been twice to the Living Water, so he knows the best way for us to go there. The tracks are too rough for chariots so we shall use pack-donkeys. The six servants who always travel with us will join Hiboe in the cave above the Valley of the Dead between sunset and dawn tonight. Only four of the men are trained litter-bearers, but the others will soon learn to keep in step . . . two to each litter and two to relieve them when we have to make forced marches."

"I don't need a litter," I protested.

"But Meena does. Think how she'd grumble if she had to walk for days and days."

"You haven't sent your own litter?" I asked quickly.

"My love, I have grown up since yesterday. Hiboe will provide litters suitable to our disguise; only two bearers, curtains of coarse linen and pallets stuffed with straw."

"How far do you expect us to go before we are recognized? Prince Nebunefer and his wife are not entirely unknown in Egypt."

"How many people have seen us as we really are? Do you think that even I could recognize you from a carving on one of Seti's stelae?" She ran her fingers through her hair and swept it back from her wide forehead. "Do you think they would recognize me if they saw me now, however often they had seen the little Princess Sensen, determinedly smiling although her ceremonial wig had given her a headache?"

"Even a very minor noble would travel with more than a few pack-donkeys."

"But they will be quite suitable to a fairly prosperous trader who is on his way to Punt, with his wife and his mother, to find merchandise suitable for barter in some of the smaller towns."

"His mother?"

"Meena: if you prefer it she can be my mother. That will allow you to grumble about her when you exchange a few rather nasty beads for enough to feed us all until the next village. My love, I have been most efficient! I even remembered to give Hiboe three gold armlets to exchange for things that a merchant would be likely to take with him to please village women!"

She was so confident that it was only with the greatest reluctance that I said, "The moment that Tuaa discovers we have escaped from Thebes she will *have* to find us. I don't want to frighten you, but you must realize that our flight will prove that we have discovered her plot. She will think I have gone into hiding until I can raise the North against her. Every house that might give us shelter will be searched, every track followed by soldiers loyal to Ramoses."

Instead of being dismayed, Sensen laughed. "It takes a queen to outwit a queen . . . so I have earned the White Crown even though Nefertari will wear it. Tuaa has let it be known that she would like every one to believe we had died by drowning, but she was far too clever to give a direct order to any one . . . though the unspoken bargain was that whoever implemented her intention would not lack the Royal Favor. When the boat in which we sailed so innocently down-river is found capsized, no one will be suspicious, for the sail is too big and Ramoses capsized it himself only three days ago . . . luckily for him it was close to a barge and he was pulled out of the water before he had swum more than a few strokes."

She laughed again. "It is a delightful comedy, Neb. Bakur will look at her husband, yet be too discreet to ask, 'Did you do it so that I should not reap the Royal Favor?' The Captain will stare at the priest, the scribe suspect the fanbearer; but Tuaa will be content as a cat who does not care whose hand flung the throwing-stick so long as her dish is filled with raw meat. At Tuaa's order search will be made for us, a magnificent reward offered to the first who brings news that will assuage the queen's anguish. Every clump of reeds up and down the river will be trampled flat, but no one will search more fervently than those privy to the plot, for each will feel he *must* find us in case another had blundered and one of us were still alive . . . even a spark of life in our nostrils, so they will argue, would be enough to set the Palace intrigue in flames that would roar louder than fire in a straw-stack.

"When we are not found there will be the greatest crocodile hunt in history . . . for Tuaa will insist that our remains receive honorable burial. The embalmers will search through the records trying to discover a precedent by which they can decide which piece of crocodile can properly be placed in our canopic jars. When your armlet, the one you are now wearing that Seti gave you when he declared you the Royal Heir, and my favorite necklace, are found in the belly of the same crocodile, the embalmers will have yet another problem. Four canopic jars or eight? What ushapti figures, if any, should be included in a mummy that is no more than hundreds of cubits of bandages round a core of crocodile bones?

I found my admiration of Sensen increasing with every moment, but I still suspected her of letting her imagination outrun her acceptance of the facts. "How will you get the crocodile to co-operate?"

"Have you forgotten that the Gods expect us to use our intelligence?" she said in mock severity. "Your armlet and my necklace will be carefully embedded in a chunk of meat. We will drop it over the side of the boat when we see a crocodile large enough to provide a suitable sarcophagus. Bother, I've forgotten something. We must have *rotten* meat, or the crocodile may leave it to ripen in his larder under the bank."

I was glad to be able to prove myself not entirely useless. "Ramoses, fortunately, is over-confident in the boy who looks after his lion cubs. I noticed this morning that the stench coming from the store-room next to their kennels was overpowering—to save a lion from having to eat food fit for a vulture is a kindly gesture."

I had already decided that whether I raised the North, or waited until Ramoses had proved himself unworthy to rule, was of secondary importance to Sensen's immediate safety. Father wished her to go to the Living Water; it was my duty to take her there. The evening wind rustled the leaves of the mulberry trees. "It will be sunset in an hour," I said. "Does Meena come with us?"

"She will leave here before dawn with the pack-donkeys that take our personal things; one of the servants goes with her, and the top layer of each pannier will be fruit or vegetables. Any one who notices them will think Meena is taking farm produce to sell to the tomb-workers. When she reaches the defile leading to the Valley, Hiboe will be there to show her the way up to the cave."

She kissed me. "I must see she has got everything ready, and you must fetch the lion's meat."

VI

FOOD FOR A CROCODILE

THE setting sun poured flame across the sky as Sensen and I walked together through the Palace garden for the last time. That everything was so ordinary seemed curiously unreal. A gardener, who was watering a clump of orange lilies, bowed low as we passed; a boy, the son of a court official, smiled shyly at Sensen as she paused to pat the tame gazelle he was holding by its scarlet leather collar.

The soldiers at the River Gate gave me a royal salute. For the first time I realized that I no longer had the right to receive the homage due to the Royal Heir. I felt cold, as though I were suddenly stripped naked on a winter night.

"Smile, Neb," said Sensen in a low voice. "People are watching us."

She stooped to pick a scarlet poppy that had forced its way between the paving-stones of the river-walk. Her air of unconcern was already producing an effect. I noticed a woman smile at the man beside her, and whispers rippled from person to person like wind through a cornfield. They ceased pretending they had come only to enjoy the cool breeze from the river, and pressed forward to watch us. Sensen smiled and waved her hand to them. A child ran forward and she gave it the poppy she carried. A petal fell to the white limestone of the quay, bright as blood on a handkerchief. I glanced quickly at Sensen, but though her eyes were brilliant it was only with excitement.

Her Nubian page put a basket covered with a white napkin in the stern of the boat, and arranged cushions and a woollen cloak for Sensen to sit on. He acted the part well; no one could have guessed he knew why one of the cushions was so heavy, and that the others were stuffed with clothes instead of feathers.

I exchanged a few words with the Royal Boatman, telling him that if my wife felt so inclined we might spend the night at the house of the Captain of the Bodyguard. He looked surprised and then nodded eagerly, taking this as proof that the rumors of Pharaoh's illness had been greatly exaggerated.

37

I unfurled the sail and the boat slid smoothly out into the current. The little crowd watched us and then began rapidly to disperse.

"Each wants to be first with the good news of Pharaoh," I said. "There will be a brisk trade in the wine-shops tonight."

It was still luminous on the water but already the Palace windows glowed through the dusk. There was a light in my father's room too, though paler than the others. Was Tuaa with him, or had a lamp been lit because even Pharaoh wanted a flame to watch so that he could forget that a tomb is dark?

Looking back across the years I realize that our chances of making Tuaa believe we had been murdered were so tenuous that I could have agreed to Sensen's plan only because, unknown to myself, I wanted it to fail. The Gods, however, had decided that it should succeed.

Perhaps Sebek, the crocodile-headed, sent one of his servants to swallow the hunk of rotten meat that contained our armlet and necklace, for I have never seen such a large crocodile near a city.

The moon obscured herself in a cloud while I landed Sensen on a wooden platform that led out from the reeds to a fish-trap. Then, while I was wondering how to capsize the boat, a sudden gust performed this office for me: the current swept the boat into midstream yet allowed me to reach the bank without having too long to think about the possibility of meeting a less helpful crocodile.

After burying our clothes, we put on those Meena had hidden in the other two cushions, and finding ourselves unexpectedly hungry ate some of the cold roast duck, bread, and lettuce she had packed in the basket.

We walked for about three hours and then slept in a stack of clover until dawn. We kept to paths between the fields until it was no longer possible to avoid going through a village.

I admit to feeling a little indignant that because I wore only a loin-cloth, sandals with toestraps of plaited straw, and a greasy forehead thong, none of the few people who saw us gave me a second glance. The men stared at Sensen, but only with the interest they would have paid to any young and beautiful woman.

Sensen, instead of being annoyed that she was so easily mistaken for the wife or sister of a man of no importance, seemed to find it amusing. She made herself a wreath of flowers that grew at the edge of a patch of corn, and returned so warmly the smile of a man leading a yoke of oxen that he let her ride in the cart among the jars of wine which he was taking to the priests in charge of Hatshepsut's mortuary temple.

Hiboe, obeying Sensen's instructions, met us at sunset with a donkey that she could ride up the steep track to the high desert above the Valley of the Dead. I found it increasingly hard to accept the new roles that the others seemed to find so natural. Meena, the nurse who must be cajoled or placated, had suddenly become efficient as the storekeeper of an army on the march. Hiboe, whom I had known only as the man to whom the pleats of a royal kilt were of supreme importance, to whom a hair out of place in Pharaoh's ceremonial beard would have sealed disaster, had become the competent leader of a caravan.

A cave had been made ready for Sensen and myself: a mattress with woollen covers, a jar of water and a towel, a flask of rubbing-oil in case Sensen's muscles were sore after her unaccustomed exercise.

The narrow wadi provided such excellent shelter, the fall of the ground being less effective than the reputation of the place, which was considered to be haunted by a particularly offensive type of demon, that Hiboe had allowed a fire to be lit over which Meena was roasting a young goat. The pack-donkeys, their forelegs hobbled, tore placidly at the dry herbage. Beyond the circle of firelight our six servants, all that was left to me of the cohorts of Egypt, ate bread and onions while they waited for their share.

Meena again basted the roasting meat with salted water; then stood back to allow Hiboe to carve it. Before bringing it to us, he arranged the slices on a dish of unglazed pottery with the same care he would have given to crane's breast served on gold. To my profound relief, Sensen displayed an eagerness of appetite which I would have paid a foreign physician five collars of gold to inspire in her. Only when we had washed our hands in a small bowl of warm water, scented with jasmine, did Hiboe and Meena cut meat for themselves, carrying it to a rock midway between us and the servants; a rock which in their eyes had acquired the status of the room of the personal attendants. In due course the remainder of the carcass became the central point of a noble's kitchen; each man cutting off a portion with his hunting-knife, no doubt following a rule of precedence already decided among them.

I began to muse on the deep-rooted urge in all of us to give and to receive homage. Sensen and I still kept the loneliness of royalty, having no one between us and the Gods even though we sat on a blanket of undyed wool and had eaten collops of goat's flesh from a wooden skewer.

As I stood up, one of the men threw a bundle of thornbush on the embers and I saw my shadow on the sheltering wall of rock. The servant feeds the fire; the fire reveals the master. In each man is the child and the God: the one who worships, the other who must discover in himself the worshipful virtues. I learned then, though I had not the wit to express the knowledge in words or even to understand it, that no man can refuse his rung of the ladder of generations unless he foolishly condemns himself to the futile service of himself.

But that night I longed to show that though I was no longer the Royal Heir I was a man who could stand alone. I wanted to tell Hiboe that I, not he, could find the best way to the Living Water; to tell Meena that I, not she, would decide where Sensen would sleep most soundly in my arms; to tell the six servants, my little Egypt, that I who had driven a chariot with two stallions jealous of a mare knew better than they did how to hobble a pack-donkey.

The fire flared as Hiboe stirred the embers with a long branch. As though a priest greater than those who serve Amen read aloud, I seemed to hear an echo from one of the Great Assessors who weigh men's hearts in the Scales of Tahuti. "Hast thou seen thy shadow on the wall and thought it mighty?"

I longed to flee from my pride into the close circle of ordinary people by the same small fire. I was no longer the Royal Heir, so surely I had the right not to be set apart? I was a man and Sensen a woman: at last we had the right to enjoy freedom from responsibility. I could be a brother to all the people of my little Egypt . . . if I thought of myself as Sensen's brother I need no longer feel I had betrayed her because the Gods had chosen not to allow us a child.

Sensen leaned back against my shoulder. "I thought," she said, "that we might find it difficult to keep faith with the Gods if we allowed ourselves to become real people. When I made a wreath to wear of little dusty flowers that grew among the corn, I pretended I had the right to a crown that neither demands nor gives allegiance. But there is no such crown, dear Neb, and he who wears it is a fool posturing before Gods who smile only in pity."

"I am not likely to play Pharaoh to a court of eight . . . or eighteen, if you include the pack-donkeys."

"What is Pharaoh except the symbol of man's link with the Gods? We are all Pharaohs, Neb. The pack-donkey is Pharaoh to the sagebrush, the sagebrush Pharaoh to the rock."

I tried to smile. "So I may still prove useful to some one —an encouraging reflection!"

"It is not for us to question the wisdom of the Gods. I used to think I could make people happy just because I would find it so easy not to be horribly gracious like Tuaa. But this morning when I smiled at the man with the ox-cart it gave *him* the chance of helping *us;* we began to be real. I walked farther than I have ever walked before; I ate not because it would please Meena or make you less anxious—I was *hungry,* Neb."

"Then how can I mind leaving Thebes?" I said, and meant it.

"We both mind much more than we dare admit even to ourselves. But one day we shall be glad, because it will teach us how to leave our bodies without regret. . . . Oh, Neb, I am so glad I need not be buried in a tomb!"

I knew she must be tired though she would not admit it, so I yawned and said that Meena would be fretful if we kept her awake any longer.

A blanket had been hung as a curtain across the mouth of the cave. I marveled again at the adaptability of women as I heard Meena insisting that the ritual of hair and nails, of cleansing with oil then with fine linen wrung out of toilet-water, should not be curtailed by so trivial a matter as sleeping in a cave instead of a palace. At last I was allowed to take my place beside my wife.

Sensen soon fell asleep. I lay awake, knowing that unless I walked under the stars until some of my tension lessened I should have nightmares, and disturb her by shouting before I could force myself to wake.

Long ago I had promised Sensen she should not be buried in a tomb. Was her fear no more than the natural result of her feverish terrors which were part of the illness that followed her only visit to the Royal Tomb: or had her instinct a deeper significance?

The Amen priests declare that the *Ka,* the link between body and soul, even of a Pharaoh lingers in the place where the body is buried until such time as the soul has completed its journey through the Underworld. This I had never believed; but if it were true? I had not been allowed to stay with my father until he died, but could I not seek him now where he might be in greater need of company?

I tried to tell myself that I was indulging in false pride. His soul was in the care of the Gods; they did not need me to help them.

The need to go to the tomb became more insistent. I tried to combat instinct with logic. I might be recognized by one of the guardians of the Valley and so endanger Sensen; but I could climb down the cliff so that I need not pass the watch-fire. It was a difficult climb at night: but in the brilliant moonlight every crevice would be as clearly marked as lines of bitumen between the deck-planks of a ship.

I woke Hiboe and told him that if I had not returned before Sensen discovered my absence he was to reassure her and say that I was in no danger and would soon return. He looked surprised, as well he might, but the habit of accepting the Royal Word, even the word of a prince, was too strong for him to question.

I too felt that I obeyed a Royal Word, though as yet I did not know what it told me to do.

VII

A VOICE IN THE DARK

I FOUND the tomb-workers' lamps in a hut outside the entrance; one was still lit, by which the others in the morning would be kindled. The tradition which demands that the same flame shall live from the first day when the reflected rays of the sun cannot penetrate far enough until the final closing of the outer door was serving me well.

The wick sputtered and then settled to a small steady light as the oil warmed. The broad steps of the first staircase were partly blocked by sacks of stone-chippings that had not yet been collected by the men who are not considered worthy to enter further than the first gallery. Even the workers on the Royal Tomb jealously guard their privilege.

On the ceiling vultures of Ma-at spread their wings and the power of Amen watched me from the walls. I felt very young and humble, for the Boat of Ra reminded me that I had considered it a matter of supreme importance that not I but Ra-moses would stand at the steering-oar of Seti's funerary barge.

A temporary bridge, the split trunks of palm trees, crossed the pit that had been made eight years earlier to carry away the water of a spring which had risen after a season of heavy thunderstorms. This pit had been deepened as a further protection against those who might dare to desecrate the Royal Sleep.

If my father believed, as he had so often told me, that death was as much a rhythm of the Gods as the rise and fall of the Nile, why had he made such elaborate provisions to protect his body? Surely he did not expect even his *Ka* to linger here, the caretaker of an empty house whose owner has chosen a new estate? Or was it Tuaa who had insisted that it was his duty to leave in the living rock this impress of his power so that men of the future might in need be reminded of the wisdom of Seti?

I found it increasingly difficult to subdue my emotions with the whip of intellect. I was in the tomb of my father and had come here alone at night because I felt he needed me for

43

some purpose greater than filial sentiment. Fear touched my skin, insistent as the feet of blow-flies, as I went through the Hall of the Four Pillars. I remembered seeing the last of those four pillars cut free of the rock and Father saying to me, "They represent the four doors of the house of mortality; the East door through which a man enters into birth: the West door of death: the North door which opens into the Underworld; the South door through which the free man enters into the Love of Ra."

I had asked him why this could not be written on them, and he had smiled, a little sadly, and said it would offend those Amen priests who clung only to tradition, and be considered too blatant by the few who understood the reality beyond the symbols.

Another flight of steps, a longer passage: now I was in the ante-chamber to the Hall of Gold where my father's body would lie in his great sarcophagus, because the gallery beyond, nearly two hundred cubits in length, would never be completed.

A pale glow was coming from one of the offering rooms. I held the lamp high to see whether I had been frightened by no more than a chance reflection from the light I carried. I tripped over something which a careless workman had left in the doorway and the lamp slipped from my hand.

I was alone in the dark with fear, fear so strong that I could not move even when the spilt oil licked my foot with a hot tongue.

Like a child begging for reassurance, I said, "Father, can you hear me?" Though I tried to speak in a loud voice, a whisper rustled from my dry mouth.

"Father, can you hear me?" I tried to believe I heard only an echo, but I knew another voice than mine had spoken.

It came again. "Father, can you hear me?"

Suddenly I knew who had spoken, and fear was swept away by shame.

"Yes, Ramoses, I can hear you. Why have you come to seek me here?"

I was so jealous of his courage that I tried to break it. "Put out your lamp, Ramoses. Why should you be afraid of the dark when you visit your father's house?"

I heard him gasp, and the light flickered so I knew his hand was trembling. He failed to blow it out until his third attempt.

"I am very glad I came here to find you," he said, so calmly that I thought he had recognized my voice. Then I realized that my wish to speak in the manner of Pharaoh had

44

become so deeply ingrained that my voice could easily be mistaken for Seti's.

"Would it not have been easier to talk to me in the Palace?" Until that moment I intended no more than to show him that his elder brother was even more self-assured than he: I hoped to forget my own cowardice in the pleasure of having so easily deceived him.

"I tried to see you there, but Mother told me that your soul had already flown from your body although your heart was still beating. She said that by tomorrow the physicians will have to admit that Pharaoh is dead. That's why I had to come here tonight, to make sure she has not lied to me."

"Why should you doubt your mother's word?"

"Because she wouldn't let me tell you about her plan. She made me swear on the Crook and Flail that I would never tell any one living."

"Yet you would tell me now?" I tried not to sound too eager. Was I about to be given proof that Ramoses thought his brother's life worth more than Egypt?

"Of course, Father." He sounded surprised. "Now that you are dead I am not bound by my oath—she said 'any one *living*.'"

"You are a brave son." And in that moment I knew that my jealousy of Ramoses had sprung from the same dark root which makes women envy the daughters in whom they have not the wit to see the renewal of their own beauty. In him were the qualities of leadership which I had longed to discover in my child born to Sensen.

"I am very proud of my son." And in my voice I heard the judgment in love of Pharaoh.

"I am not really brave, Father. I was so frightened when I entered the Valley that I nearly turned back . . . it was much more difficult than pretending to enjoy my first lion hunt."

I said, "I also nearly turned back." Only just in time did I relinquish the easy luxury of confession. Sensen had said, "We are all Pharoahs." I would not try to betray her.

"You mean the physicians are wrong?" he said eagerly.

"I mean that I too found it difficult to visit my tomb. I can assure you that I have no intention of lingering here, so do not feel anxious about me during the eighty days' mourning."

"Have you ever been afraid of the dead, Father—before you were dead, I mean? I wasn't, until Mother sent me to watch the embalmers, to cure me of being sick when I saw entrails bulging through the slit in a man's belly. It was after one of the village people was clawed when he was driving a lion out of a patch of thorn-bush. Of course I know she was right, for if I had been only the Leader of a Hundred, my men would have been ashamed if I had let them know I was afraid of seeing even foreigners hurt."

"Yet you were not afraid to seek me here, though I might have appeared to you as a corpse not yet prepared for the decent obscurity of mummy-wrappings?"

"I was sure, or very nearly sure, that your soul would look almost exactly like you did when you were alive. I didn't understand that I would be able to hear you but not see you. Father, please forgive me if this is a question I have no right to ask, but did you ask me to put out the lamp because you were afraid I should not like to see you?"

"Why did I think it easier for us to talk in the kindly dark? For the same reason that I used to draw the curtains when I came to sit beside your bed before you went to sleep . . . we felt closer to each other because our eyes could not remind us that you were a child and I a man who had begun to realize that his muscles were not so obedient as they used to be."

His sigh of relief was refreshing to me as cool wind to the forehead of a desert traveler. "I am sorry that I let myself believe that death was frightening. You always told me that it was a trivial experience, to be feared only by those in whom Tahuti will be disappointed when he weighs their hearts. I am sure Tahuti will never be disappointed in you, Father."

"Thank you, my son. Your confidence will give me added courage when Anubis asks me the name of the prow and of the oars of the Boat of Millions of Years, and your wisdom will increase mine when I answer the questions of the Forty-two Assessors."

"Shall I tell you about Mother's plot now?" The eagerness in his voice warmed my heart . . . how good it was to hear his impatience to tell a story, even though he thought the audience was one of the illustrious dead. Surely it is this urgency that the Gods long to hear in the voices of their children?

"You have my full attention, and my profound gratitude for bringing me this vital news."

"Four days ago, Mother told me you were going to die very soon. She made me promise not to tell any one, because she wanted to protect you from all the people who would expect to be allowed a last audience. She said I must be especially careful not to let you know, otherwise your peace would be disturbed by having to comfort me."

His voice became more confident. "Mother said that even Neb and Karaden had not been told, but she could trust me because she had taught me to hide my real feelings. She might have been ashamed of me if she had guessed I couldn't help crying as soon as I was alone, but I did it in my boat so that no one would know. I deliberately pinched my finger between the sail-rope and the mast so that I had an excuse in case she noticed my eyelids were puffy. She said it was clever of me to sail as though nothing terrible were happening . . . it made me feel rather a fraud. But that kind of fraud doesn't count with Tahuti, does it, Father?"

"Tahuti considers such translations of mere fact to be a filament of the Feather of Truth," I said with very real conviction. "Is there more of the plot, except your mother's kindly wish to spare me the anxiety of wondering how my death might affect others?"

"Much more." Then he paused and added diffidently, "Ought I to be as brief as possible?"

"Why be brief? Eternity at least has the advantage of not being measured in hours."

"I thought it might be difficult for you to make me hear you . . . of course I ought to have known it would not be at all difficult, now that you are One with the Gods."

In case he asked me some awkward question, such as whether the voice of Anubis sounded like a man or a jackal's bark, or whether Hathor mooed as a greeting, I thought it wise to show that Seti was still fully concerned with corporeal problems.

"I think I can promise that our conversation will impose no undue strain on either of us. Why not sit rather than stand while we are talking? There is no need for formality."

"Thank you, Father. There is some straw here, I noticed it before I blew out the lamp. I expect one of the stone-carvers brought it to kneel on when he was doing the lowest bit of the wall."

I heard straw rustle as he pulled it into a heap. "Being dead makes people beautifully unremote," he remarked contentedly. "I have always been so much in awe of you that I have never found it so easy to talk to you as I do now . . . which was entirely my fault."

"The fault was mine. How curious it is to find that death is also a cure for pomposity! Why were you shy with me?"

"Because I wanted to be your favorite son, and although I tried to do what Mother said would please you I was never able to think of the right thing to say when we were alone together . . . and we were so seldom alone."

So Tuaa had been too jealous even to allow Seti privacy with her children. For the first time I realized how lonely Ra-

47

moses had always been; he had had no Sensen to share his childhood.

"Even before I went to the House of the Captains I decided I was going to lead your armies when you were too old to want to do it yourself. I never told you in case you thought I was only boasting . . . I *do* boast rather a lot, especially when I'm shy, but I was going to conquer the Hittites if they became rebellious and even set your stele beyond Babylon. Hatshepsut did, and she was only a woman, so I thought I could manage it too."

"One must not underrate women: they have a fund of subtlety which it is difficult, when in a male body, fully to comprehend."

"I know," he said fervently. "That is why I am going to marry Nefertari. You do want me to marry her, don't you, Father? She is nearly as good as I am with a throwing-stick, and yet she is so pretty that when she asks me to do something for her I can almost always manage it. I don't *have* to do it, I just like making her happy. I even let her steer my new sailing boat when the wind was so strong that Mother had forbidden us to take it out. She thinks it is weak of me to be so obedient to Mother."

"And I agree with her."

"Do you, Father? Oh, I wish I had known!"

"Obeying Tuaa becomes a habit, and habit is a bad overseer. You will, of course, give her the respect due to the Royal Mother, but you should accept her advice only after due consideration."

"*Advice* from Mother!"

"You will find, my son, that when you wear the Double Crown even Tuaa will not openly give you orders. The only order you will obey is the voice of your conscience which, unless you deliberately cripple it, will continue to act as the honest messenger of the Gods. Tell me, does Tuaa approve of your choice of a queen?"

"She had to give her consent, because I told her that I wouldn't agree to her plot unless she also swore on the Crook and Flail that I could marry Nefertari before the end of the year."

My respect for Ramoses continued to increase. Tuaa's power as the first woman of the Two Lands would be more difficult to sustain when Egypt had a new queen . . . and a queen who, for I had complete faith in Sensen's judgment, would soon be loved by the people who had never felt more than awe of Tuaa.

"Nefertari will undoubtedly provide me with grandchil-

48

dren in whom I shall be greatly honored. If any one tries to prevent your early marriage I would remind you that the words 'Pharaoh has spoken!' are sufficient to make even a murmur of disagreement the confession of a traitor. You will find this usage a most comforting reflection when you have to make a pronouncement which is unpopular with some opposing faction. Does Nefertari play a part in the plot, except as a bribe?"

"She wasn't exactly a bribe, Father. If I hadn't loved Nefertari I would never have believed that Neb had refused to be Pharaoh. When Mother said that you wanted me to rule after you I told her that I wouldn't believe it until either you or Neb told me."

"A most natural and proper decision. How did she cause you to change your mind?"

"I saw I was wrong after she explained. She said there was still a chance that you would recover, but that if you started thinking about who would be the next Pharaoh you would feel that you were ready to die . . . so if I said anything about it I would be as wicked as though I had killed you on purpose."

"Your mother is a woman of remarkable subtlety; however as I have warned you of that already we need not labor the point. And what reason did she give for your not discussing the matter with Neb?"

"She said that Neb loves Sensen even more than I love Nefertari. You once told me that no one can be loved more than they love, and the other way round. Nearly every one loves Neb and Sensen, but I have only got Nefertari; and the boy who cut a bird-arrow out of my shoulder when he wounded me by mistake in the reeds; and my hunting dogs, the two who sleep in my room; and the soldier with one leg who looks after my horses. He was going to be sent home to his village after his leg had been kicked so badly by an unbroken colt that it had to be cut off just below the knee, but I made such a scene with the leader of his Hundred that he was allowed to stay with me."

"Neb and Sensen both love you," I said gently. "And you are my favorite son."

There was a long pause. I heard a strangled sob. "But I was telling you about Neb," he said, fighting for self-control. "Sensen will never be able to have a child . . . I don't know why but Mother says all the physicians are quite sure about it. Neb has refused to take a secondary wife or even a concubine, for he is sure that if he did, even for Egypt, Sensen's cough would get worse and worse and she would die. Mother says that if Neb thought that Sensen died because he had made her unhappy he would become so absorbed in grief that he would be a worse Pharaoh even than the Heretic. I couldn't go to Neb and tell him that I knew he had lost Egypt because the Gods didn't think him worthy of a child, could I, Father? Mother had to explain how much that would hurt him before I understood."

"Neb once told me that if he were still childless after my death he would take another woman, with Sensen's full approval."

"Mother told me something else, which I wouldn't even tell you, Father, if you were not already with the Gods. Neb won't take a concubine because his seed can't quicken. She told me last year, when I was fourteen, and she said it was my duty to prove to her that I was blessed of Osiris. She chose the girl I had to prove it with and told me exactly what I must do . . . being told by Mother was almost worse than having to watch the embalmers. But I didn't know then that it was *right* to disobey her, so when the girl was sent to my room I pretended that I had done it often before. She was more frightened than I was, but I didn't know it then. I thought she was secretly laughing at me, so I pinched her arm until she began to cry. Then something horrid in me began to feel strong because she was frightened of me, instead of my being frightened of mockery. I never saw her again, but not very long afterwards Mother said she had protected me from yet another fear." There was a long pause. "Unless you had told me not to obey Mother I would not dare to say what I'm going to say, so please forgive me if it sounds terribly impertinent."

"Between us there can be no need of forgiveness," I said, with fervent hope that the Gods would hear and shrive me of my earlier lack of understanding.

"Father, when you talk to the Gods will you try to remember that it would be good if men asked questions instead of only trying to think of the right answers? When Anubis asks you the name of the oars, couldn't you say, 'You know the answer as well as I do, but why do you ferry children to people who don't really want them and forget to send them where they would find friends on both sides of the river?' It might be very dangerous, Father, but even if Anubis were offended and left you in the Underworld, surely *one* of the Gods would hear about it and give you an audience? Then you could tell them how difficult it is to be human. Sometimes the Gods seem like very wise parents who have been too busy thinking about more important things to have time to remember how it feels to be a child. You were too busy with Egypt to remember to tell me not to obey Mother: perhaps the Gods are too busy quelling rebellions among the stars to remember that the priests of their temples have forgotten why people are born."

"Why are they born?" I asked in real humility.

"But, Father, you told me that when you said I must obey only my conscience. Didn't you mean that we have to come to this side of the River to learn how to train our hearts to be true messengers of the Gods?"

"You are wise, my son."

I heard him sigh. "I wish that you had had a lot of children, so that I could be sure that I was not going to be Pharaoh only because there was no one else."

I found it surprisingly easy to admit the truth that I had at last accepted. "You will be a great Pharaoh, Ramoses. Neb would never have been more than a name among many."

"It is not Neb's fault that he hates killing things. He is better with a throwing-stick than any man in Egypt, but if he doesn't enjoy wild-fowling, how could he like slaughtering barbarians? I once saw him holding a dying gazelle in his arms—he had wounded it with an arrow, and he looked as I will feel when my favorite dog dies. Mother knows I love Neb, and she asked me how I could be so cruel as to make him choose between conquering our enemies and making their women weep and *not* conquering them and seeing *our* women weep."

"Would not their men or ours weep also?"

"How could they, Father? You told me there is no sorrow beyond the Great River and surely even foreigners would not think of defeat until their bodies were dead."

I then asked him a most vital question. "So it is not because you despise Neb that you are willing to depose him?"

"I *love* Neb! I can't lie to you, now that you are dead and we don't have to pretend. I love Neb more than I love you, he has always been the person I would like to be. But I shall never be Neb; I am ambitious like Mother; I *want* to rule."

I heard the catch in his voice even when he spoke such bold words. "Then why are you unhappy, my son?"

"Because now you are dead and Neb is going away with Sensen there is no one I can really trust. It is lonely being a prince, but even fewer people are honest with Pharaoh. Mother promised me that Neb knew about our plan, and Usermentu and the Captain of the Bodyguard both promised me she was telling the truth. I tried to believe her, even when she refused to let me say good-bye to Neb or even to let Ne-

51

fertari say goodbye to Sensen. Please, Father, don't be angry with me for not trusting Mother."

"I am far from angry. Have I not told you that it is the duty of Pharaoh to see the color of the heart and not hear only what is said with the mouth?"

"When I hold the Crook and Flail, Mother will be my responsibility. I *must* know whether I can trust her. Sometimes she says things which are the opposite to what you would say . . . such as telling Usermentu that Neb has neither the wit to accept expediency or the strength to make it unnecessary. Of course Usermentu was pleased, because he hates Neb for advising Karaden not to increase the temple tribute."

"You have not yet told me what arrangements your mother has made for Neb."

"That is what I came here to ask you about. At first it sounded so reasonable, and then I began to be suspicious, and the suspicion grew stronger and stronger until I knew that I should have to break my oath if I couldn't make you hear me. Mother said that Neb would be afraid that people might sneer at him if they knew he had given up Egypt for Sensen, so he was going away for a year or two until there was no chance of the North making trouble because they didn't understand Neb *wanted* to give the Throne to me. She said it had been arranged for Neb and Sensen to borrow my boat, and it would be found capsized. Every one would think they had been drowned, but they would really be on their way to a place which is healthier than here so that Sensen's cough will get better. It was only when the people began to wail in the streets because they had heard that the Royal Heir was dead that I suddenly remembered the way Usermentu smiled at Mother when he was pretending to console her. She didn't know I was watching her, but there was something in the way she looked at him, as though they shared a horrid secret."

His voice, which he had managed to keep under strict control, grew shrill. "Father, did Tuaa arrange for Neb and Sensen to die? If she did then I have murdered them. If she killed Neb so that I could take his place I will revenge him. Even if it takes years and years I will kill everyone, *everyone* who shared in the plot! Oh, please, Father, tell me what to do!"

When I heard his hard, difficult sobs it was all I could do not to take him in my arms. I forced myself to speak with the authority of Pharaoh in judgment.

"Ramoses, it is my wish that you take the Crook and Flail. There is no blood guilt on your forehead, the forehead from which will shine the Golden Cobra. You have taken nothing

52

from your brother except a burden which was too heavy for him to carry."

"Thank you, Father, oh thank you so very much. You are not even ashamed of me for crying?"

"Is the warrior in the press of battle ashamed because he sweats? Remember, my son, that even when I have crossed the River and you do not hear my voice, I shall still be very proud to be remembered as the father of Ramoses."

His sobbing flowed into tears that were healing as water to parched fields. Then in a small voice he said, "Father, could you give me a sign to hold on to when talking to you like this seems too unlikely not to have been only a dream? Mother has so often told me not to believe in magic that it has become a habit for me to distrust everything I can't see and touch."

I knew he longed for me to kiss him, yet I dared not. "Your heart will never forget what I have told you tonight. My flesh is growing cold, a clean, kind cold like ash that has given its fire to light the darkness: but you shall not lack for a sign that you can see and touch. Wait here a little while, and be not afraid for I shall be with you although you will not hear my voice. It will be a preparation for the many times I shall give you counsel, perhaps in a dream or only as a sudden flash of insight . . . what does it matter now that I share your heart? Leave the Valley before dawn, and at sunrise you will find my messenger waiting for you at the Well of the Three Sycamores. To him you will ask the question, 'Have I betrayed my brother?' and he will prove that you are Pharaoh in truth."

"I shall try to sleep while I am here so that I may be able to see you. I'm glad now that Mother never let me have a light in my room, because it has taught me not to be afraid of the dark. It isn't dark for you, Father? No, of course it isn't, or you wouldn't be able to see the paintings on the wall."

I heard the straw rustle as he drew it round him. "Good night, my son," I said; and prayed until the sweat ran down my face that he would find himself in the arms of his father.

VIII

THE WELL OF THE THREE SYCAMORES

MORNING light poured across the cultivation, making a patch of cabbages green as malachite and gilding ripening wheat into a collar of gold for the Well of the Three Sycamores.

I was thirsty, and began to regret that I had chosen the meeting place because the well was dry, and so would be un-frequented. I knew it was dry, for Sensen had been here with Ramoses only a few days earlier. When he had noticed that one of his dogs was panting excessively he had tied his chariot-horses to a tree and gone in search of water. She had watched him bring up an empty bucket from the well, then stride off along the path to Hatshepsut's mortuary temple. He had returned carrying a pitcher which he had filled from the pool in the priests' court, and only when his dog was comfortable did he suddenly become angry that no one had recognized him. Sensen held the dog in her arms while he drove at full gallop to the house of the overseer of the temple tribute and ordered him to supply the village with water until such time as his servants or the prayers of the priests had effectively replenished the well.

The shadows of the sycamores drew slowly nearer as I sat on the well-head. Time passed so slowly that Ra seemed to drive the sun at the pace of a scarab beetle rolling a ball of dung.

I began to torture myself with anxiety. Had the high courage of Ramoses failed to withstand the dark? Had he called out to Seti and, hearing only the drumming of lonely blood in his ears, fled in panic and slipped from the narrow bridge over the pit? What bitter irony if Seti's favorite son had fallen into the trap designed for tomb-robbers!

My capacity for imagining disaster now used a merciless flail. I could see Ramoses returning from Thebes, embittered because he thought even his brother had found it amusing to deceive his courage. I could see him with a broken spine, un-able to make himself heard, even when the stone-workers passed above him, because his mouth was too dry from calling to a father who seemed indifferent to the pleas of a crippled boy.

When I saw him coming towards me along the narrow path I concealed myself behind one of the trees, so that I could snatch a moment in which to seek composure. It was not an old tree, so he knew a man stood there though my face was hidden.

"Are you waiting for me?" he asked.

I turned towards him. "Is it really you, Neb?" he said slowly. "Oh, Neb, are you safe!"

He flung his arms round me and we hugged each other as we had done only once before, when he was a little boy sobbing in a hayloft because Tuaa had made him kill his kitten that had scratched her.

His fingers clutched my shoulder blades. "Neb, you are solid! I know Father would be disappointed because it matters so much that I can feel you, but it is difficult for me not to be afraid when some one hasn't a body you can touch."

He hugged me again. "Neb, there is so much to tell you. Do you know where I have been all night? You will never be able to guess so I had better say it at once. Neb, I went to the tomb, and Father was there! We talked to each other much more easily than we've ever done before . . . and I *know* it wasn't only a dream, his talking to me I mean, because I knew how difficult it is for me to believe in real things so I asked him for a sign and he said I would find it there—and the sign is you!"

"You went to Father's tomb alone?"

"I did, Neb; I promise you I did."

"Then you have more courage than your elder brother," I said, hoping that my voice sounded as though I gave the rather grudging praise which is always the most convincing to those who are too humble to realize that praise is their right.

"When I tell you everything you'll understand why I *had* to go there . . . it is not brave to do something when everything else is even more frightening. I am not really brave, Neb; I just chose the smallest fear."

"When a boy of thirteen insists on driving the most unruly pair of stallions in the Royal Stables and kills three lions on his first lion hunt, he is unlikely to lack courage."

"But, Neb, surely you understand? That is one of the thousand reasons why you are the person I measure myself by. When every one else was saying how brave I was, you only smiled and refused to come to the banquet Mother gave in my honor. You knew, though she didn't, that I chose the new stallions to prove that *my* groom, the man with one leg I

55

brought back with me after my first season at the House of the Captains, was more skilled with horses than any of the others whose fathers and grandfathers had been trained in the Royal Stables."

"I too have driven stallions that were not yet familiar with harness, but I have never killed three lions in an afternoon."

"I only killed three because I was so terrified of killing one. I thought that when I had killed a wild lion, even though it had to be killed because it was old and ate villagers when it was hungry, my own lions would know and turn against me. And I was also very frightened of being clawed . . . don't you remember the man whose face was ripped open? Father had driven his spear deep into the lion's side, but when the man ran up to proclaim it Dead to the Royal Spear, it suddenly stood up and slashed its paw like a flail across his face. I was only eleven then and everyone believed that I suddenly ran into a patch of reeds because I wanted to squat—even Father was amused, for he thought it would teach me not to eat too many honey cakes. I vomited, because seeing the man's eye slowly sliding down his cheek was choking me as though it were a huge lump of phlegm in my throat. So I *had* to kill three lions, to prove to myself that I wasn't afraid of thinking that I could not even play with a lion cub now that I knew I had been an enemy of its kindred."

"There is a certain skill required before any one can kill a lion with a spear thrown from a chariot moving fast over stony ground."

"Skill!" said Ramoses a little scornfully. "Any one can teach his body to be obedient if the fear of being betrayed by it is worse than having to punish it."

To show he was not boasting he held out his right arm: dried blood was dark as onyx in the deep pits his teeth had scored in the muscle. "My body is horribly disobedient, so I have to treat it as though it were a foreigner who refuses to realize he is fortunate to be allowed to pay tribute to Egypt. I had to bite my arm because it wouldn't hold the lamp steady when Father told me I didn't need a light to see him by." He looked at his arm attentively. "I didn't realize it showed so much. Usually when I have to punish myself I can hide the mark with some stuff I stole from Tuaa's toilet-chest."

"Did you see Father?"

"Well, I did and I didn't—it is rather difficult to explain, but it's all true."

"I am sure it is."

"Oh, Neb, it's so lovely being believed! I ought to have

known you would, even without Father telling me you were the Sign."

"You saw Father?" I tried to conceal my eagerness.

He sat on the wall of the well beside me. "At first I only heard him. We talked as though we were both alive, and quite soon I wasn't even shy. Then he told me to try to be aware of him even though I couldn't hear his voice. I remembered Sensen telling me that real and beautiful things could happen in dreams, not just nothing or nightmares which usually happen to me, so I tried to sleep. I heard Father say, 'Good night, my son,' very gently as he used to when I was so young that I was allowed to take a toy to bed. I'm not quite sure even now whether I was awake or asleep when I felt him take my hand—the odd thing was that though I was lying on some dusty straw it smelled like fresh clover. I stood up, and hand in hand we were walking through a cornfield, tall corn with poppies and moon-daisies among the stalks. Father looked younger than I have ever seen him, and he wasn't wearing a wig or his ceremonial beard. I knew we talked, but it wasn't in words . . . at least I can't remember any. We went to his new temple and suddenly, instead of pillars that make everyone feel small and insignificant, there were trees soaring up with birds singing among the leaves and very green grass instead of stone under our feet. It was a dream, Neb, but it was real. . . . Neb, you are crying!"

"Because I am happy. Now I can go away with Sensen and not feel guilty."

"You are *sure* you want to give me Egypt?"

"If I were Pharaoh and promised to let you marry Nefertari tomorrow, wouldn't you be sad if I changed my mind?"

"It will be very difficult to rule Mother without you to help me. Couldn't you stay here? Father said that I must remember that she will not dare to argue if I say 'Pharaoh has spoken.' " He scored a line in the white dust with the toe of his sandal, trying to find a tactful way of telling me news that he feared might hurt my pride. "Mother tried to murder you and Sensen. How should I punish her?"

"By proving to her that although she could rule her husband she cannot rule her son."

"It is terrible to discover I hate her," he said slowly. "It's like hearing the murmur of a crowd but suddenly knowing what each of them is saying against you. I have always believed that she was much wiser than I am, but now I know she is only much more clever. She wanted me to be ruthless so that I would never refuse to obey her . . . Oh, Neb, what shall I do?"

"It has been said that the fowler who tries to snare a wild swan becomes entangled in his own net. She thinks I am dead; so your enemies are already divided because each is jealous of the other who may claim the favor of the Royal Mother for having implemented her secret orders. It is our secret that she has been outwitted: and knowing how easy it was to deceive her by so simple a device as feeding rotten meat to a crocodile, you will have no reason to be awed by her subtlety."

"Crocodile? What crocodile?"

"The one that was so obliging as to swallow apparent proof that Sensen and I are dead . . . a necklace and an armlet, garnished with putrid goat's flesh."

"I shall never forgive Mother!"

"That is a remark unworthy of Pharaoh!" I smiled to show him I spoke only in affection. "It is your duty to honor loyalty in all its manifestations. If you pause to consider whether each individual soldier of an invading army deserves to be killed, Egypt will again be insecure. A time may come when only the horizons fence a pasture where all flocks can graze, but in our day there is need of shepherds, and their dogs. You have seen your mongoose teaching her young to kill snakes: Tuaa gave you a similar education, not having the wit to know that it is better to wear the uraeus on your forehead than to fear a cobra under your bed. You have also seen Father's hunting-cat kill a dog which came too near her kittens. To protect one's young is a very proper instinct. Had Tuaa been more richly endowed with insight she would have known that her elaborate plans for my disposal were redundant."

"I still think she was wicked not to let me talk to you about it."

"Wickedness is another word for stupidity, and she at least had the courage to do what she considered best for Egypt. She has never loved anyone more than herself, so how could she believe I would not soon grow bored with Sensen and return to lead a revolt against you?"

"Mother despises people who think it is important to be lovable. She says it is a weakness which should have been outgrown by those who are Royal and Egyptian."

"In due course she will revise her opinion. Perhaps when she is born in Babylon; a drab little girl with a squint, pounding pig's fat to grease a Zuma's beard." I said this with considerable feeling.

Ramoses stared at me in astonishment and then laughed until he got hiccoughs.

"Think of Mother fat, and young, and silly! Neb, whenever I am frightened of her I shall try to think of her like that—and I'll tell Nefertari, so we can both think of it so hard that it will probably come true."

"One must not underrate women . . ." I broke off, dismayed that I had used the same phrase when I was speaking as Seti.

He smiled. "That is just what Father said . . . and now that you have reminded me I shall never forget it. You don't believe all women are dangerous? No, of course you don't or you wouldn't love Sensen." He slid down from the wall and sat cross-legged looking up at me. "Neb, I shall never be the person I want to be until a woman really loves me. I am going to tell you my most secret secret. I wish I had been born a woman, because the two people in history I admire most are Hatshepsut and the Heretic's queen . . . now that I'm Pharaoh I shall refuse to say 'the Heretic's queen' when I mean Nefertiti—it's sillier than calling the Hyksos the People-whose-name-shall-never-be-spoken."

That Ramoses feared women was natural to the son of Tuaa, but that he would have liked to be female I found startling. "Why did you choose Hatshepsut?"

"Because she was betrayed by both her husbands yet neither of the great Thothmes dared do more than cut her name from her monuments after she was dead. She was a much greater warrior than either of them, and our captains still drink a toast to her before battle; she lives in the hearts of both men and women. Didn't you know that every woman thanks Hatshepsut whenever she colors her nails or her hair with the henna that the Warrior Queen brought to Egypt?"

"And Nefertiti?"

He looked embarrassed. "Sensen had a dream—it was when we were sailing together and she went to sleep while we were becalmed. We had been talking about Nefertiti, and when Sensen woke up she said there was something very important she had to tell me about the People-whose-name-shall-never-be-spoken. I've always wondered about them ever since my nurse used to threaten that they would kill me in my bed if I was disobedient, so I listened very carefully." He hesitated. "Sensen said I wasn't to tell anyone because they would only laugh at me."

"Sensen knows I never laugh at her dreams."

He nodded. "She told me that, too. Well, first she said that Nefertiti could have ruled instead of her husband, and ruled much better than he did, if she had told anyone—anyone important I mean—that he hadn't really invented a new religion but only adapted a heresy that came originally from Sumaria."

"As the Sumarians have always been a tiresomely warlike nation I fail to see how they caused Akhenaten to carry pacifism to the point of idiocy."

"I know it sounds unlikely," he said anxiously, "but if you had been with us and heard her talking while the dream was fresh, I'm sure you would have believed her. Even the history scribes don't know who the Hyksos really were, except that twice they conquered Egypt for more than two hundred years, because all the records of our shame have been erased from the monuments. Sensen says that the Hyksos were the Northern Princes—who are still only prosperous shepherds though they pretend to be kings, and that they invaded us when Egypt had already been conquered."

"Conquered by whom?"

"By an idea. A Hebrew idea! Until they thought of it Hebrews were ordinary Sumarians, but this idea was so wicked that they were exiled even from Babylon. The idea is about an imaginary god called Yahveh—he must be imaginary for they don't make statues of him because no one knows what he looks like. People who believe in Yahveh think it wrong to kill other people even in war. So they have no temples and no army. They told our people about their idea, in secret, of course, and as everyone loves having a secret to tell, the idea spread and spread throughout Egypt until the weaklings and the fools who believed in it began to think that Yahveh was a better god even than Horus. It was easy for the weaklings to believe, Neb, because the ones who were cowards could refuse to fight without admitting even to themselves that they were cowardly, and those who were mean and greedy could refuse to pay temple tribute. The idea was like a terrible pestilence: first the army revolted, and then everyone ceased to respect even the priesthood, when they saw that they could keep everything for themselves without suffering the wrath of the gods."

"Why did not our priests challenge theirs to a magical battle?"

"They have no priests! Neb, think what would happen to a country without a priesthood!" He hesitated. "I know some of the Amen priests are corrupt but I suppose even Usermentu is better than nothing. Hebrews think that every one, at least every man, I am not sure about women, should obey only Yahveh and allow no one else to direct his conscience. What arrogance! Each of them pretending that they are an intermediary of the will of their god; each of them pretending that he is as good as, or better than, a Pharoah!"

He was so hotly indignant at this last heresy that my lips twitched, though fortunately he did not notice.

"And you think this idea of the Hebrews has already, on two occasions, caused Egypt to be overrun by foreign shepherds?"

"How else could Egypt have been conquered? We have the best soldiers, the best chariots, the best ships . . ."

"And the best kings."

"Now you are laughing at me, Neb," he said reproachfully. "It makes sense, really it does, if only you will believe that the People-whose-name-shall-never-be-spoken were nothing more than an idea and some Hebrews. Akhenaten's Vizier was born a Hebrew, everyone knows that, but what they *don't* know is that it was the Vizier who persuaded Pharaoh to let the Northern Garrisons starve so that the Egyptian soldiers wouldn't be able to kill any one."

"The New Religion worshipped Ra in the form of the Aten," I said mildly. "You may well disagree with Akhenaten, as I do, but he was sincere in his belief that mankind should follow love rather than hatred."

"He didn't really love Nefertiti, even though he had horribly undignified pictures made of her, kissing him and sitting on his lap. Hebrews don't even *like* women, for they have a law against concubines. I know this is true, for one of Mother's physicians is a Hebrew and he told me himself, when I offered to give him one of Nefertari's maids if he would tell Mother that I should get ill if I had to spend so much time memorizing the balanced numbers contained in a pyramid."

"So Nefertari need have no fear that, through the influence of Hebrews, you will fail to love her enough."

"But will she love me enough? Neb, I am not easy to love," he said, suddenly forlorn. "Sensen does, and you do—I never knew you did until today—and Father does."

"And Nefertari does."

He looked up at me and his eyes were troubled. "I *think* she does—and she thinks so too. But it is difficult for her to be sure, because she doesn't like her mother, and she wants to be married, and she wants to marry a prince. But I want to be loved for what I am and not for what I pretend to be." He sighed. "It is very hard to be really loved, Neb."

I felt that curious sense of authority which is insistent as the rising Nile and as unconcerned with logic as the flowering of a lotus.

"One day, Ramoses, you will find love."

He questioned me eagerly, but I, much as I longed to tell him of the time, and the place, and the circumstance, could say no more.

IX

PHARAOH HAS SPOKEN

IF, my dear Nephew, you have reached this point without becoming unduly impatient with my story, would you prefer to read next of my journey with Sensen to the Living Water, or to learn something of Ramoses' first day as Pharoah?

You may well ask yourself, for I am unlikely to be available for questioning, how I am in a position to offer you these alternatives. How could I know what he experienced while I was occupied with teaching untrained litter-bearers to keep in step, and subduing my impatience at the implacable independence of pack-donkeys?

Truth, being real and therefore intangible, cannot be tested in a crucible or weighed in a merchant's scales. It shares, however, the needs of the goldsmith, who demands complexity in service of his simplicity. If Pharaoh wears a pectoral, even one so conventional as a hawk with outspread wings, he knows that the materials of which it is constructed have come from sources separated by many days' journey: lapis lazuli and haematite, malachite and glass, amethyst and cornelian.

It is in this same tradition that I shall attempt to give you the truth concerning Ramoses. Some details of the pattern came to me out of his own mouth, and often his heart also, many years later: some were described by Sensen, whose dreams were often clearly cut as the inscription on Hatshepsut's obelisk at Karnak. Karaden provided certain useful material—he can always be relied upon to be entirely factual, which frequently diminishes the value of his evidence. I have done no more than disregard the petty confines of precedence and set, in what little gold I have, certain emotions of a man who closely concerns you and appears to be in increasing danger of being judged as a man by the Gods and as a God by men, instead of as Pharaoh.

Whatever your inclination, I shall now tell you what befell Ramoses after I watched him take the path to Thebes—and Egypt.

"Pharaoh has spoken!" declaimed Ramoses, as though the standing corn were a hostile crowd he must subdue to his will. A small breeze rippled the field and the tall stalks bowed their heads. He walked on towards Thebes, feeling more confident.

"Pharaoh has spoken!" said Ramoses, to a bull calf. He spoke mildly, as a Captain might speak to an over-zealous Leader of a Hundred who must be reminded that there are occasions when the right of a subordinate to give his opinion shall not be exercised.

"Pharaoh has spoken!" he said to a white goat whose twin kids played at her side. Now he was Ramoses the husband, indulgently admonishing his queen for expecting him to flatter her by argument when he was preoccupied by matters of grave importance.

Beside the path was a block of granite that, two years earlier on the way to Karnak, had slid from its greased rollers, killing two men and so been abandoned. Even though it had sunk during the inundations to a third of its width it still dominated the placid fields.

"Pharaoh has spoken!" the boy shouted. But the crushing weight was implacable as his mother, so his voice seemed no stronger than the cheep of a quail chick.

"I hate you!" he cried out, and kicked the invulnerable stone. Then he began to sob, because the pain of a splintered toenail was not sharp enough to dull his increasing fear. He saw a stick that some herd-boy had dropped. He broke it in two and crossed his arms on his breast, as though the pieces of smooth wood were the Crook and Flail, while he vowed that from the granite he would cause to be made a statue of himself, so large that in seeing it he would forget that he had wept because it challenged the Royal Foot.

As he drew nearer to Thebes he became increasingly lonely. The field-workers' huts were deserted, and not even a child watched the cattle that strayed across the road. In the distance he heard a thin sound as though a thousand thousand birds were lost in sorrow. It was then he realized that the people had gone to the city to join in the lamentation for the death of Pharaoh.

He looked down at his scratched and dusty legs, the thin legs of a boy for all that he was tall for fifteen. He longed to let them do what they wanted to do—to run, very fast, to find Neb. Before he could stop them they carried him a few swift paces and he had to force them to a standstill as though they were horses almost too wild to hold.

"I cannot follow Neb," he said aloud. "If Neb knew I had

run away he would have to come back and then Sensen would die. If I killed Sensen because I am a coward it would be worse than Mother killing them—for at least Mother is brave. Perhaps the Gods are not very angry with wicked people who are also brave."

He came to the river and saw a trading-barge. It would be easy to hide among the jars of grain. He was strong and intelligent. If he stayed with the barge until it reached one of the smaller Nomes he could easily earn his food by looking after horses—or even cattle, if there was no one rich enough to own a chariot.

He heard some one crying. A girl, her leg wrapped in a dirty rag, was staring at him from the doorway of a hut at the end of the quay.

She stopped crying and rubbed her cheek with the back of a small and grimy hand. "Are you hurt too, boy?"

He knew she must have noticed his toe which had begun to bleed again. "It's nothing," he said hastily. "What is the matter with your leg?" He did not want to know, but it was the kind of question that Sensen would have asked.

"There is a sore on it, so I cannot walk very far, that is why they would not take me with them to the city."

She began to cry again.

"Does it hurt you much?" he said anxiously.

"No, I am used to it. When the bandage falls off it looks horrid, but this one is nearly new and will last many days."

"Then why are you crying?"

She gazed at him in astonishment. "Everyone is crying. Don't you know that our father is dead?"

He nearly said, "My father is dead too," when he suddenly realized they were both thinking of the same man.

So that is what the common people felt about Pharaoh! He wasn't remote, and wise, and all-powerful, as Seti had been even to his own children—or had been until he was dead. To this girl, Pharaoh was a father for whom she wept real tears when there was no audience to see her weep. So the Eighty Days Lamentation was more, much more, than a formal gesture of respect.

"Pharaoh has a son," he said diffidently.

She wept afresh, rocking herself from side to side as though she held a broken doll in her arms.

"He who would have been our new Father is dead too. He and his wife, the Princess-who-makes-the-heart-sing, were eaten by a crocodile and there is no longer anyone to protect us from the barbarians."

"Pharaoh had a younger son," said Ramoses.

65

She looked round to make sure they were alone, then whispered, "He is said to be like his mother—and no one will weep in their hearts for the Queen Tuaa. You must never tell anyone I said that, though I have heard people whisper it up and down the river. I live on that barge with my brother and my uncle and I have been to many places," she added by way of explanation.

"You must not believe all you hear about Prince Ramoses," he said fervently.

"You know him?" She said this only to tease him, for how could a boy who looked so tired and dusty know a prince?

"His lion boy is a friend of mine."

She looked awed: obviously it was an event of importance to speak with a boy who knew someone who had spoken to a prince.

"The prince has killed three lions in an afternoon: if Egypt is ever in danger he will kill many barbarians," he boasted.

She shrugged. "If the Queen tells him to do so I expect he will obey her. Everyone says that even the great Seti, the Son of Horus, let her rule him."

"No one ruled Seti!" he exclaimed with a flare of anger. How dare this child presume to judge his father!

"There is no need to be cross," she said gently. "Grownups are so often cross; it is silly for children to make each other unhappy."

"I must go now; will you be all right alone?" He wanted to run away again, but this time from a girl who kept on reminding him of the slow, agonizing battle of youth against blind age.

"I am used to being alone." She said it to put him at ease, but her quiet acceptance made his own fear of loneliness seem more unbearable.

"I have to go or my mother will be worried." He despised himself for not having the courage to admit that every moment he delayed would arm Tuaa with fresh anger.

She smiled. "You had better tidy yourself or wash before she sees you. When my mother was alive she was pleased when I tried to keep clean."

Before Ramoses reached the outskirts of the city, he stopped by a boundary stone which bore the cartouche of Seti and touching it said, "Thank you very much, Father, for sending me to that girl so that he could tell me I must try to look like Pharaoh before any one will listen to me—even when I say 'Pharaoh has spoken.' Now I understand how you will tell me things even when I do not hear your voice."

He wanted to be like Neb, but a Neb who could enjoy killing barbarians who needed killing, so it was right that he should wear Neb's clothes.

It was very important that no one recognized him before he was ready. Would Tuaa have sent people to search for him? She would have to pretend he was in the Palace, except to those who knew her secret plans. But how many knew? Surely very few could be trusted with such dangerous news . . . was it Neb or Father who had said that his enemies were already divided against each other by jealousy?

He was hurrying along a narrow lane when ahead he heard the regular tread of soldiers. On each side of him were high walls that enclosed the gardens of court officials. He saw an overhanging branch and pulled himself up until he could scramble to the top of the right-hand wall. He lay flat, until the soldiers passed below him. There were ten of them: too many to have been sent to search for him.

He heard a woman weeping and, peering down through heavy leaves which had already begun to droop with the morning heat, saw Tausert, wife of the Keeper of the Royal Granaries, sitting on a folding stool in the shade of a small portable awning.

Tears, large black tears, slid smoothly as onyx beads from a greased string down her immobile face. She was studying the effect in a silver mirror held by one of her maids. Another maid stood ready with a bowl of steaming water and a linen towel.

"Too much kohl, you fool," said Tausert petulantly, holding up her face to be washed and dried. Then she snatched up the kohl-stick from a table that was covered with ointment pots and flasks of unguents and carefully outlined her eyes again.

"Pharaoh is dead!" intoned the girls, their shoulders heaving in simulated sobs.

"Louder!" snapped Tausert. "If you cannot cry for Pharaoh you shall have something else to cry for!"

She blinked her eyes rapidly, but the tears refused to flow to her satisfaction.

"Cry until I cry too," she demanded, then pinched the arm of the girl holding the mirror, who began to sob in earnest.

Ramoses felt more cheerful. He had always disliked Tausert and been surprised that his mother trusted her.

"Cry louder, you fools! Are you such ingrates that you wish your mistress to be shamed because she cannot weep properly at the lamentations?" Her voice became shrill with self-pity. "Do you wish to be sneered at by the servants of

67

the wife of the Chariots, or the Royal Barges, or even those who serve that pallid creature who contents the chief scribe! *She* could weep easily enough if she thought how her face resembles a bowl of sour milk!"

The other girl giggled nervously, then squealed as Tausert's hand left a reddening print across her cheek.

"You dare to laugh when Pharaoh is dead! Shall you be whipped, or must I tell your master that you have dishonored our house?"

The girl flung herself on the ground at Tausert's feet, imploring mercy.

Ramoses was so angry that he nearly betrayed his presence. Then he realized that a similar performance must be usual at Tausert's toilet, for the girl with the mirror looked bored instead of frightened.

"Get up, you misbegotten daughter of a hippopotamus, and stop groveling in the dust!"

The girls sobbed louder and louder, and Tausert's expression became intent, as though she were trying to catch a tune she was expected to sing and had no ear for music. Her eyelids flickered like the wings of a bat, she leaned forward, the muscles of her jaw and neck taut with effort.

She seized the mirror, peered into it, then flung it at a cat that was basking in the sun. The cat screeched and ran up a tree.

"Fetch me an onion," she shrilled. "And if either of you let it be known that I hid an onion in my mourning flowers I shall sell you both—to a Nubian, old and fat and horribly diseased!"

Ramoses felt happier when he swung down into the lane. It was comforting to learn that he had been wiser than Tuaa, even in so small a thing as judging the quality of Tausert.

He went through an orchard, keeping in the shadow of mulberry trees that bordered the central water-channel. Neb's garden was so familiar that for a moment he expected to see Sensen there. He noticed that a towel trailed in the water among the stalks of broken lotus and wondered who had fallen into the pool.

He looked into Sensen's room and saw it was meticulously tidy. Had Meena tidied it before she left with the pack-donkeys, or were the other servants in her confidence? He wished he had thought to ask Neb. Surely Neb's servants could be trusted, or must he be on his guard aganst every one?

He went quietly through the ante-room into the main hall. He heard voices from the kitchen quarters, cheerful voices. If whoever was speaking believed that Neb and Sensen were dead, surely they would be lamenting? He crept closer to the half-open door and listened.

A woman and a man were arguing. He recognized the voice of Kia, the chief cook and kinswoman to Meena. "You can stay, but I'm going to follow them, desert or no desert," she said.

"The boys won't want to come with us," her husband grumbled. "Why should they, now that we have all got enough to live on without working for the rest of our lives?"

"Buy your land, and may your radishes wilt and your wine sour before it reaches the storeroom, but I am not going to let Meena look after their kitchen. It is only my broth that she fancies when she is ill, and he likes my cooking."

"Wouldn't you prefer a house of your own?"

"With only you to grumble at? You, who don't know the difference between my cakes and the things any one can buy from a market stall!"

"Then I suppose I shall have to come with you—me and the boys and their wives. You are a good woman, though don't remind me I said so when next you plague me when I don't wake early enough to pick your lettuce before the sun dries the dew."

Ramoses heard the chuck of liquid being poured. "Pity we shan't be able to take this wine with us," said the man. "Try as I will to use it, there will be years of good drinking left when Hiboe comes to fetch us."

So they knew about the Living Water! Ramoses pushed the door wider, and while the old couple stared at him open-mouthed, he filled a cup with the wine and raised it in a toast: "To the Prince and Princess—may they live long to the sweet singing of their hearts."

He sat on the edge of the table, between a hunk of cheese and a platter of broken meats.

"Do not be frightened," he said cheerfully. "I saw my brother this morning and they have made a safe start on their journey."

"You *know?*" the woman gasped.

"Yes, but don't talk so loud another time or someone we *can't* trust might overhear."

"Does—does the Queen know?" The man's voice trembled as he asked the question.

"No," said Ramoses briskly. "And if she ever finds out it will be annoying—to say the least of it, so watch how much you drink unless your door is barred and the shutters too."

He paused and took another gulp of wine to show them

that he had too strong a head to fear it could ever betray his tongue.

"Have you—have you heard that Pharaoh is dead?" faltered Kia.

There was a pause in which was no movement or sound.

"I am Pharaoh," said Ramoses.

Less than an hour later he was ready to go to the Palace. At first he had intended only to make himself presentable, but with the help of the two who had proved themselves so much more than Sensen's servants he had dressed himself in the ceremonial clothes that his brother had worn when representing Pharaoh in Audience.

The kilt of fine linen was embroidered with gold bees, and the hilt of the short dagger was inlaid with lapis lazuli. The pectoral was also richly inlaid, the outspread wings of the hawk brilliant against his smooth skin. He chose a warrior head-dress striped in blue and gold, and his sandals were of gilded leather with studs of turquoise.

"You should have a standard-bearer," said Kia, already as easy with him as she had been with Neb.

"Shall I? No, let Pharaoh be guarded only by his lions. Tell my lion boy to bring them here."

The man ran off to obey the first command of his new Pharaoh.

"Is there nothing I can do for you?" asked Kia.

He thought a moment, then said, "I wish I felt as confident as I hope I look—but I am hollow as a gourd. Do you think if I ate something it might make me sick?"

"Hunger takes the heart out of the bravest," she said, and hurried away to return with some of the cold meat and bread.

He ate with vigorous appetite, and then took a little more wine which warmed his courage.

"Now I am ready for my lions—and my mother," he said.

Kia fell on her knees and tried to kiss his foot. He raised her up and patted her affectionately on the shoulder. "Tell Neb," he said, and swallowed convulsively. "Tell Neb that I shall not betray the honor he has conferred on me."

Outside the door leading to the Palace garden the lion boy waited. The lion and lioness purred a low thunder of welcome to their master. He caressed them until they were content to follow him.

There were no gardeners to be seen, for during the first days of mourning no one except an embalmer may follow his usual occupation. The shutters were closed in every window of the Palace. No pennants fluttered above the entrance pylon. Even the lamentation of the crowds outside the wall seemed dulled by the noonday heat.

On the flagstones of the outer courtyard the tread of his sandals and the heavy paws of his lions sounded unnaturally loud.

The great bronze doors which led into the central hall of the Palace swung slowly open.

Tuaa stood watching him. "She looks old," he thought. "Did she really love my father, or is it guilt which makes her look so old?"

"He is dead," she said, and her voice was flat as water stored too long in a jar.

"He told me that he had died," said the boy. "He told me that I am Pharaoh."

She pretended not to understand what he claimed, but now there was fear in her eyes.

"Where have you been? How dare you leave the Palace when he was dying!"

"Pharaoh does not explain his actions to any one."

"You fool!" she said bitterly. "Must you spoil all I have done for you by trying to pretend you no longer heed me? When did you leave the Palace?"

"Last night."

"Before Neb . . . *before* Neb and Sensen went on the river."

"Before Neb and Sensen . . . were drowned."

"Who told you they are dead?" The question flicked out like a snake's tongue.

"A girl who lives on a grain-barge." It gave him fresh strength to be able to deceive her with the truth.

"I have trained you well, my son—almost too well. It is an ill omen for the enemies of Egypt that the heart of Pharaoh is so cold that he can amuse himself by dressing up in the clothes of his dead brother, while the embalmers grow impatient because his father's body must await his pleasure."

She began to laugh, laughter harsh as the sound of bone splintering.

"And I used to mock you for being weak! Is any woman born who has the wit to judge the quality of such a son?"

She seized him by the arms, shaking him in a passion of fury—fury, or what was it? Her eyes were hard as black glass: her tongue ran to and fro over her dry, pale lips, as though she had fever. He was more afraid of her than ever before: then revulsion was stronger than fear, and with revulsion came pity. He had seen a woman look like that before

—a woman clutching at a soldier in the doorway of a hovel near the Warriors' Quarters.

He was no longer only her son, he was a man: and the man was Pharaoh.

Not until he was alone with the body of his father did he allow his heart its freedom. With a gesture he had sent the fanbearers and the attendant priests from the quiet room. Lamps at the head and foot of the bed burned with a strong aromatic scent.

He shivered, remembering where he had encountered the same pungent odor before, when Tuaa had made him watch a corpse prepared for its purification.

Already death had touched Seti's face with faint blue bruises. A fillet of sacred linen held up the jaw, and on the eyelids were gold discs inscribed with the names of the prow and the oars of the Boat of the Dead.

Seti wore the Double Crown, and in his hands rested the Crook and the Flail; until his son should carry them to Egypt's honor.

"Father," whispered the boy. "Father, can you hear me?"

He fell on his knees and pressed his forehead against the feet that now wore their Golden Sandals beyond the Causeway of the Gods.

He heard only the beat of his own heart and the buzzing of a blow-fly that was drowsy with incense.

"Don't come back here, Father," he said in desperate urgency. "Stay in your tomb if you can't find Neb's mother yet."

He stood up, trying to feel very tall and independent. How could he have been so cruel as to ask his father to come here to comfort him, to come back to the body which might send to his soul an echo of the knives and hooks of the embalmers?

"I am not afraid," he said. "You need not worry about me, Father."

He took a breath and prayed that his voice would not tremble. "Pharaoh has spoken," said Ramoses, and knew he spoke the truth.

X

THE LIVING WATER

IT is unnecessary to describe in detail the route we took to the Living Water, for you, my dear Nephew, will not be obliged to go there in secrecy. It is probable that you already know the place, for I have instructed Karaden that it is to be held by him for your use and on your fourteenth birthday is to become your personal property, provided that in his opinion you will maintain the traditions which I have tried to foster. Although its boundaries are so restricted that you could walk round them between dawn and sunset, it will prove refreshing to have at least one property where you rule because you are chosen only in virtue of affection.

The first nine days proved an increasing drain on Sensen's energies, and I was greatly relieved when Hiboe announced that he considered it wiser for us to continue the journey by river. He left us encamped near a village, and returned the following night with the news that he had arranged for all of us, including the pack-donkeys, to join a train of empty barges which were returning to the stone-quarries near the First Cataract.

He told the overseer that I was going South to choose bulls required by the Keeper of the Royal Herds, but I soon realized that the unspoken sympathy we received was due to the belief that we were nobles who had incurred the Queen's displeasure.

I rebuked Hiboe for what I thought must have been lack of discretion, and at last made him admit that he had deliberately given this impression because our original plan of posing as petty merchants had already proved so unconvincing as to arouse dangerous suspicion.

"It is bitter," I said to Sensen, "to find that I am not only a failure as a prince, but also in the insignificant role you and Meena have chosen for me."

She was always gentle, even when jealousy of Ramoses poisoned the wells of my understanding until I had to go for long, solitary walks, striving through physical effort to free myself from the claws of hatred. Sometimes I almost believed

73

that it was not jealousy but the goddess Sekmet who tried to drive me back to the North where I could still hope to rally the Army of the Reed to my standard. Had there been a local temple with a sanctuary dedicated either to Sekmet or her dark consort Set, I should probably have attempted a blood sacrifice, of some black animal, that might induce her to destroy not only Tuaa but Ramoses. Fortunately the lack of facilities made this unpleasing gesture impracticable.

In my defense I must point out the subtlety of Sekmet's arguments. When I thought of Ramoses with tenderness, Sekmet rebuked me for having delivered him into the hands of Tuaa. When I honored his courage, she asked how I could bear to live with myself, knowing that he was snared in the net of conspiracy from which I had escaped like a thief who has greased his body to evade the grasp of honest men.

I became increasingly morose, until Sensen wept in secret —and Sekmet told me she wept because through loyalty to so weak a husband she had sent herself into the exile only he deserved. I even tried to belittle Sensen, pretending that I was a sacrifice to her ill-health: and though it shames me to write this even after twenty-four years, there were times when I drank deep of the curdled milk of self-righteousness—a horrid draught which lies uneasy in much stronger stomachs than mine.

As work in the stone-quarries was suspended during the Eighty Days, the overseer, being a kindly man, took the opportunity to rest his rowers. Every night we tied up near a village and I, eager for news of Thebes, used to visit the wine-shop either alone or with Hiboe. I learned to drink beer and date wine as though I enjoyed it, but I envied Hiboe his ability to talk as an equal with the common people—Hiboe who used to amuse me because to the other servants he had seemed almost more royal than Pharaoh!

Fact and rumor, a few words in one village, fragments of a longer tale in another, began to form a pattern. Sensen did not have to pretend that she was happy, but sang because joy had begun to bud in her heart, and I, albeit grudgingly, recognized that I had no excuse to regret my decision . . . I even made myself believe that it had not been made for me.

The people had expected Ramoses to be no more than a puppet, and every incident which showed he stood firm against Tuaa excited their admiration. For instance, the story of how he offered the wife of the Keeper of the Granaries refreshment, and then set before her a bowl of onion soup, lost nothing in the telling. Had he in fact caused onions to be planted in her flower-beds, or was this an embellishment of

74

the tale? There seemed no doubt that her two maidservants had been given, in obedience to a Royal Request, to the Princess Nefertari, and that their despondent donor had, on the pretext of illness, withdrawn to the seclusion of her sister's house near Memphis.

Though there had been no proclamation, it was already known that Pharaoh intended to marry the Princess Nefertari on her fifteenth birthday, a month after the sealing of Seti's tomb. Somewhat to my surprise, Sensen received this news half-heartedly.

"But you seemed so sure they loved each other," I said.

"I am sure they do." She hesitated. "Neb, am I really sure, or do I think it only because it ought to be true?"

"He will never be able to rule Tuaa unless he has a wife he can trust. Sensen, how could I ever have been jealous of him when I have you!"

"I have always had you," she said, "which is why it has been very easy not to be jealous." She laughed ruefully. "Oh, Neb, how easily one lies when one dares to boast! Of course I have been jealous! Every time I saw Nefertari use a throwing-stick or drive a chariot I was bitter because she had never been so tired that even loving was a weariness. It even pleased me that sometimes Ramoses preferred to talk to me instead of being with her."

"Why did Ramoses choose her?"

"He did not have a wide choice."

I smiled. "Egyptian princes do not usually lack women's favor."

"I meant girls whom it would have been possible for Ramoses to choose. Don't you see how difficult it was for him? The daughters of women who are acceptable to Tuaa are all pale shadows of their mothers. Consider your half-sister, who hardly dared to speak in case she said something foolish, and was detested by her servants whom she bullied in a pathetic attempt to restore her self-respect. Were Tuaa not her aunt, Nefertari would never have been accepted at Court."

"They are both very young for marriage," I said, forgetting that I had been only a year older when I married Sensen. "Will she be clever enough to pretend a little awe of him?"

"Pretend?"

I kissed her. "My love, am I unaware that all fond wives cherish their husbands as children?"

She blushed. "How foolish you are, my Neb—but we were talking of Nefertari. I wish I had warned her before we left Thebes. To Ramoses she must symbolize the Crook while he is the Flail, the female and the male: only together can they make of Egypt a strong family."

On the seventeenth day we left the barge, to the surprise of the overseer who obviously wondered why persons who had lavishly rewarded him for his hospitality should disembark at so obscure a town. Knowing that he would inquire about us we took the track leading South. There were several small estates near the river which might reasonably have been our destination, and only after sunset did we turn up a dry wadi leading into the hills. Here we camped for three days, while Hiboe took the pack-donkeys loaded with water-jars and fodder, which he left at the places he chose for two overnight halts, so that we could travel easily instead of having to make a forced march through lack of wells.

The track we followed was seldom used, for the mines which it had served had been abandoned during the reign of Horemheb. The country became increasingly arid, and only Hiboe's assurance that we would be pleasantly surprised checked Meena's mounting disapproval.

I knew that the same architect who had supervised the chain of wells along the trade-route to the Narrow Sea had found underground springs which had made possible this place that was now mine, and had once been my mother's. Five hundred freemen had worked on a dam for five years, and the secret that it belonged to Pharaoh had been kept faithfully. Yet as the barren rocks shimmered in the heat my anxiety increased. I concealed it as best I could, but Sensen's determined gaiety showed that I had not done so with much success.

On the morning of the third day we left the trail and clambered over loose stones up the bed of an ancient stream. It was too steep for the litters, but Sensen said she was eager for a chance to climb with me, and even insisted on helping to urge the donkeys by cajolery instead of a stick applied with monotonous regularity to their hindquarters. Meena plodded behind us, tight-lipped when she was not muttering forebodings I tried not to overhear.

The cliffs narrowed: far above us a solitary hawk seemed painted on the hard blue sky. I shivered, reminded of the outspread wings of vultures on the roof of the passage leading to Seti's burial chamber.

Hiboe, who was leading, turned towards the towering wall of rock at whose foot were several large boulders. He thrust against one much larger than the rest, which rolled smoothly aside to disclose the mouth of a tunnel.

"There is another way," he said, "but it is steep and difficult. This was cut as the entrance of the Queen. She used to say that it was the gateway to her little heaven."

He gave me a lamp and then stood back to allow Sensen and I to lead the way together. I heard him tell Meena not to be impatient to follow us.

Sensen took my hand, and as we went along the sloping passage I almost expected to see mulberry trees painted on the wall.

"It is not at all like the entrance to a tomb," she said. "I think it is much more exciting than an ordinary way to a house. It will be fun, living in a cave."

"With donkeys?" I asked, pointing to a pile of fresh droppings on the sandy floor.

"I like donkeys," said Sensen firmly.

The passage kept to an easy gradient: only later did I discover that it could have been much shorter if steps had not been impractical for the horses and pack-donkeys which also used it. In front of us we saw sunlight like a gold door.

For a moment we were both dazzled, and I knew that Sensen shared my sense of being suddenly caught into a vivid dream.

Instead of lion-tawny sand and the bleak thorn-bush we saw a lake, the vivid blue of polished glass. Behind us were cliffs; before us, like the rim of a cup, a barrage of dressed stone enclosed the bright water.

A broad path led down in a half circle between water and rock. We had found the Living Water, now for the first time we saw the place it had brought to life.

In a natural amphitheater was a village set among pastures and gardens, neat and beguiling as a child's toy. The smoke of cooking-fires rose placidly in the still air; shade trees were green as the neck feathers of a mallard, rows of vegetables meticulous as smoothly combed hair.

An avenue of flowering acacias led to a long, one-storied house painted the color of the bud of a pink lotus, and the forecourt was thronged with our people who were singing to welcome us home.

It is not easy to remember what I had expected to find at the end of our journey: a modest house, a patch of cultivation sufficient for the needs of a few old servants, a small herd of goats. We had decided that Pasar the steward would probably resemble Kia's husband; honest, faithful, a little garrulous: anxious to please but secretly dismayed that we had come to disturb his placid routine.

The real Pasar looked no more than thirty though he was fifty-three: he spoke like a Royal Scribe and had the quiet authority of a Nomarch. He made us feel that he was both our host and our servant, and equally content in either role.

On the first morning he came to ask whether I would like to visit the High Village, saying that at Meena's suggestion he had delayed the formal presentation of the people until Sensen had rested.

We took a narrow, zigzag path up the face of the Eastern cliffs and came to a wide plateau with low hills on the horizon. In the middle distance were groves of date palms and I could see both large and small cattle pastured in their shade.

"Is there no end to the surprises you have in store for us?" I said.

He smiled. "The Queen, your mother, loved the Living Water. It was the wish of Seti that nothing should be spared to make it even more pleasant in her sight."

"It is not for me to question the wisdom of priests, but surely it is better for a place of happy memory to have new delights for the soul to visit than to be unchanging as the wall painting of a tomb?"

He pointed to the groves. "They were planted because once the Queen said that shade would be pleasant when she came here to watch the sunset. So I looked for another source of water. For two years I found none, though many wells were dug, but in the third year the sand was moist at thirty cubits, and the springs of sweet water are sufficient for three wells."

As we came nearer I could see houses among the trees. He pointed to them. "Here live the herdsmen, and those who make the date-wine we barter for grain in the riverside villages."

"If you barter with the villages, surely our arrival may arouse unwelcome curiosity?" I said with a sudden return of anxiety.

"I take only a small quantity at any one time and place, such as would be sufficient for the needs of the thirty who live up here. Only our own people know we are more than thirty—to be exact we number one hundred and fifty-two, or one hundred and fifty-three if the Potter's wife has had her baby since this morning."

"How are we so many, Pasar?"

"It was the Queen's wish that no work should be done here except by freemen. Is a man free if he is sent into exile? And to those who felt the peace of her memory there could be no other place which did not seem alien."

"Then how is it that there are not thousands trying to join us?"

"When a child is born provision is made so that there shall be food and work for it without another receiving less than before. We had no need of many workers, so each man or woman I chose was skilled, and willing to teach his skill to whoever wished to share it. Our woolen stuffs, and our glazed pottery, are eagerly sought in the marketplaces of Thebes, though none know where they are made. Seti gave into my keeping much treasure to fulfill the Queen's wishes, but it increases year by year." He smiled. "The tallies are painted in five colors on slips of ivory, for even the scribe enjoys his work."

We shared the noon meal with the people of the High Village: a kid cooked with dried figs, a soup of lentils and garlic, cakes flavored with sesame. The men were strong and clear-eyed, the women gentle, the children gay as young gazelles.

While I inspected the stalled cattle, Pasar said tentatively, "There were horses in the time of your father, though only two pairs, a black and a red. They had the intelligence of women and the courage of lions."

"You love horses?" He had no need to answer, so I said, "Then we must have horses, for Sensen enjoys riding in a chariot and I can see that the desert is firm and not too stony."

Nothing would content him, though he tried to conceal his eagerness, until we had paced out the ground for new stables and marked with pegs where walls would be built to protect the yard from leopards.

"There are very few leopards," he said, "but it is not wise to let horses run free at night."

I noticed a quantity of mud-bricks neatly stacked beside an unfinished house. "We can start on the stables tomorrow—I am glad that among our people there are some who are not so talented that it would be a waste of their time to set mud in molds."

Pasar smiled. "Ptah makes the hair of a man, not only his eyes. Is it for us to decide whether the goldsmith deserves greater honor than the stonemason, providing each keeps an appropriate standard of perfection?"

"I am rebuked—and most rightly."

"Your words remind me of those your father spoke when I suggested a different site for his house from the one he had selected. At first he was a little annoyed. 'Pasar,' he said, 'is it you or I who will enjoy the view from the Queen's window?'

79

I replied, 'It is your nostrils not mine which will be offended if there is not sufficient gradient for the water-channel to run swiftly through the drain under your privy-room.' "

I laughed, the first real laugh I had felt for many days.

"Pasar," I said, "you will do much more for us than protect our nostrils: you will keep our hearts free from the cobwebs of complacency."

XI

THE GIRL FROM THE GRAIN-BARGE

FOR the first three days of his reign Ramoses did not see Nefertari alone. He longed to open his heart to her, for he was exhausted by the effort of ceaselessly maintaining his role of sudden maturity. But Nefertari was more eager to become the wife of the new Ramoses than to console the boy: perhaps she thought that if she allowed him to admit, even to her, that he still lacked self-confidence, he might revert to his habit of obedience to Tuaa.

Before he realized she did not want to listen, he told her about the girl who lived on the grain-barge.

"She was sent by my father," he said eagerly. "If I had not talked with her I might never have thought of wearing Neb's clothes."

She was hurt because he had not turned to her instead of to a stranger, and so in a voice sharper than she intended said, "Seti would not be likely to use a crippled girl as his messenger—nor to be pleased that his son takes advice from one of the common people."

"So you refuse to believe I spoke with my father after he was dead?" His temper flared. "I suppose you also think I lied about going to the tomb! No doubt I hid in a hayloft because I was afraid of seeing him die, and then stayed there all night like a child in dread of punishment."

"Of course you went to the tomb," she said hastily. "No one but you could have been brave enough to sleep there. . . ."

"So you think it was only a dream! Did I dream Neb too, or is he only another figment of my fevered imagination?"

"Of course Neb was real!" She flung her arms round him. "Dear Ramoses, please stop being horrid. What does it matter if you were awake or asleep when Seti said you were the new Pharaoh? You *are* Pharaoh, nothing else is at all important."

"It is odd that Father did not send me to you . . . or perhaps it is really not so odd as I thought," he said coldly.

"Then if you like that girl so much you had better show your gratitude!"

Nefertari was close to tears, though too proud to shed them. When he did not answer she tried to make him more angry, for they had often quarreled and found swift reconciliation. "The Royal Treasure is now at your command. What would she like? A roll of linen for a clean bandage every day, or a string of beads so that her brother will not be ashamed to show her to his companions?"

Until then Ramoses had intended to do no more than make some suitable provision for the girl—a small farm for her family, or a new barge, with permission to trade in the larger towns, if she preferred living on the river.

"She will need far more than a roll of linen if she is to be suitably dressed among the women of your household. As to the bandages, whether they are to be used will depend on the advice of my physician."

"Ramoses, don't be ridiculous! How could a grubby child find a place among my women? Or do you mean she can work in the kitchens? I will arrange that to please you, but I think she would be much happier among her own kind."

"You flatter me, Nefertari! Since when has one who has earned the gratitude of Pharaoh been unworthy to peel onions for your soup?"

"I don't eat onions!"

"Then I suggest you seek advice from Tausert, as you have not the wit to weep for your own stupidity."

He stormed out of the room, and Nefertari wept.

The quarrel might still have left no lasting scar if Tuaa had not found her crying, and been clever enough to get the angry girl to tell her what had happened. For the first time she realized that it would be wiser to use her future daughter-in-law than to oppose her.

"I will go to Ramoses," she said consolingly. "He is a little intoxicated with his new power, but in domestic matters he will still listen to me. Together, but only together, we can save him making foolish mistakes."

"It was mostly my fault," said Nefertari forlornly, suddenly afraid that she might have said far more than she intended.

"Who is this girl, and why does my son feel grateful to her? If she is the one I chose for him as a concubine, two years ago, you have no cause for anxiety—her child died and if he is still thinking of her she can easily be removed."

With profound relief Nefertari knew that she had not said too much—though already she regretted saying anything. Why had she been so foolish as not to ascribe her tears to grief at the death of Seti? In future she must be far more careful.

"The girl is not important—the sister of one of the boys with whom Ramoses used to set snares for wild-fowl. He wanted me to take her into my household. It was silly of me to take offense: she could join the sewing-women, or learn to make garlands, if she shows any special skill with flowers. Please don't mention it to Ramoses . . . he will be angry with me if he thinks I run to you with our petty quarrels."

"It is of course as you wish, dear child," said Tuaa, then hurried away to seek out her son.

She found him at last in the room where the tallies were kept. He had been wondering whether he could, without loss of dignity, consult Karaden as to how much he should give to the girl without being absurdly over-generous. What *would* be wealth to them? A collar of gold, or three collars? What was the value in *utens* of a farm, with animals to stock it? Why had no one taught him the value of things? In imagination he saw himself choosing a bunch of radishes in the market-place and in exchange offering a tusk of ivory while the bystanders tittered.

The door opened. "So that is where you are!" said Tuaa. "I have been looking for you everywhere."

"I regret, my honored Mother, that I dared to move freely in my palace without first asking your permission."

"Now don't be tiresome! You have already upset Nefertari, but I have no intention of letting you disturb *me*."

He sat on the cedar-wood chest which held the scrolls which recorded the revenues of the Royal Estates of the South.

"I think," he said smoothly, "that we should come to a more exact definition of our rival authority. Let it be understood that although you will have jurisdiction in your own household you have none in mine. I asked a favor of Nefertari. She preferred not to grant it, so I will make different arrangements. The Little Palace belonged to Neb, who left no direct heir, so it has now reverted to me. Tomorrow it will have a new owner. Anyone who inquires into her antecedents will incur my personal displeasure, and have to make a substantial restitution—a tenth, say, of all they possess."

"Ramoses, how dare you insult Nefertari! Or have you changed your mind and decided that you are too young for marriage?"

"A man is old enough to marry when he cannot be dominated by women. It seems that few men achieve this desirable condition, but I consider myself to have been successfully weaned."

"You have been remarkably sly," she said, but there was pride of him rather than anger in her eyes. "May I venture to ask the name of the woman who has so cleverly taught my son the art of manhood?"

To his acute embarrassment, Ramoses realized that he had no idea what the girl was called. "She will be known as . . . the Lady Iri. It will depend on Nefertari whether she becomes one of the Queen's Women or holds some more enviable, if less official, position."

When his mother had left him, his anger cooled. He felt ill at ease. He had been a fool, and somehow he must prevent any one finding out how much he regretted this extra responsibility he had put upon himself.

He had intended to send one of his servants to the girl, with some appropriate gift, but now he would have to go himself, for no one must ever know that the Lady Iri came from a grain-barge. It had been difficult enough to enter the Palace as Pharaoh: it would be harder to leave it without being seen.

It was easier than he expected, for he went to the Little Palace and took Kia and her husband further into his confidence. Wearing the kilt which Kia had carefully mended he set off at dusk. There were lights on the barge, and he waited until the owner and his nephew took the river-walk towards the city. The girl came out of the living-quarters in the stern and threw a bowl of fish-heads into the water. He gave a low whistle. She turned and saw him.

"Oh, it's you!" she said. "Was your mother cross?"

"She tried to be, until I said 'Pharaoh has spoken,' and then she knew I was in no mood to be argued with."

She giggled. "It's lucky your mother hasn't a proper respect for Royalty or she'd have given you a proper scolding. Even when my uncle is very drunk he won't let anyone make fun of Pharaoh . . . he used to be a soldier before Father left him the barge and sometimes he still boasts about what he did in the Army."

"Would you ever break your word to Pharaoh?" he asked.

"How could I—not that I'd ever have the chance."

"Why couldn't you?"

"Come into the light, I want to look at you," she said.

He jumped down from the quay and walked along the gangway between the grain-jars.

"You're not a foreigner," she said. "When you asked me why I wouldn't break my word to Pharaoh I thought you

84

couldn't be an Egyptian. I suppose your mother thought it so obvious that she didn't bother to tell you. Anyone who breaks his oath of allegiance stays in the Underworld forever and ever because the Gods know he can't be trusted."

"Do you ever think what you would do if the Gods gave you a wish—or several wishes?"

"Of course, don't you? Sometimes I wish I was beautiful. . . ."

"You are," said Ramoses, "so that wish wouldn't make any difference."

She blushed. "Tell that to my brother, and hear him laugh! Then I wish my leg would heal. . . ."

"That will soon happen. There are ointments which take the poison even from the wound made by a leopard's claws."

"And who would give it to me?"

"A physician."

She smiled. "Your family must be much richer than I thought or you would know that physicians don't want fish or grain for barter."

"You don't wish widely enough; it is more fun if you think of very unlikely things. What do you really want—really, not just what seems possible?"

She sat on a sack of millet and looked up at him, her eyes dark silver in the lamplight.

"I should like always to have enough to eat, without having to gut fish or grind millet for gruel. I should like to have clean clothes every day and hot water to wash in. I should like a garden where I could grow flowers. I should like a dog to sleep in my room, and to have a room to myself, and a woman to be kind to me when I am tired—Mother was always kind even when she was ill."

"All these things belong to you," he said.

"Only when I am asleep—but sometimes the day seems very long, especially when I have to stay awake until my uncle comes back from the wine-shop. Once, when I didn't hear him, he fell off the quay and nearly drowned. He beat me because he thought it was my fault, but he was sorry afterwards."

"I am not exactly who you think I am," he said hesitantly. How was he going to tell her without making her frightened?

She patted his knee. "I knew you weren't rich," she said consolingly. "My leg will heal without ointment, so please don't be sad about it."

"I can give you the ointment—and the house, and the garden, and the dog . . . I can give you everything."

"Why do you mock me? It is only a game we are playing

—the game will be spoiled if you claim it will really happen."

"It is more than a game. Will you come with me, so that I can show you the house and the woman who will look after you?"

"Your mother will not like you to bring home a stranger," she said, still afraid to believe she could be welcomed by a woman so fortunate as to own ducks and goats and a patch of vegetables.

He took her hand and helped her up to the river-walk.

"You were right about the new Pharaoh," she said. "My uncle says the wine-shops are buzzing with talk, like bees when the bean-fields flower, and every one believes that Ramoses is not going to be ruled by the old Queen."

"What do you think Ramoses is like?"

"He is very handsome, and brave, and clever. He is the Son of Horus, so the hawks wait in the sky to watch him pass, and lions trot behind him as dogs follow other men."

He looked up at the moon and laughed. "But what do you think of me?"

"You are the kindest boy I have ever met . . . and I am sure you are very brave and clever too."

He kissed her lightly on the forehead. "You would never break your word to Pharaoh. Would you break your word to me? For if you are sure you can keep it I will tell you a secret."

"I will never break my word to you. You are my first real friend."

"I can make all your wishes comes true," he said gently. "You see—my name is Ramoses."

Tuaa would have made an excellent Captain of Captains, for instead of stubbornly keeping to a prearranged plan of campaign she was prepared instantly to modify her strategy when unforeseen factors appeared.

So long as she could treat Ramoses as a child, she did not want him to marry, but now he was proving intractable the sooner he had children the better, for as a grandmother she could hope for a new sphere of influence. She respected Nefertari and hoped to find in her an intelligent pupil: therefore the girl must not be allowed to hear about Iri until after the Royal marriage.

She found this surprisingly easy to arrange, not realizing that her arguments would have carried little weight if Ramoses had not been too preoccupied to notice that Nefertari was still brooding over their quarrel.

Tuaa's reasons would have been difficult to refute even by

someone more assured than her chosen daughter-in-law. . . . "If you are here during the Lamentations Ramoses will not be able to conceal his joy at your forthcoming marriage and people may think him lacking in filial piety." . . . "There are so many officials he must see during the early days of his reign and he will grudge the time spent with them if he could be with you." And, even more subtle, "Until now he has thought of you only as a companion with whom he sails a boat or goes wild-fowling: give him a little while in which to realize how greatly he misses you and then return as a woman. He will love you more than ever before."

So Nefertari went North to the house of her father's sister, and tried to believe that choosing clothes to wear as the bride of Pharaoh was more important than being with him when he most needed her.

After she had gone, Tuaa defended her to Ramoses until he began to think she needed defense. "You cannot blame the poor child for being jealous of Iri, but you are wise, my son, not to permit her to become overpossessive."

To her intimates, Tuaa hinted that her son was so virile that his Royal Wife would not be neglected even if he took a secondary wife or many concubines. So the mothers of daughters took heart, and gave them new dresses and even necklaces and bracelets. Men, both in the houses of nobles and in the wine-shops, boasted that their Pharaoh was lusty as a young bull and would lead the Armies of Egypt to fresh conquests.

Almost the only person who for a time remained unaware of his growing reputation was Ramoses himself.

He thought Nefertari had left Thebes only because she was sulking, and so became increasingly determined that she should accept Iri as one of the Queen's Women. Before Iri would be ready to face her future companions she must be taught the etiquette and speech of the Court—and who else could he trust to teach her?

So every day he spent at least an hour with her, even though it meant curtailing an audience with some important official. No one was allowed to enter the Little Palace without his permission, and the food she ate, except fruit which he himself picked for her, was brought from the market by Kia's husband. Even the soldiers at her gates were selected from those who had been with him at the House of the Captains and whose personal loyalty was well proven.

With Iri he never had to pretend to be older, or braver, or wiser, than he felt at the moment. She was refreshing as spring water and as undemanding as a pigeon. She had dreamed many dreams of what heaven would be like, so she did not question the bounty of the Gods when they showed her that the same joy could flower on both banks of the Great River.

Ptahmas, the young physician who had saved the life of Ramoses' friend and charioteer, came to live in the house. until his skill and his ointments cleansed the open sore and she no longer walked with a limp. When there was nothing more he could do for her he expected to return to the Southern Garrison where he looked after the women of the soldiers' village, but instead Ramoses gave him the title of Personal Physician to Pharaoh.

Iri did not miss her uncle or her brother, for they had never been linked except by blood. They were told that she had been taken into the household of the wife of a minor noble; and were more than willing to accept the value of a second trading-barge instead of an extra mouth to feed.

She was nearly as tall as Sensen, and so able to wear the clothes that still filled many of the chests. At first she found it difficult to walk gracefully in a long dress of pleated mistlinen, and she wielded a fan as though the ostrich-feathers were a fly-whisk.

Ramoses told one of Tuaa's women to provide him with every unguent used by the Queen, and these he put into little alabaster jars, their lids inlaid with lapis lazuli, and took them to Iri in a gold and ivory toilet-chest which had belonged to his father's first Queen.

They laughed together like the children they still were when he showed her how to draw a line with the kohl-stick from the corners of her eyes towards the curve of her ears, and both discovered how difficult it is to get the eye-line in exact balance with the lengthened eyebrow. He practiced until he discovered how to grind malachite for her eyelids and then showed her how to put it on with the tip of a finger dipped in oil.

Her voice was already sweet, but he made her repeat poetry after him so that any rough inflection was smoothed away. Though she was docile he rejoiced that she was never subservient. She accepted everything he told her as though it were natural as dawn and sunset; and she had no fear of the future, for it did not occur to her that Nefertari could be anything but fond to one who so dearly loved her husband.

"You will not mind when I marry?" he asked, a little disappointed that she was never jealous, for all the women he had known thought love could be limited, as though it were a bowl of figs from which if one is taken there are fewer for the others to share.

"How could I, when you will be happier? It is sad for you that the Princess has had to visit her kinsmen, but soon she will return and then you will never again be lonely."

"You will be happy as one of her women?"

"Of course," she said, "for unless you had known I would be happy you would not have brought me here."

"Nefertari is a little jealous—you must not be hurt if at times she is impatient."

She laughed. "Oh dear and silly Ramoses, how could your wife be jealous of a girl who only a month ago knew nothing except how to make soup from fish and onions?"

"You must never let her know you lived on a barge," he said quickly.

"Doesn't she know?" Her eyes were troubled. "Ramoses, surely she knows all about me?"

"She doesn't," he reluctantly admitted. "I tried to tell her, but she wouldn't listen."

"Then I had better go back to my uncle."

"You said you would never be disloyal to the boy who was your first real friend—must you also desert Pharaoh?"

"You will very soon forget me. Kia said that I must always remember that I am not important to you as a person, only as a kind of doll that it pleases you to dress because you mended it."

"Then Kia is a fool! Don't you realize how much it means to me to have someone with whom I never have to pretend? Except when I am with you, or asleep, I am always Pharaoh. Hour after hour, day after day, I have to listen to people drone on about tallies, or treaties, or new roads, or the plans of architects. And I have to give judgment on matters which I do not fully understand. Only by the eyes that watch me can I guess whether I have been just or unjust, too lenient or too harsh. Iri, you can't leave me just because you may find the other women difficult!"

He paced up and down the narrow garden, while she watched him compassionately.

"Iri, because I was able to bring you here and give you things you never had before, you think Pharaoh can do anything. But he can't, Iri! Even my father couldn't talk freely to his son until after he was dead. We all honored him, but none of us really loved him. Nefertari loves me, or I think she does, but already she sees me as Pharaoh. If I tell her I am afraid she will be ashamed, as though I squatted in the public highway. I will let her share my throne, and she will

89

give me children in exchange—barter, honest as any in the marketplace—but still barter."

"Then why marry her?"

"Because at least she will not be able to forget that we were children together—it will be easier with her than with any other woman."

"Easier?"

"To secure the succession," he said bluntly. "Iri, I must be honest even if you hate me for it. Mother thinks you are my concubine, and she will warn Nefertari about you—if she hasn't done so already."

"But the Princess will believe you—of course she will believe you."

He avoided her dismayed eyes. "I shall encourage their belief—shall I tell you why? I warn you that it is not a pretty confession."

"You can tell me anything, and if you wish it shall be instantly forgotten."

He ceased his restless pacing, and sat leaning back against her knee so that his face was hidden from her. "I have only once taken a woman—do you know what that means?"

"I know," she said gently. "You cannot help seeing a lot of things if you are poor and the house has only one room—we lived in a house before Uncle took to the river."

"The woman might have mocked me, until I pretended she was only one of many and then she was more frightened than I. Afterwards I never wanted to see her again. I want Nefertari to think I know all about it—I couldn't bear her to be sorry for me. I hate pity! How dare any one pity Pharaoh!"

"You pitied me and I don't hate you, Ramoses."

"Don't you realize," he said slowly, "that you are the only person whom I shall try never to hate?"

And Ramoses wept, but did not try to hide his tears.

XII

FUGITIVE

As an illustration of the difference between my life at Court and my life at the Living Water, I will describe the acceptance of a gift from a craftsman.

One of my duties as a prince had been to represent my father when a Master of Craftsmen brought what was considered to be the year's finest product of his craft to Pharaoh. It was seldom that I did no more than express the Royal Pleasure in the gift, for the audience was private, and the Master of Craftsmen took the opportunity of putting forward any grievance of the hundreds, in some cases thousands, of people for whom he was the spokesman.

The last time I fulfilled this particular duty I received a roll of woolen stuff, sufficient for two winter cloaks, yet the audience lasted over two hours. No specific complaint was made during the conversation; yet much was implied, and had to be carefully sieved so that no chaff of personal grievance was mixed with the grain of honest indignation.

While apparently discussing only such harmless matters as the texture of various types of weave, the setting of looms, the carding of yarn, I learned that there was dissatisfaction in three cities of the Delta because minor temples had demanded double their usual tax from the weavers; that fleeces from Aleppo had been poor in quality and would never have been accepted unless one of the officials of the Royal Treasure had been open to bribery; that several flocks in the high desert opposite Abydos had been decimated through the negligence of another official, against whom I should have to take appropriate, and stringent, action.

So when Pasar told me that each family of the Living Water wished to make us a gift of welcome I naturally asked him what he advised me to say in reply, so that I could use the opportunity to make it clear that I had their interest at heart.

He looked surprised. "I do not think that any of the gifts will be so unacceptable that you will feel it incumbent to conceal your distaste."

91

"But surely you expect me to show that at least I know more than they do? Between you and me, I am sure I shall have much to learn before I can speak with intelligent appreciation that does not need your prompting."

"Perhaps we may appear over-simple, but here it is considered a courtesy to ask for information rather than to pretend that one is too weary to learn."

"Forgive me," I said coldly. "For a moment I had forgotten that I am no longer expected to be Royal."

I hope he never realized that I had taken offense, for without him I should have taken much longer to discover the pleasure of being taught the complexity of things so apparently simple as the pressure of a thumb against clay on a potter's wheel, the drive of a hand-plough through soil, the action of the outflung arm which scatters grain evenly across the field, the smooth sweep of a sickle.

And if I had not had Pasar's example to follow I would never have earned more real friends than I had ever remembered as a prince, for I would have been too proud to let them see how unskilled I was at the occupations which seemed so easy to them.

I was more proud of the first bowl I made than I had ever been of the masterpiece of a Royal Goldsmith. I gave it to Sensen, and every day she filled it with flowers . . . it is on my table as I write, though the marigolds, the last flowers she ever picked for it, are no more than a handful of yellowish dust.

Time passed swift and brilliant as a dragonfly. We had been at the Living Water just long enough to love it in every season of the year when for the first time we could no longer remain entirely separate from the world we had escaped.

It seemed a very ordinary day, quiet with the manifold incidents of joy known only to happy people. Sensen was watching me paint an inscription on a small wine-jar. As she bent forward her hair, smooth as water and scented with jasmine, brushed my cheek. "You are doing it very well," she said. "No smudges, and the green paint looks much gayer than black. Is my name, perhaps, a little crooked?"

I regarded it critically. "It is surprisingly difficult to make neat hieroglyphs on a curved surface. Obviously there is no drawing-scribe in my immediate ancestry for he would have starved to death before I had a chance to be born! However, you must be tolerant, my love, for it was your idea that we should make our own wine. As your hands picked the grapes, and your delectable feet trod out the juice, this wine should receive the same honor as that famous royal vintage which

92

had on its jars only 'Nefer! Nefer! Nefer!' in a cartouche. Thrice beautiful—what could be more appropriate?"

"I love you exaggerating about me! It is a pity there are only seven jars of our first vintage, but Pasar has promised to make me a vineyard. He says the grapes we used are better for eating than for wine so he is going to try another kind; he thinks they should grow well here."

She picked up one of the finished jars and read aloud, "Wine of the First Year of Sensen and Neb." She kissed the top of my head. "It has been a good year. Can you understand why any of the nobles go to Court when they could live as we do?"

"You are happy?" I knew it but loved to hear her say so.

"Happy, and clever, and useful. So happy that I can't remember ever being sad; so clever that I wove two thumb-joints of wool this morning without breaking the yarn; so useful that I can make a honeycake that tastes almost like Kia's."

"I wonder if Hiboe will bring us news of Kia."

"He may not bother to see her." She spoke a little too quickly, and I knew that she did not want to admit why we had sent Hiboe to Thebes. Or did she think that he had gone only to choose my light hunting-chariot, and rolls of linen and embroidery threads for women's dresses?

She was silent for a moment and then said, "Pasar expects the red mare to foal tomorrow." In her sudden change of subject she betrayed that she too was thinking of the child that this month would be born to Nefertari.

"Tomorrow? Oh, the mare. Pasar is a genius with horses."

We could see him in the distance, opening the sluice-gate which regulated the flow from the artificial lake into the elaborate system of water-channels.

She put down the jar rather too carefully. "Pasar is a genius at everything. Architect, herdsman, farmer, potter, treasurer, what should we do without him?"

"I was so foolish that at first I used to wonder why he was content to stay here."

"What made you cease to wonder?"

"Is a man who has found contentment surprised that another knows its value?"

"Dear Neb!" She kissed me. "My *dear* Neb."

Someone was coming down the path from the tunnel, but I could not see who it was until he paused to speak with Pasar.

Sensen stood up, shading her eyes with her hand. "It's Hiboe! I didn't expect him back yet."

"Why so excited?" she said over her shoulder. "You know he wouldn't have come unless there was news."

She began to run down the path. I called after her, "If Meena sees you running while the sun is still high she will scold me."

With an effort she concealed her impatience while Hiboe approached. Even before he spoke I knew he was troubled.

Sensen cut short his formal greeting. "You bring news of the Queen?"

"Thank-offerings have been made in all the temples."

"Is it a son or a daughter?"

He hesitated. "The thank-offerings are only for the safety of the Queen."

"You mean . . . ?"

"The son of Ramoses was stillborn."

"What happened, Hiboe? Both of them are so healthy, so young. Oh poor Nefertari!"

There were tears in Sensen's eyes, and trying to comfort her I said, "She will have other children. It is a disappointment, but next year the Gods will relent."

"Neb, don't be so horribly reasonable! It was this baby she wanted, not just any baby. Hiboe, is she terribly unhappy?"

"How should I know the Queen's heart?"

"You have many friends in the Palace. You must have heard something."

"It is unwise to rely too much on servants' gossip." He was obviously reluctant to say more, but could not long withstand Sensen's insistence.

"There are rumors," he admitted, "but when have there not been rumors where there are too many to do too little work?"

"And the rumors say?" I prompted.

"That Queen Nefertari has quarreled with Pharaoh. It should have been only a trivial quarrel, but the Royal Mother made it grow faster than melons on a dung-heap."

"Who, or what, is the melon, Hiboe?" I asked.

"The Lady Iri, the girl who Ramoses put in the care of Kia."

"She would never have joined Tuaa against Nefertari. Hiboe, the whole thing is ridiculous—false as a water-rat befriending a quail-chick!"

"I did not suggest that the Royal Mother befriended the Lady Iri, only that she made use of her so that the Queen would refuse to allow Pharaoh to send his mother into retirement."

94

"The name of Tuaa stinks like a rotting crocodile!" I exclaimed, too angry for discretion.

"It is sad that Queen Nefertari does not share your insight —forgive me if I sound presumptuous. Very few know that it is the Royal Mother who causes the Queen's unkindness: the rest cannot understand why the Lady Iri is one of the Royal Women, why she is chosen more often than any other to attend the Queen, who takes every opportunity to make her unhappy."

"But it is all so *unlike* Nefertari!" exclaimed Sensen. "What does she do to the girl?"

"Nothing that Pharaoh would notice, but a thousand sandflies can be more distressing than a single hornet. It is said that the Lady Iri becomes increasingly clumsy: every one knows that she spilled a flask of rubbing-oil on the Queen's dress, that she broke a favorite flower vase, that she left a wig too near a lamp and never noticed what she had done until she smelled the burning hair."

My sympathy was for Nefertari. "I am amazed that the Queen keeps the girl near her. She was never over-tolerant of fools—why should she be?"

"Perhaps the Lady Iri is not sent away because everyone would take it as proof that the Queen has cause for jealousy."

"Jealousy is sour fruit, but I never heard it could poison an unborn child," I said, finding the conversation more than a little distasteful.

"Perhaps jealousy was the whip which drove the young Queen from her husband's room after his voice had been heard raised in anger," said Hiboe reprovingly.

"To seek sympathy from Tuaa? An action more futile than trying to draw water from a sand-pit, but surely in no way lethal?"

"The Queen did not go to the Royal Mother." His voice was grave. "Before anyone could guess her intention she seized the reins from a groom who was standing at his horses' heads in the Palace forecourt. Thebes will long remember the sight of their Queen lashing the stallions of a hunting-chariot to full gallop down the Avenue of Sphinxes. No one dared follow her, for with her hair streaming in the wind, her robe disordered, they thought she was possessed by demons. Only behind closed doors do they whisper of what they saw, yet every one knows of it."

"Did the chariot overturn? Was she seriously injured?" I tried to hide my mounting dismay.

"The horses, one of them lamed, returned to their stables several hours later. The Queen was in her room before dawn,

95

her birth-pains already begun. It is said that her hands and her knees were deeply grazed: perhaps she climbed over the Palace wall, for none of the guards saw her." He paused, and then added slowly, "The people hope Pharaoh will take another Queen who will cherish the Royal seed more carefully."

"Hiboe, you must return to Thebes immediately and bring the Lady Iri here," said Sensen.

For a moment I was too astonished to speak. Bring Iri here! Iri, who had brought not only misery but death to my family! My indignation further increased as I heard her say to Hiboe, as though she gave a trivial order, so trivial that my opinion was needless even in courtesy, "From what Kia told you, the first time you went to Thebes, I am sure the girl is not to blame. She stays only through loyalty to Ramoses, and his pride keeps her there. Once she has gone he will be happy with Nefertari."

For the first time since his return Hiboe looked less worried.

"Your charity has relieved me of a heavy burden. I had to obey Pharaoh although I knew that I should not do so without asking your permission."

"I am not sure that I understand," I said coldly. "Explain more clearly."

"The Lady Iri will be here by sunset."

"And if she tires of our company she can go back to Tuaa with interesting news to sell! No doubt she has carefully memorized the route, for a spy is more valuable who can bring a careful plan of the enemy's defenses."

Sensen caught hold of my arm. "Neb, you are being unjust."

"Unjust! Unjust, when I protest against our safety being imperiled because it pleases you to trust a girl who has already brought misery to my brother and killed the heir of the Two Lands?"

Sensen ignored me and turned to Hiboe. "Tell the Lady Iri that we will make her very welcome."

He looked at me to see if I upheld Sensen's order.

"Tell her that if she comes here she will stay until Tuaa dies," I said.

"You need not fear her." He spoke calmly. "I too have given my word to protect the peace of the Living Water. The Lady Iri will never be able to lead anyone here: she does not know the way even to the wadi."

I was a little mollified. "I should have known that you would take the precaution of blindfolding her. Tell Pasar to have her carefully watched. It can be done discreetly so she will suffer no embarrassment."

It is not pleasant to recall that I avoided further discussion because I wanted the full responsibility for Iri to be shared by Hiboe and Sensen, so that if my forebodings were fulfilled I could lay the blame on them with magnanimity.

Mumbling something to the effect that I had promised to meet Pasar at the stables, I strode off without giving Sensen a chance to speak.

My mood was so dark that the mare sensed it, and rolled her eyes wildly when I entered the stall. Her flanks were steaming with sweat, and Pasar was sitting with her in the straw, soothing her with his voice and gently pulling her ears.

"Hiboe has returned from Thebes, and brought Kia and a girl with him," I said abruptly.

"The wife of one of Kia's sons?"

"No, one of the Queen's Women who is out of favor at Court."

I expected Pasar to display concern, but instead he remarked, "Your wife will be glad of someone to talk to when you are busy. I have often thought she must be a little lonely."

The mare began to struggle. "She knows you are upset," said Pasar. "Perhaps she will quieten if you leave her with me."

I walked morosely along the top of the cliff and then, having made sure there was no one in sight, lay down on a narrow ledge from which I could watch the house. Sensen was picking flowers in the garden, lupins, by the color, and either white poppies or marguerites. Then I saw Meena carrying a mattress across the courtyard to the room which I sometimes used if I wanted to work late without disturbing Sensen. So I was not even to be consulted as to where Iri was to sleep! I was beyond considering that I had given Sensen little opportunity to ask my advice.

Children were weeding a field of lettuces, their voices rising up through the still air like bubbles from the mouths of basking fish. Smoke plumed up from the kitchen quarters, and in imagination I could see geese being plucked, ducks stewed in honey, cauldrons of broth to tempt the uninvited guest who would take so much of Sensen's time that I should soon fill the shabby role of neglected husband. So determined was my gloom that I did not even consider myself ridiculous.

What right had Ramoses to send his discarded concubine to me! Or did he consider himself so powerful that Tuaa could no longer endanger us? He might be able to trust Iri, but what of her litter-bearers? Why had I failed to ask Hiboe who else she had brought in her train?

The voice of reason piped, thin as the cheep of a newly hatched duckling, but still audible. I listened, and had to admit that I had probably misjudged Hiboe. He would have brought Kia and her family with him, and they had carried Iri's litter—and I hoped she had received a thorough jolting.

Evening shadows were beginning to flow down into the bowl of cultivation before I saw Sensen leave the house. She walked slowly down the avenue; even in the distance I knew she was forlorn that I was angry. When she reached the lake she took off her sandals and sat on the wall dabbling her feet in the water. She wore a blue dress and a wreath of white flowers held back her hair. No doubt the Lady Iri would be wearing some of Pharaoh's more lavish gifts, in case we had heard that she came from a barge. What role would she play? The innocent child sorely misjudged, or would I be expected to prove that I was more difficult to please than Ramoses?

At least I need not behave like a sulky boy afraid to return home because he has offended his elders. I made my way back to the path and descended it briskly, whistling as though Iri's arrival was a matter too trivial to concern me. Without fully intending to do so I found myself hurrying to join Sensen.

"I'm so glad you've come back," she said. "I thought you were cross—you aren't cross, are you?"

"I was—but I'm not any longer. She can't do us any harm —we wont let her."

"Dear, silly Neb! I'm not Nefertari and there is no Tuaa here."

"Unless Tuaa is disguised," I said and stamped on a scorpion that darted from a crevice in the rock.

Sensen shivered though the evening was warm. "I didn't see it," she said. "If you hadn't come it might have stung me."

We hard the dry patter of hooves echoing down the tunnel. Sensen slipped her hand in mine. "If she pretends to be grand you mustn't be angry with her. She will only be trying to behave like a Lady of the Court."

Hiboe was leading a donkey which carried the Lady Iri. She wore a yellow cloak and over her head was a fall of blue linen that shielded her bandaged eyes.

"Welcome to the Living Water," I said, and the stilted words made me feel foolish.

The girl put out her hand, groping towards us.

"Shall I untie your bandage?" said Sensen. "You must forgive Hiboe for bringing you here blindfolded—later we will explain why he thought it necessary."

"You are very kind," she said. "I have heard so much about you from Kia—otherwise I should not have dared to intrude upon you."

Kia came from the tunnel and whispered urgently to Sensen. I caught only the word "bandage," and could not understand why Sensen went suddenly pale.

"You must be tired, Iri," she said gently. "We shall soon be at the house." She took the donkey's head-rope from Hiboe and led the way down the path to the avenue.

Kia plucked at my tunic to prevent me from following them. "The Lady Iri must not take off the bandage, for something is wrong with her eyes. She is very brave, but the light sears like fire and I think she will soon be blind."

Hiboe had brought me a letter from Pharaoh. The writing-signs were carelessly formed so I knew it was not the work of a scribe, but of Ramoses himself. I still have it, so I will give you a faithful copy, omitting only the preliminary inquiries as to our health and well-being.

"Iri tells me that you will have already heard from Hiboe how she came to live in your house at Thebes and later became one of the Queen's Women. I ask you and Sensen to cherish her for the sake of your brother, who is Pharaoh of the Two Lands yet cannot himself protect the girl who has afforded him a refuge in her heart.

"When you gave me the Crook and Flail you said that my enemies were already divided against each other by jealousy. Tuaa is more subtle than I feared, for she has used jealousy to divide me from my friends. If this were all, I should not be forced to appeal to your charity nor to disturb your peace.

"One of my first acts as Pharaoh was to visit Abydos, where I found our father's mortuary temple to be still unfinished and all the works he had ordered, including the temple to Za Atet, grossly neglected. Karaden warned me not to make pertinent inquiries regarding the misappropriation of the revenues, but I was determined to assert my authority.

"The guilt lay with Usermentu who, as you know only too well, was privy to my mother's plot to murder you. I took considerable pleasure in informing him that instead of the increased tribute which he was demanding he would be held responsible for the completion within a year of the new temples at Abydos. I was proud to have made him my enemy.

"Usermentu still exerts so great an influence with the

whole priesthood of Amen that I dare not have him either exiled or otherwise rendered harmless . . . in fact I doubt whether death would do more than increase the venom of this particular scorpion if that death were hastened by mortal hands.

"On Karaden's advice I placated the priesthood by commencing several new temples, which when completed should prove more enduring than anything yet built, with the possible exception of the greater pyramids. It is solemn evidence of the influence of Amen that even Karaden encourages me to burden the treasury with enormous extra expenditure.

"Usermentu, however, is still fully aware that I distrust him, and that I wait impatiently for the time when I need no longer be influenced by him or his kind. He also knows that my increasing popularity with the common people is due to Iri having helped me to understand some of the problems which affect their daily lives. For instance, the tax on salt, wool, and barley has been decreased by a fifth part; and the market tax of a tenth has been rescinded; to the benefit of thousands of the poor and the annoyance of the temples who counted these as part of their revenue.

"Nefertari approves my reforms, though recently she has been less interested in matters which do not personally affect her. The physicians tell me that this attitude of mind is natural to her condition: though I had hoped that she would prove a notable exception, in the great tradition of women such as Hatshepsut and Nefertiti. No doubt disappointment will become more acceptable when I am older in years! I already feel far too old in heart; I have almost forgotten the joy of sailing a boat, and instead know the river only when a rhythm of rowers punctuates the interminable speeches I deliver to the crowds assembled to watch a Progress.

"Usermentu, possibly at my mother's instigation, told me five months ago that Iri was in the power of Sekmet and that her presence in the Palace would prove a malign influence on my unborn child. He spoke of this after a particularly long and tiresome audience, so I answered him without the modicum of tact which lately I have used to temper my more forthright statements. Somewhat bluntly I told him that if he could not protect us from the Dark Gods, without trying to foist the blame for his inadequacy on an innocent girl of fourteen, I should be forced to believe the allegations which suggested that most of the priesthood were growing fat and lazy and that their cure would be effected only by healthful fasting. This did not please him.

"Three months later he returned to the attack, pretending

100

that Ptah had appeared to him in person, to say that as Iri persisted in looking to the Dark Moon for power he had reluctantly decided that I must be given proof, in that Iri would slowly become blind.

"When Nefertari complained that Iri was increasingly clumsy you can imagine my dismay. At first Iri refused to admit that her vision was blurred, but I forced the truth from her though I did not tell her that my alarm was due to more than pity for her affliction.

"Of one thing I am sure: Iri is entirely innocent, and her blindness is not due to the intervention of Ptah. Is she suffering only from one of the eye infections which are unfortunately only too common in Egypt? My personal physician, an excellent man who cured Iri of the sores on her leg, says that the symptoms are unusual in a girl of her age. The progress of the disease is slow but relentless: her eyelids are no longer inflamed, though strong light causes her acute pain which neither ointment, lotions, nor magical healing appear to relieve.

"Is her affliction due to some subtle poison, either in her food or introduced as dust into her room? I suspected Tuaa's hand in this, but she seems genuinely frightened that the girl is a source of danger to the household.

"I have given much anxious thought to these two alternatives and have reluctantly rejected both and come to believe that she is under a curse put on her by Usermentu or one of his priests. Undoubtedly some of the Amen priests have the power they claim—and are not scrupulous in using it in ways which are utterly at variance with the traditions our father upheld.

"You may well ask why I do not attempt her cure by getting some beneficent priest to break the curse and then to heal the damage already caused, if indeed her release did not produce a spontaneous recovery of sight. But how can I find such a priest? I cannot! That is the stark truth of the situation in which I find myself.

"I am determined that my successor must be himself a fully initiated priest, a Winged Pharaoh. There is no other way in which Pharaoh can rule without being subservient to Amen, unless he becomes a tyrant who denies his people their rightful intermediaries with the Gods. Nefertari's child will be born within a few days. She is convinced that it is a son, but my concern is only, 'Is he one whose Jar of the Ma-at is already so clear that he can become Initiate before I appoint him my Royal Heir?'

"Having confessed myself helpless to protect Iri you may

101

well ask why I should inflict her upon you. Perhaps there is one thing which you do not know about the Living Water. Why did Seti build no temple there? He told me the reason when we were with him at Abydos, four years ago, though at the time I did not know the place to which he referred. He said that every man, especially those of Royal, and therefore semi-divine, blood should have somewhere in which he sought personal awareness of the Gods. He advised me, I remember, to look up to the sky when I was alone, or to seek some hidden place in the reeds where I could find that solitude in which I might feel myself truly in company. I asked him where he went to be alone with the Gods, and he smiled and said he had made such a place for your mother. He called it the Living Water as a symbol of the spring that gushes from the Jar of the Ma-at to bring the flowers of rejoicing to the arid heart. I did not then realize that he had found actual underground springs to bring fertility to some remote desert valley. Because he intended to build no temples there, he asked a certain priest whom he greatly honored to make the whole area of the Living Water into a sanctuary.

"I could protect Iri with walls seventy cubits high and forty cubits thick. I could set five thousand men to guard the gates, and still Usermentu would mock my pitiful defenses. But no priest of Amen, unless he be of the merciful Gods, can prevail against her while she is in the sanctuary that was given to you and Sensen by our father.

"If you agree to receive Iri, as I pray you will, she must on no account be told that I have sent her away through fear of Usermentu, for knowledge of the curse might increase its potency. I have told her that through no fault of her own she has been the cause of quarrels between myself and Nefertari, and that I think it wiser for us to part. Let her continue to think that I value her so lightly that I allow petty jealousy to deprive me of her solace . . . such thoughts will make it easier for her to forget me.

"When you read this, ask Sensen if together you will grant my request. Then send Hiboe to me with your reply and tell him to travel swiftly."

Here the letter continued on a different roll of papyrus and was obviously written in much greater haste.

"Usermentu came here at sunset and demanded that Iri be given up to him before my child is born. He claimed that he would exorcise 'the demons which possess her.' I refused, for I knew he would throw her to the sacred crocodiles or choose some other hideous death. I thought I had convinced him that I was adamant, but he went to Nefertari and told

102

her that unless she could persuade me to let him take Iri, then the curse would kill the child in her womb.

"Nefertari came to me and pleaded on her knees that I let Iri go with Usermentu. She was hysterical and refused to listen either to reason or charity. We quarreled most bitterly. She has just stormed out of the room, I suspect to seek sympathy from Tuaa.

"I have no alternative but to send Iri to you immediately. She will travel with only Kia and Hiboe—the Gods are merciful in that Hiboe is here tonight. He says he can hide her on a barge going South with a cargo of hides. How pitiful is Pharaoh when the woman he honors must journey in such disgusting conditions!

"As soon as they are safely out of the Palace, I shall go to make my peace with Nefertari. In the joy of the child she will soon forget our quarrel.

"To prevent Usermentu finding Iri by some diabolical means before she reaches sanctuary with you, I shall tell him I have killed the girl myself. As I am Tuaa's son he should find it easy to believe me capable of murder for expediency.

"My heartfelt prayers and gratitude be with you always—Ramoses.

"Send news of Iri only by Hiboe, put nothing in writing—I trust no one here!"

XIII

THE RIVER

I KNEW it was futile to try to keep my thoughts secret from Sensen, otherwise I should not have shown her my letter from Ramoses. I expected her to be even more alarmed by it than I was myself, however, I should have known her better.

"I always thought Usermentu was evil," she said cheerfully. "I hope he did the curse himself."

"Why?" It seemed a reasonable question.

"Because it will be better for Ramoses to get rid of him than one of the other priests who isn't in Tuaa's confidence."

"I don't understand."

Sensen sighed. "Neb, aren't you being a little obtuse? Iri is safe here, so the curse will turn back on the person who put it on her."

The idea of a curse bouncing back to the sender as though it were a *checka* ball thrown against a wall struck me as more than unlikely, but I pretended to agree with her.

"Do you think she will recover her sight at once?" asked Sensen.

"You must not be too hopeful. I am inclined to think that Usermentu noticed that there was something wrong with her eyes and used it as an excuse to make his threat more convincing. Anyway, you must not let Iri guess there is anything odd about her disease."

Sensen smiled. "Neb, my love, you are as guileless as Ramoses. Tuaa made certain that all the Queen's Women knew about Usermentu's prophecy, so that they were afraid to be nice to Iri. Of course they told her about it with a wealth of detail."

"Then she ought to have left the Palace months ago."

"She only stayed in the hope that Ramoses would conquer his fear of the priests until he could find a way of restoring good ones to power. There *are* good priests, especially in the smaller temples, but he hasn't a way of finding them yet."

I found that a wound I had thought healed was still raw. "I suppose what you really mean is that if I had only continued my temple training instead of giving up before I reached even the first stage of initiation I could still be of real use to Egypt."

"Neb, don't be so touchy. You were perfectly right to tell Father about the horrible things they expected you to do— and he fully agreed." She shuddered. "Fancy making a boy of fourteen read chapters of the Book of the Dead by the light of a putrescent corpse. Of course it was evil!"

"Usermentu maintained that it was done only to help the pupil overcome repugnance and so strengthen his will to pass the ordeals."

"You left the temple and married me. We are both very glad about it, so why worry about what would have happened if everything had been different?"

I knew her view was more robust than mine, but I still wished that I could have been better equipped to protect the Living Water from Usermentù, should he breach our defenses.

I have never been entirely sure whether Iri recovered her sight because the curse could not follow her into our sanctuary, or whether her happier environment produced a more ordinary cure. Within seven days she did not need to cover her eyes even in strong sunlight, and before she had been with us a month Sensen was teaching her to do fine embroidery.

I sent Hiboe to Ramoses with this encouraging news, and he returned to say that "a certain person," whom I knew must be Usermentu, was suffering from a series of particularly painful boils. This may or may not have been coincidence, but it was inconclusive for his eyes remained unaffected.

A house was built close to our own for Iri and she lived there with Kia, whose husband came back with Hiboe. Sensen made a close friend of her, and any regrets I may have had were soon dispelled by the pleasure the two found in each others' company.

If Iri still wept for Ramoses she did so in secret, and I began to hope that she would soon fall in love with one of the young men who tried to gain her favor.

I sometimes left the Living Water for a few days, usually with Pasar when he went to different villages to barter our products for the grain or wine which we did not grow in sufficient quantity ourselves. It was on one such occasion, when Iri had been with us nearly three years, that I heard of a Royal Progress in which Ramoses would pass up-river in the near future, on his way to inspect the progress of a great temple which was being carved from the living rock at Nubyt near the sandstone quarries.

I shall never cease to regret that I mentioned this news to Sensen, though at the time it seemed a harmless topic of conversation.

I ought to have known that Iri's sudden gaiety was due to something more than the fond glances of Qen, the eldest son of the Chief Coppersmith. The boy was handsome and intelligent, he would make her an excellent husband. I even felt a little smug when she and Sensen informed me that they had exciting news to impart. My benign thoughts of suitable wedding gifts were abruptly scattered by Sensen's opening remark.

"Iri and I have decided that you are to take us to watch the Progress."

I made excuses, but even to me they sounded unconvincing.

"He is afraid that Usermentu will attack me again," said Iri, and her shoulders drooped with the weight of disappointment.

"Nonsense!" Sensen frowned at me over Iri's bent head. "We stay here because it is so much nicer than anywhere else, but if we dared not go outside then we should be no better than prisoners."

I took Sensen's cue reluctantly. "If you both want to go I have no real objection. I only thought that it would be rather tiresome for you—the inns are most unsuitable so we shall have to camp in the wadi."

"I like camping," said Sensen firmly; before Iri could protest, as I knew she would, that she did not want to cause any inconvenience. "Iri and I want to see the new queen. It is said that she and Nefertari get on quite well together and are nice to each others' babies."

Ramoses' second queen was a subject I had carefully avoided discussing either with Sensen or Iri. He had sent me several letters by Hiboe but had taken no notice of my advice. Nefertari had accused him of deliberately murdering her child and for several months had refused to allow him to give her another. Ast-nefert had been one of the Queen's Women, though not until Iri had left the Court, and it is much in her favor that though she became first a concubine and later queen she was instrumental in reconciling Nefertari and her husband without losing the respect or affection of either.

Sensen said, "I suppose that Nefertari being the Great Royal Wife still gives her a comfortable advantage over Ast-nefert, even though she has only one child to Ast-nefert's two."

"Will the queens be with Ramoses?" Poor Iri, she tried so hard to sound as though she were unconcerned.

I told her that as Ast-nefert's son was only two months old she would probably stay with him in Heliopolis. I also pointed out that we should only see Ramoses in the distance even if we forced our way to the front of the crowd.

But Sensen had made up her mind that if Iri saw Ramoses again she would realize he was no longer a part of her life, and would turn to Qen for happiness.

So what could I do but give my consent, when Sensen sat on my knee and beguiled me?

I tried to put off my sense of foreboding. What could be more natural than that two women should be excited at a break in the placid routine of their lives? Surely I was not afraid that the sight of a Progress would make the Living Water seem circumscribed, even a little dull? Or was it the sight of Ramoses with his children that I feared?

I dreamed of Usermentu, but only as I had often seen him, walking with his hands hidden in the sleeves of his robe, his shaven head gleaming as though the skull shone through the yellow skin. I almost convinced myself that his curse was no more than another priestly trick by which the uninitiated are held subservient: surely the dream was no more than the rotting shreds of an old fear from which I had fled without daring to give it decent burial?

Because my consent had been grudging I tried to make amends by suggesting that instead of watching the Progress from the nearest village, where we should only have seen the barges pass in midstream, we should go to a town where Ramoses would speak to the assembled people.

I sent Hiboe and Qen ahead with the portable pavilions, which I had had made the previous year so that I could take Sensen with me when we went to the hills, a day's journey by chariot, where I pastured some of our goats in the early spring. Each pavilion was light enough to be carried by two pack-donkeys, for the framework was of acacia-wood poles which could easily be taken apart for transport. The hangings were wool except on the fourth side where a gauze curtain let in air but kept out moths and biting flies which were particularly troublesome during the inundation or before one of our rare thunderstorms.

I had considered taking Sensen and Iri in a chariot, but then decided that an ox-cart would be more appropriate to the clothes we intended to wear, which would be suitable to the family of a moderately prosperous farmer.

I knew the town for I had already been there with Pasar, so had no difficulty in finding the place where Hiboe had made our camp. It was near a well, but secluded from the main highway by a grove of persea trees which, being evergreen, afforded pleasant shade so early in the year. Qen had food ready for us, and after we had eaten, Sensen announced that she was going to bed so that we should be able to find good places on the waterfront soon after dawn.

I made a mild protest that we need not get there so early for the Progress was not until noon, but the mist was still rising from the river when we reached the marketplace. Many of the people must have been traveling through the night for they were still streaming in through the town gates. Every inn and beer-shop was crowded, their yards filled with carts and chariots while stable-boys threw armfuls of fodder to the horses and oxen or groomed them with wisps of straw.

The houses which formed three sides of a square that led to the quay were decorated with swags of leaves and sheaves of green wheat. Masts flying yellow or scarlet pennants lined the principal streets; and at every corner stood a wine-seller, dipping one cupful after another from the jar beside him, while his rival poured sweet beer or syrups from a row of pitchers.

Sensen pointed out that we had disguised ourselves too well. "Women look at Iri and me with sympathy, thinking you might have been more generous on this famous occasion. Every one else is wearing every necklace and bracelet she owns or could borrow!"

I took them to the booths which sold trinkets and bought them necklaces of faience beads which Sensen said were a much prettier blue than turquoise. Qen, emboldened by my example, gave Iri a copper anklet. We paused to watch acrobats, and a juggler who conjured a quail-chick from Hiboe's ear. At the food stalls we chose slices of goose wrapped in a napkin, three-cornered rolls of bread sprinkled with poppy seeds, a jar of curds and another of honey. The crowds began to drift towards the quay and we jostled our way forward so as to be in the forefront of spectators. I found good places for us, beside a heap of garlands which children would later throw before Pharaoh's barge. The poppies had begun to wilt, and scarlet petals trodden in the dust were bright as blood. I shivered as though the wind blew suddenly cold.

Voices raised in the name of Pharaoh rippled towards us as the Royal Barge drew slowly into sight. The song in his honor swelled into an arc of sound as though we were closed in a temple whose pillars were praise. The rowers slowed their rhythm and eager hands caught the scarlet ropes that guided the barge towards us, proud as a swan.

The steersman held up his hand for silence. Ramoses spoke to his people.

I found myself deeply moved, for though reason told me that his words were polished smooth as a rubbing-stone by constant repetition, they sounded as though he spoke to each of us from the heart.

Tears were running down Iri's face, yet she was smiling. "He looks happy," she said, so low that I knew she was speaking her thoughts aloud. "Now I know he is happy I can make Qen happy too."

Nefertari and Ast-nefert were in the second barge. They were smiling together and each had a child on her knee. The eldest prince was trying to catch the shadows cast by the ostrich feathers which six fanbearers waved above the raised platform where the Queens could be seen by the crowd.

Nefertari took a lotus from her head-dress and gave it to her son, helped him to wave it to the people, who shouted their pleasure. Ast-nefert's daughter, not to be outdone, held up her gold rattle, chuckling fatly.

"Now none of us need worry about Ramoses," said Sensen, yet her voice was wistful. "I wish we could ask him to come to the Living Water . . . it would be good to talk with him again."

"He is Pharaoh," said Iri. "Only a queen can really talk with Pharaoh."

The Rhythm Keeper struck the silver gong which hung in the prow of the Royal Barge. The rowers leaned to their oars. They quickened their stroke. Slowly the train of barges drew away until the sun on the water was too bright for us to see them any longer.

That night we joined the townspeople who danced in the marketplace and ate and drank as Pharaoh's guests from the long tables which had been set up in the main street. It was dawn before we returned to our pavilions. Sensen was so sleepy that I had to guide her steps, and Iri clung to Qen's hand as though she were afraid of being lost.

I noticed that Iri seemed very tired on our way home, but thought it was due to the unusual excitement. She went straight to her own house on her return, and I did not see her the following day.

"It's odd that Iri hasn't come to tell us about Qen," said Sensen. "She has promised to marry him, for he has told Pasar and Hiboe."

Kia woke us in the middle of the night. "Iri is ill," she

said. "She has a high fever and when she breathes it sounds like dry palm-leaves rattling in a wind."

Sensen insisted on going to Iri though I tried to go alone. Iri did not recognize us. She thought I was Ramoses and kept pleading with me to send her away before she brought danger to the Palace. Sometimes she stared at the wall and seemed to see something which filled her with terror. Was it Usermentu? I shall never be sure, though she cried out that the lamp was searing her eyes.

Her skin felt brittle as dry grass and her lips cracked with the heat that flailed the moisture from her parched body. We wrapped her in wet linen to try to bring her coolness, dropped wine through a hollow reed into her mouth, rubbed her with lion's fat to give strength to her wasted muscles.

Sensen refused to leave her except when she was too exhausted to keep her heavy eyelids open. Even Qen had begun to lose all hope when, on the tenth day, there came a blessed change. Sweat began to pour from her, as though a spring had broken into a dry well. She recognized us and smiled, spoke like a child, saying she was hungry. She swallowed sips of milk mixed with raw egg and honey.

Then she fell into a gentle sleep, holding Qen's hand.

That night I slept, a deep sleep dark as bitumen. I was lost in a desert on a night without stars, yet a black sun blazed down on the torrid rocks in shafts of shadow cruel as a charring brand. I tried to cry out, for Sensen was also lost and trying to reach me. But my tongue was dry as a stretched hide, powerless as though my mouth were filled with the natron of embalmers.

I struggled to escape from this black net of nightmare, forced open my eyelids. Had I cried out and frightened Sensen?

I took her hand: it was hot as the sand of my desolate dream.

I cannot write of the days and the nights which followed. I was sustained by hope because Iri had survived this cruel ordeal.

On the evening of the ninth day Sensen's pillow was also drenched, but not with the beneficent sweat of healing. As I raised her to ease the anguish which racked her lungs, blood gushed from her mouth.

All through the night I held the body of my love in my arms, while her heart's blood slowly stiffened until we were wrapped together in its scarlet shroud.

XIV

MASTER OF EXPEDIENCY

You may have noticed that the box which contains this manuscript is divided into two parts. The central partition, though apparently only a strip of cedar-wood, in fact represents eighteen years.

These years do not directly concern you, for during this period of my life I learned nothing which might bring you more intimate understanding of Ramoses. So I take up my story on a certain day of late summer, to be precise, six thousand seven hundred and twenty-four days after the death of Sensen.

The arrival of a stranger at the Living Water was no longer an unusual occurrence, so when Qen, who at Pasar's death had succeeded him as overseer, told me that a noble from the North wished to see me I was not particularly interested.

"Does he seem ill in body or only in mind?" I asked, for Qen had considerable experience in judging the quality of those who sought advice from us.

Qen laughed. "The affliction appears to be inflammation of an overdeveloped sense of his own importance. His litter-bearers found the wadi road too steep and he objected to riding on a pack-donkey."

"Then you can look after him until I have been to the stables; it will be salutary for him to cool his impatience."

Meena met me on my return from the High Village. She was wearing the woolen wig which usually appeared only on feast days and the carnelian necklace of which, for some imponderable reason, she was particularly proud.

"I have invited the guest to eat with you," she said in conspiratorial tones intended to inspire curiosity. Her eyse were bright as a bird's that offers a grub to its fledgling. "I am sure you will both find plenty to talk about."

It was unusual for Meena to ask anyone to the house without my permission, but I was no more than mildly interested.

111

"There is plenty of meat, for Qen had a young bull killed yesterday."

"This will be a proper meal," she said briskly. "And you had better put on a fresh kilt, for Prince Karaden has always been fussy about the formalities."

She had achieved her objective for now I was really startled. "Karaden? Are you sure?"

"The Vizier of the Two Lands himself: and not finding it easy to pretend he is no more than a minor noble."

"Then we had better serve the wine of the twelfth year."

"It is already cooling. Now hurry along and don't keep him waiting any longer."

I patted her affectionately on the shoulder. "Don't try to deceive me. What you mean is that you will be restless as a flea on a hot bed-brick until you find out why he has come here."

Karaden was pacing up and down the paved walk under the vine pergola. He appeared agitated, or was it only that he was offended at being kept waiting?

"What brings you here, dear brother?" I said. "Dare I hope that it is only the proof of fraternal affection?"

"What is more natural than that I should seize this rare opportunity of visiting you?"

I laughed without rancor. "Surely the Master of Expediency does not have to wait twenty years for opportunity to serve him?"

He avoided a direct answer. "Neb, you look remarkably young for your age; no one would think you were forty-two —but of course your life has been far less arduous than mine."

"Obscurity has its compensations."

"Then you have no regrets?"

"None. You need have no fear that I harbor any resentment for my somewhat precipitate decision."

His short-sighted eyes became less wary. "You are happy? It has been worth it, even since she died?"

"We had four years together. I think I have been useful here in my small way: at least it pleases me to think so."

"I am sure you have done very well," he said, like a scribe encouraging a backward pupil. "I have already observed many proofs of your admirable influence. The houses are excellently planned, the water-channels would do credit to a palace garden, every cubit of land is under cultivation."

"And the people?"

"All in remarkably good condition. And so are the cattle, not a blemish on any of them, I made particular note."

With a smile I led him to the table that had been set under one of the shade trees which Sensen had planted. I saw that the appointments pleased him and wondered if he could be surprised to learn that everything from fringed napkins to alabaster drinking cups had been made by my own people.

"I am most flattered that my small estate meets with the approval of one so well qualified to judge," I said smoothly. "But I think you did not come so far only to compliment me."

"Neb, you were always too direct for comfort. Why should I not come to see you? From what I hear, people come a long way to consult the Lord of the Living Water."

"You exaggerate my small success."

He leaned forward, his thin hands tightening on the arms of his chair. "Neb, why do they come to see you?"

"It is a long story; we had better eat first or Meena will say the food is spoiled."

"Meena is still with you? She must be over seventy."

"Seventy-three to be exact, but still capable of scolding either of us if she thinks we deserve it. Had it not been for Meena no trace of me would exist except in the memory of a few people here, and as a carving on some of our father's less important monuments."

Karaden seemed embarrassed. "Your name has been replaced by the name of Ramoses. You must not blame him, for it was done at Tuaa's order." He sighed. "Ramoses is far too inclined to take the credit for what other men have built. I protest vigorously, but he only says that to build everything new would over-burden the treasury."

Meena came in with the first dish and he greeted her cordially.

"A remarkable woman," he said when she had made sure we approved of the goose stuffed with artichokes and green almonds and had gone back to chivy the cook. "You say that she saved your life?"

"When Sensen died I fear that I did not behave with a seemly acceptance of tragedy. To be honest I considered killing myself."

"It would have been a most disgraceful example to your people," he said in a voice which would better have expressed his disapproval had his mouth not been filled with goose.

"I congratulate you most warmly, O wise and illustrious brother, for it is obvious that you have never been driven to the brink of an action against which your reason protested. I was not so fortunate. I endured my grief for a year, convinced that the Gods would take pity on my separation from

113

the woman I loved more than I loved Egypt. The door did not open, so I was foolish enough to think that I could enter by forcing the bolts. So that no one would know that Sensen's husband was a coward, I went alone with the goats to a distant pasture, telling a herd-boy to join me there at the next full moon. I intended to open a vein in my wrist. Vultures would have removed the evidence and my people would have thought I had been killed by a leopard while defending the flock: a decent, if somewhat mundane, demise."

"I should have known you would not disgrace our family. Forgive me for misjudging you. Would it be impertinent to inquire what made you change your mind?"

"I was about to tell you, but first you must try the second course of our humble meal."

"Your cook is a genius. I must see her later and compliment her in person. I always insist on encouraging the servants of my host when they deserve it. These little courtesies are too often neglected."

"Your manners have always been impeccable, Karaden. Even when we were children you seldom grabbed the last cake before offering it to your juniors."

He laughed heartily. "Knowing that their nurses would be shocked if they took it in the presence of the eldest son! Always expedient, was I, even as a boy? It serves Egypt well, for Ramoses is far too apt to rely on chariots instead of treaties. But you were telling me what made you change your mind."

"On what I thought would be my last night as Neb I had a dream. I stood by the dying embers of the fire over which I had heated water to wash my body for death. I drew my hunting-knife across the veins of my wrist. Blood spurted on to the sand. I was surprised that there was so much blood. It formed a rivulet which widened into a darkening river, yet I felt neither pain nor faintness.

"I heard Sensen's voice, 'Neb! Neb, do not let your blood divide us.' Beyond the red river I could see her and there were tears in her eyes. I tried to wade towards her, but my feet were trapped as though they were held fast in mummy wrappings. I cried out, 'Sensen! Sensen, help me to reach you. I bring you my life. I have no other gift to offer.' She shook her head sorrowfully. 'You must share your life with others until the Gods decide I may share mine with you.'

"With the sound of her voice in my ears, I woke. The desert was silent, except for the bark of a jackal in the far distance."

Karaden appeared to find my story disconcerting and

coughed to hide his embarrassment. "A most remarkable experience, Neb. Most remarkable. I presume this dream was the reason why you have acquired certain priestly attributes."

"It made me determined to train myself to become frequently aware of Sensen's presence. At first I tried many false avenues: I was foolish enough to think that I could burnish my soul by weakening its link with my body. I alternatively fasted, or drunk inordinate quantities of wine until I became plagued with fantasies. I tried several concoctions containing poppy-juice, and dreamed dreams which in my saner moments I knew to be unreal. I invented ordeals of physical endurance, and found myself trapped in a net of pains which prevented me even thinking clearly. I then entered a hell whose existence I had not previously considered: I found myself to be a most ordinary man.

"The shock of this recognition was so terrible that had it not been for Meena I should undoubtedly have died. She treated me as a child, convalescent after a long illness. I defy any one to retain his sense of righteous indignation against the Gods when his nurse treats his outbursts of grief as an ailment which must be cheerfully endured until it is cured by time; or to be pompous after she has supported his tottering steps to the privy-room."

"Neb, I consider it very charitable of you to keep Meena here. There are few men who would like to be served by some one who must be a constant reminder of an unfortunate experience."

"Perhaps I am lacking in pride, my dear brother; or you in understanding. It was because Meena had helped me that I conceived the idea of offering my services to those who have been able to make use of them. Meena helped me to find myself, and who was I? I had to ask myself this very searching question."

"And the answer?"

"I was not the Prince Nebunefer who had given up his right to the Crook and Flail for love of a woman. I was a man who had shown himself to be a reed that broke under the stress of bereavement, a man who could not rejoin his wife until he had fulfilled his obligations. Gradually, I became more interested in others than in myself. A most salutary experience. Probably at the instigation of Pasar, my invaluable friend and overseer, people began to consult me when they were troubled. There is no temple here, so I filled the role proper to a temple counselor. In solitude I found answers to their questions which had an authority unknown to me as Neb: they seem to find me adequate."

"You mean that you have developed the faculty of intuition, usually more acute in women, to a remarkable degree?" He sounded disappointed. "I expected something more startling."

"I fear I have no tricks to offer such as would be likely to astonish the Amen priests, nor do I exact thank-offerings from my followers. Sensen taught me the power of affection. I use it to the best of my ability."

"Would you, for instance, be able to tell if a newly born child were in any way remarkable?"

It was a curious question, and I saw he waited anxiously for my answer. "I presume you do not mean could I recognize signs of congenital weakness? No, I thought not. I have, on three occasions, been told by Sensen when some child of unusual talent was born here. I dream of her frequently: we discuss even trivial matters. She told me that Iri's second son would be a goldsmith—I will show you a pectoral he made recently which is a proof of her foresight. She also told me that the third daughter of one of our herdsmen should be given to a foster mother as the woman to whom she had been born was linked with her only by hatred."

"Did this also prove correct?"

"Regrettably I did not take Sensen's advice; it seemed so unreasonable that a baby could contain such bitter enmity. However, at eight she stabbed her mother in the arm and the mother retaliated by beating her over the head with a waterpot. The whole matter was most unfortunate."

"Excellent!" exclaimed Karaden with real enthusiasm. "I am delighted that I took my wife's advice. It was she who persuaded me to come here."

"I heard that you had married again. I am sorry you did not bring her with you."

"To be honest, I was not too sure of my welcome. I always thought you were very badly treated, though Ramoses said you came here of your own free will. Horrible woman, Tuaa! I gave five thousand large cattle and a hundred collars of gold to the priests when she died. I thought it might encourage them to make sure she did not return to haunt me. Mind you, I did not know she had planned to murder you or I should have felt impelled to make a very vehement protest."

"You must have thought our accident unusually convenient to Tuaa."

"But I didn't *know* anything. I gave several very strong hints to Ramoses, but he never admitted you were alive until he heard about Sensen. Her death distressed him very much: I have never seen him so upset even when his first child was stillborn. He is a good-hearted man, in spite of all his bombast and wrong-headedness." He gave me a piercing glance from under his heavy eyebrows. "Why didn't you come back to us as he suggested? He would have given you any Nome you wanted, given you anything. Why didn't you even answer his letter?"

"He was fighting against the Hittites. Had he been killed I should have had to rule until his son was old enough to take the Crook and Flail."

"You could have told him your reasons."

"Blame my pride for my silence. I still had too much of it to admit that I dared not risk having to rule anyone before I had learned to rule myself."

"But now you would take a different view?"

"Why should I?"

"Neb, you always were a difficult person to understand. Here am I, after a most uncomfortable journey, asking you to come back and play your part, a great part, for Egypt; and you look at me as though I were a huckster trying to sell you stale fish!"

"Karaden, you are inimitable! Not a word has been said about my being able to help you, much less that I can help Egypt. What am I to do, lead an army or depose the priesthood? Or have you some easier post for me to fill? Try some more of my wine, it might suggest to you that I become the Keeper of Pharaoh's Vineyards, a most suitable occupation for a man with small ambitions and a good palate."

"I should not have come here for any frivolous matter," said Karaden severely. He permitted me to fill his wine-cup. "I must remember to give you glass to drink from. Ramoses no longer uses gold or alabaster except on formal occasions, he thinks it spoils the flavor of a great vintage."

"Am I to be Pharaoh's wine-taster? It would afford magnificent opportunity for learning the niceties suitable to my birth if not to my present circumstances."

"Now don't take offense, dear boy. Personally I like the old ways best; I always use alabaster myself when I am alone with Penpi."

"Penpi?"

"My wife. You will like her, she is a beautiful woman and has a better brain than most men, but she uses it well, and doesn't try to meddle in affairs which are above her head." He blushed. "She is twenty years younger than I but she seems to like me."

"Karaden, much as I enjoy hearing of your domestic felicity, I insist that you tell me why you have come here. My

117

curiosity bubbles like soup on a brazier and unless you cool it with a speedy explanation I shall shout for Meena to bring me a basket of eggs. I shall then emulate Ramoses as a boy, when he used to relieve his feelings by throwing eggs at the scribe whose painful duty it was to teach him history."

"I came here because I want you to prevent Ramoses making a fool of himself. He won't listen to me, he won't listen to anyone, but he always had a very real affection for you. He says you are the only man in Egypt who has given him everything and asked for nothing in return. That is why he didn't insist on you leaving here years ago: he said it was your right to forget Pharaoh if you wished. He sounded genuinely humble, which is very unlike him I can assure you. Arrogant, proud, bombastic—I know all those moods only too well, but humble!"

"So even the Vizier of the Two Lands does not find it easy to control our young brother."

"Control him! I would rather try to drive unbroken stallions on a linen thread—not that I can see well enough to drive anything except a pack-donkey! In some ways he resembles a pack-donkey—when he gets an idea nothing can equal him for stubbornness. For instance, consider his attitude to Hebrews. They are kept in walled villages and are not allowed land on which to grow their own food, so we have to feed them. This would be a matter of minor importance if there were not Hebrews in positions of influence throughout Syria. I need wool from the king of Naharin, and have to pay too high a price because his adviser is a Hebrew. It is the same with Arvad, with Kode, with Carchemish; everywhere there are Hebrews, shrewd men whose subtlety I am forced to admire, who feel it their *duty* to cheat Egypt because of the fanatical attitude Ramoses maintains towards their kindred."

"What excuse does he give?"

"Ramoses never finds it necessary to excuse his activities. When I try to make him see reason he refuses to discuss the matter except to reiterate that until Hebrews repudiate their god, Yahveh, they shall never be allowed to mix with Egyptians lest they infect us with their heresy. Since when has Egypt become so poor in spirit that we need to fear foreign gods! And a foreign god who is so servile, if he exists at all, that he has no temples and no priests!"

"Ramoses believes that Yahveh was the power behind our two invasions by the Hyksos."

"Then Ramoses has even less grounds for his folly than I suspected. If he dislikes Hebrews why not send them out of

Egypt? I have repeatedly implored him to do so, and I am not unskilled in argument. He says they are useful to us as craftsmen, and in captivity may even learn, when Yahveh has proved to them that he is powerless to release them from bondage, that their skill may be used to the greater glory of Egypt. 'Tell the Hebrews,' he says grandly, 'that when they are willing to sacrifice to Ra and to swear allegiance to Ramoses, they are free to stay or to go in peace.' "

"Hardly the utterance of a tyrant," I said, "and I am very doubtful whether I could persuade Ramoses to alter his policy."

"But I did not come here to discuss Hebrews," he said testily, "I came for a far more urgent reason."

He paused only long enough to sip his wine. "Neb, you had your happiness even though it lasted only four years. Ramoses needs you. If he doesn't find some kind of peace in his private life he will plunge us into another war so that he can escape out of Egypt without loss of dignity. Now wait and don't interrupt me! Ramoses already has a hundred and forty-five children. The Queens, secondary wives, and concubines, all live within the Palace walls. Separate households of course, but the atmosphere is about as placid as a lake of hungry crocodiles fighting over a corpse! If only he would choose his Royal Heir we might have a little peace, but he won't do it. He has a fixed idea that he is to have a divine son who will be a Winged Pharaoh. Seven of his sons have attempted temple training, but none of them has proved really satisfactory. We all hoped that he would choose Merenptah, the thirteenth son and Ast-nefert's fifth child, but he won't make the declaration until he has carried out a ridiculous experiment."

Karaden refused more wine but paused for a moment's indulgence in self-pity.

"It has always been my misfortune to be faced with a new problem when I think I have earned a respite. I am in the process of negotiating a most important treaty with Khatusil —needless to say the keeper of his Treasure House is a Hebrew. It is time we stopped fighting against the Hittites, for the booty is never worth our expenditure in men and weapons: but Ramoses says he cannot be bothered to take another wife—ridiculous of him to make difficulties, for the Hittite princess, Khatusil's eldest daughter, is still only a child, so Ramoses need do no more than be civil to her and give her toys."

"You want me to persuade him to add a new bud to his already overcrowded garden?"

"No, no! Neb, please give me a chance to speak! Ramoses had a dream—he is always inclined to have a convenient dream when he wants to overrule my objection to some plan on which he has already decided. This time he says you and Sensen came into the dream—he must have believed in it himself, for he sent a messenger to make sure that you were still alive, by relays of chariots the whole way from his new city of the Delta. If he *must* dream of you I wish he could do it when he is at Thebes or somewhere more accessible to the Living Water."

"No royal messenger came here," I said mildly.

"He met one of your people in the riverside village and relied on your still being in good health. When Pharaoh says 'travel swiftly,' no one wastes an hour in getting back to him with news! It appears that you or Sensen, Ramoses was not very sure which, said that his divine child would be born next year, and that he would see its mother for the first time on the night the child was conceived. Apparently one of you added something cryptic about the state of the moon, but as he could not remember the details he decided to take a virgin each night for a full month so as to be sure that the omens were propitious."

I failed to conceal my amusement at Karaden's expression of painted distaste. He frowned. "Neb, levity is most inappropriate. If you will indulge me by listening to the rest of what I have to say you will doubtless take the matter more seriously."

I composed my features to a more seemly gravity and leaned back in my chair. "I am all attention."

"Thank you, I will be as brief as possible. When I told Ramoses that it would be more than undignified for him to receive strange young women in his bedroom, young women moreover who had no place at Court for otherwise he might already have seen them, he said airily that he was perfectly willing to leave their selection to me. Imagine my consternation! I, Karaden, the Keeper of the Royal Seal, Vizier of the Two Lands, ordered to behave like a slave dealer! I did not trouble to conceal my anger. Was I, I said, to pinch the buttocks of girls in the marketplace to see if they were firm enough to please my master? Was I to finger young breasts and perform even more intimate explorations to assure myself that the meat for the royal table was without blemish? Would he prefer them dark or redheaded, plump or skinny?

"Did he sympathize with my righteous indignation, or consider the feelings of a man with a young and beautiful wife who might turn from a husband who showed such apparent dissatisfaction with her charms? No, he roared with laughter and said he had consulted me only so that I should be assured that his heir came of lineage on its mother's side also of which Egypt need not be ashamed. I pleaded with him. I argued with a subtlety which would have caused even Babylon to treat with us. He remained adamant.

"I found the girls. All of them are young, for he insisted they be virgin and comely—and virginity among older women is as significant as dull scales when judging the freshness of fish. At least he let me send them to his hunting-pavilion in the marshes near Tanis instead of to one of the palaces, and he has agreed that the children shall be born at a suitably remote estate which I own in the Delta. So I have done my best, such as it is, to insure that the incident will be treated with the utmost discretion."

"It seems too late for me to intervene."

"But not too late to persuade Ramoses that these are only more children, ordinary children whose unwanted presence is only an added complication. I begin to think that the Gods mock our family. Either we have no children or a plethora! I do not ask you to stay longer than is needful, but at least have the charity to convince Ramoses that he has been deceived by a demon in your shape, or in Sensen's shape, and select which of his grown sons you prefer and make him announce his heir. We must have an heir, or if Ramoses dies Egypt will be rent by rival claimants to the throne as though she were a carcass dismembered by hyenas!"

"And what of the unfortunate children?"

"You could adopt them," he suggested hopefully, "or adopt those which might prove an encumbrance to their mothers."

"You think of everything, my dear Karaden. It should comfort the paternal instincts of a childless man to be offered such a wealth of nephews and nieces. Is it too much to ask how many I may expect?"

"Not too much, but too soon. I started on my journey South three days after the moon had completed the twenty-eight nights of Pharaoh's folly."

XV

THE WIFE OF THE VIZIER

I HAD expected Karaden to ask me to travel North with him but this was not his intention. I was to send a letter to Ramoses, saying that I had recently dreamed of him and found the loss of his company increasingly hard to endure. This, as Karaden assured me, would arouse his curiosity and remove any resentment he might still feel at my previous refusal to leave the Living Water.

I was to be Karaden's guest and pose as his wife's cousin, a nephew of the Nomarch of the Oryx. Such a man had a real identity but he had died the previous year. It was a good alias, for he had been near my own age, had been named after me, and had lived quietly on his own estates and so was unknown at Court.

I willingly agreed to this plan for it meant I need not start on my journey for nearly two months. Ramoses sent me an enthusiastic welcome, adding a Royal Command that I should proceed with all haste to Tanis, his new city on the seaboard of the Eastern Delta.

I decided to travel by road, driving my own chariot, and taking a second one with Apu, the eldest son of Iri and Qen, who would act as both charioteer and personal servant. We went North by easy stages for I wished Apu to have the opportunity of seeing something of the great cities which once had been so familiar to me. The magnificence of Ramoses was proclaimed on the walls of temples, on pylons, on obelisks, on colossal statues in granite and limestone. The roads, better roads than had served Egypt even in antiquity, linked new villages, larger towns, and the distance-stones had been replaced by stelae with the Royal cartouche, which became increasingly monotonous. I began to wonder if I should recognize the boy I had known in Ramoses the Pharaoh.

At Goshen, a small town to the south of Bubastis, we were forced to spend two nights while a wheel of my chariot was replaced. The only inn was squalid and noisy, but the boredom which I should normally have felt in such unpleasing surroundings was stemmed by the increasing pleasure I found in Apu's company. Nothing was too trivial to arouse his interest, and the various foreigners he saw, who came from the trading barges on the canal, brought eager questions which at times I found difficult to answer.

On the evening of the second day he was unusually silent when we shared the evening meal in the shabby room which opened directly to the dusty street.

Then he said, "When you showed me the strange animals that are kept to amuse the children of Heliopolis I did not know that human beings were also kept caged in Egypt."

"Malefactors are only put into the town jail until judgment has been given—and never for more than seven days."

"This jail is a village, and how can children of five years old be malefactors?"

"What children?"

"I have already asked several people, but they only shrug their shoulders, or mutter 'Hebrews' and refuse to say any more. Because no one would answer my questions I spent the afternoon hidden in a dry ditch, where I could watch the Hebrews without being seen by the whip-men."

I tried to sound disinterested. "It is only with us that men work because they wish to work. Here it is necessary to make sure that the idlers do not batten on the diligent."

"But none of the people were idle. They were working too fast, as though the grain which they were gleaning was very precious to them. Some were old men, too old to have to work so hard, and women, and small children. And not even the children laughed or sang. A huckster with a string of fish came along the road and the people surged towards him but were driven back by the whip-men. They were hungry, Nebunefer. How is it possible for any one in Egypt to be hungry when there have been four good Niles in succession?"

"The people you saw have displeased Pharaoh," I said uneasily. "They blaspheme against Ra, and against Hathor and Horus—they refuse to acknowledge any of our gods."

"I still do not understand. You told me that all foreigners were allowed to worship their own gods in Egypt. Don't you remember telling me, Nebunefer? You said that a god could comprehend the completeness of another god, but men could only attempt to understand, and that most infrequently, one attribute of any god at a time. That is why we have so many gods . . . is the Hebrew's god different to all others?"

"This is a discussion suitable only to priests—and neither you nor I can claim that distinction. The subject of Hebrews is one which does not concern us. If you persist in pursuing your inquiries as to their merits or demerits, I cannot prevent

123

you, for I have always affirmed that each individual has the right to acquire knowledge on which to nourish his wisdom. However, if you will be guided, not ordered but *guided*, by me, I suggest that you find some more profitable method of slaking your excellent thirst for information than concerning yourself with Hebrews."

We finished the meal in silence. Had I known Apu as well as I came to do later, I would have realized that I could have said nothing which would be more certain to make him determined to explore a Hebrew village at the first opportunity. It is exceedingly fortunate that I was so obtuse.

We reached Tanis on the twenty-third day. I had not been there since I was fifteen, when it was distinguished only by the marshes which provided the finest wild-fowling in Egypt. I was nearly as impressed as Apu, perhaps more than he, for I knew the immense labor it had entailed to drain such large tracts of land as had been necessary to provide dry ground for the wide avenues shaded by foreign trees, for the spacious villas of the nobles and court officials, for the squares where the more prosperous merchants lived in well-built houses, two or even three stories high.

The principal streets were thronged with chariots and carrying-litters, and the people appeared even more prosperous than those we had seen in Memphis. It was obvious that although when I last saw Ramoses he was wearing a torn and somewhat grubby kilt and I the loin-cloth of a field-worker, I should have to provide myself with clothing more suitable than any I had brought with me before proceeding to a Royal Audience. The purchase of garments would be a novel experience, for a prince such matters had been the concern of the chief of my personal attendants and during the last twenty years Meena had replaced such items which she considered shabby enough to offend her sense of fitness. I need not have wasted thought on the matter, for Karaden, as I was soon to discover, had, with the greatest tact, furnished the chests in my bedroom with every garment which I could possibly need, even to thirty pairs of sandals and ten cloaks of the finest wool.

The Palace was approached by an avenue of sphinxes, whose faces, as I expected, were yet other portraits of Ramoses. There were four gates, and as my brother was in residence, yellow and scarlet pennants flew from the masts, like a rack of giant's spears, set in each side of the pylons.

So that Apu should have a chance to see the size of the Palace I drove round three sides of the outer wall, a wall

124

which enclosed an area the size of an ordinary town, until we came to an arm of the sea.

Here Apu inquired the way to the House of the Vizier and then drove ahead, down a wide, paved road bordered with palm trees, so that the guards at the entrance pylon would be ready to fling open the gates for me to enter the outer courtyard at full gallop. As I saw him rein in his horses with a flourish which would have done credit to a Royal Charioteer I knew I had been wrong to think he might find his new role a little overwhelming. It would have pleased Sensen to find that the Living Water gave its people a self-confidence which would have been enviable even to one trained at Court—I think it did please her.

Karaden and Penpi were waiting for me at the top of the steps which led to the bronze doors of the entrance hall. He greeted me with formality, for the benefit of the servants who thought this to be our first meeting. Penpi played her role equally well, kissing me on both cheeks as though I were indeed her favorite cousin whom she had not seen for five years.

She led the way to a pleasant room which opened to their private garden. "Welcome, dear brother," she said, putting her hands on my shoulders and smiling into my eyes. "I feel I already know you, for you have Karaden's ears and the nose of Ramoses. The rest is your own, and I find it very pleasing."

I kissed her warmly. "I salute you as a sister, you must not expect me to behave as though I were a mere cousin, and a neglectful cousin at that."

Cakes and wine had been set ready, and she insisted that I eat before she allowed me to ask questions.

"It is cruel to satisfy a guest's hunger only to whet his appetite for information," I said, shaking the crumbs from the pleats of my kilt. "What is the news of our illustrious brother? How many additions to our Royal House may be anticipated?"

"Twenty-three," said Penpi, "unless there are any twins."

"Which is worse than I feared," said Karaden gloomily. "I had hoped for no more than twenty. Less might have provoked Ramoses into some further proof of his virility."

"Wasn't it outrageous of Ramoses to make Karaden choose them?" said Penpi. "How dared he expose me to such barbs of jealousy!" But she smiled at her husband in a way which proved she was immune to this horrid affliction.

"Penpi helped me," he said. "I should have been lost without her advice."

She laughed. "He would have been, Neb. All he bothered about was whether their lineage was respectable. Consider Pharaoh's fury if he had been presented with the eldest daughter of the Nomarch of the Sistrum, who has a club-foot and is still a virgin at thirty, or the sister of the Governor of the Southern Garrison, who is too idle to pluck her hair to conceal that her forehead is lower than an ape's!"

"I still maintain that my paramount duty was to ensure that we shall not be embarrassed if it ever becomes necessary to record their ancestry not only for our contemporaries but for posterity," said Karaden with the pomposity which I already realized was unusual to him in the presence of his wife.

"You sound as though you had been asked to choose cows for the Royal Herds," said Penpi.

He sighed. "I wish my task had been so easy! No Sacred Bull ever caused such anxiety to its herdsmen!"

Penpi laughed. "If Ramoses were a bull he would expect Hathor to let him range the celestial fields."

"And to breed golden calves." Karaden shivered and glanced towards the window. "The wind has turned cold."

It was a curious remark, for the evening was sultry with a threat of thunder.

Penpi put her hand to his forehead. "You are not getting a fever?"

"If I shivered it is only because I am growing increasingly doubtful of my ability to protect Egypt from Pharaoh's exaggerated ambition. When I consider how I allowed myself to co-operate in this plan, I wish I had been born a goat-herd— I should have been able to do less harm."

Penpi stroked his forehead. "My love, I have not even a fleeting affection for goats. I infinitely prefer the comfort of the estates which it has pleased the Gods to give into our keeping."

Karaden managed a dubious smile. "I should have made an inept goat-herd. While I was preoccupied with thoughts of how to get the best price for our cheeses the goats would have strayed to another man's pasture."

"It must have been difficult to persuade the parents of the fortunate young women to give their consent," I said.

"That was the least of my difficulties. You must realize that they have much to gain. The mother of the divine child may even become the Great Royal Wife, a title which none of the queens has held since the death of Nefertari."

"One chance in twenty-eight: I did not realize that we had so many optimistic gamblers."

"The twenty-seven, or in my opinion the twenty-eight, who

126

fail to implement Pharaoh's ambition, will have no reason to be dissatisfied. I have given close attention to every detail: the exact amount each may expect has been set in writing with the seal of the parent or guardian."

"And the girls were not reluctant?"

"Neb, you show a refreshing incomprehension of female ambition! I believe they would have been almost as enthusiastic had Ramoses been eighty and scrofulous instead of one of the most handsome men in Egypt."

"He belongs to a very handsome family," said Penpi, tweaking her husband's ear.

"Wasn't it a little unwise to coop them up together like a bunch of broody geese?"

"I modified my original plan, on Penpi's advice. Each girl returned home when it had been established that she was with child. They go to the house I have prepared eighty days before the birth is expected."

"You appear doubtful of their integrity. Surely none of them could be so venal as to try to foist a bastard on Egypt?"

"Why should they feel loyal to a man whom they had seen only once?" said Penpi.

"Pharaoh is more than a man," said Karaden.

She wound a strand of his graying hair round her finger. "It seems that there is still much I must teach you about women. Either they thought of Pharaoh as a man, or there will be no children to worry you. Even Ramoses would not wear the Double Crown on such an informal occasion."

"My dear, such a remark is unseemly. Neb is not yet familiar with your frankness of speech."

"Then he must have opportunity to get used to it." She linked her arm through mine. "I shall show Neb the garden while you go and rest. Otherwise you will get indigestion and have another sleepless night."

We sat on a stone bench under lemon trees whose clean scent sharpened the evening air.

"You are wondering why I married a man twenty years older than myself," she said, with the forthrightness which I found so refreshing. "Shall I tell you? I think it may help you to know the real Karaden."

"I should be greatly honored."

"I married him for expediency. Don't look so startled, Neb; I shall never try to lie to you—it would be a waste of time. My mother arranged the marriage. I thought that Karaden would be a dull husband, but I wanted to get away from my parents—you'll sympathize if you meet them, and I liked the idea of being the wife of the Vizier. As you probably know, my father is the Nomarch of the Oryx and we were married at Hebnu. We went to Thebes by river on our wedding journey. The rowers were still chanting the marriage song when I told Karaden that I would not let him really be my husband unless he took me to the ghost city."

"The City of Aten?"

"Yes, and of course he was horrified because it is forbidden to go there. He refused, so I sulked for three days and wouldn't let him come near me. Poor Karaden, he was so miserable! But I wouldn't relent for I was determined to make him obey me . . . Mother had showed me how easy it is to rule even a man like my father. I told him, over and over again, how disappointing it was to find that although my husband was supposed to be the second most important man in Egypt he was powerless to grant the first request of his bride. That worried him, as I meant it to do.

"When we had almost reached the northern boundary of the forbidden ground, he halted our barge and had our traveling pavilion set up at some distance from the bank. Food and wine were put there, and he told our attendants that any one who came within five hundred paces for the next three days would be severely punished. One of my women wept and said that he would probably beat me unless I was obedient—and the other two seemed to think I ought to be flattered. I found the prospect interesting, if somewhat alarming, but I was furious because even the rowers smirked."

"Karaden has my sympathy. I should not have been so patient."

"And with you I should not have been so foolish as to demand such an inappropriate emotion."

"But you considered it no more than Karaden's due?"

She laughed. "I suppose, to be honest, I thought he had had enough of feminine whims and had decided to prove that if a woman is silly enough to engage in physical combat she will almost certainly lose. How startled I was when, instead of entering the pavilion and throwing me on the bed which my women, with sly glances, had so carefully prepared, he told me to pack sufficient food for three days in a bundle he could carry on his back, and to put on a stronger pair of sandals than I usually wore. . . ."

"A brisk walk was less than you deserved. I hope it was raining."

"No, it was the most beautiful night that even the pyramids remember. He strode ahead of me and sometimes I had to run to keep him in sight. But he knew when I really began to tire and put out his hand to me. Oh, Neb, I was suddenly so happy! Walking hand in hand with a Karaden I hadn't suspected existed; up from the river by a steep track, alone under the kind stars, to the high desert. We could hear goats running on their little pointed hooves across the stony ground, and Karaden gave me wild sage to crush in my fingers because he knew I liked the smell.

"When the sky was green as the first grass we looked down from the cliffs to the forsaken city. The sun came up as we were standing above a boundary stele . . . it was so high on the cliff-face that no one had taken the trouble to destroy it. Karaden said, 'They have broken his aqueducts and sown his fields with salt, but they have not been able to destroy the memory of the man who was proud for his scribes to record that he delighted to kiss his wife.' Then Karaden kissed me; and I found that even expediency is sometimes entirely different from what one expects.

"Together we went down into the city. Pillars had been overthrown and lay like dead men in the dust. This was the Horizon of Aten, the city of whose splendors my nurse had told me when I was a child, whispering because she told me about it only to make me afraid that I too might find myself forsaken if I disobeyed authority. I was frightened, and tried to hide my feelings from Karaden because I still wanted him to treat me as an equal . . . having not yet learned there is no equality except in loving. Then he said, 'Penpi, are you frightened too?' And before I could answer, he said, 'I am frightened because this place has shown me that I cannot protect you from the journey of Anubis even if I build you a tomb so splendid that it is as yet beyond the imagination of architects.'

"As the sun brightened we saw that across the boundary stele some one had written, 'This is the Heretic and the Foreigner who seduced him.' Karaden stared at it and then he said, very quietly as though he were speaking to someone standing at his elbow, someone who had waited a very long time to hear what he had to say, 'You who swung down at the end of a rope to paint those words, why did you rebuke a man who tried to love the unlovable? He was a crippled man who had the courage to allow his physical weakness to be cut deep in stone for all who had a greater weakness to mock. And his wife also had courage: she ordered her sculptors to show that she was blind in one eye, hoping that because of her acceptance of mortality other women would lose their shame of imperfection.'

"And then, Neb, for the second time he kissed me. Not out of duty, or in lust, or so that he could feel stronger than I . . . he kissed me. And we walked very quietly through their city, as though we must make no sound lest the fall of our sandals disturb their dreams. Close to the Window of Appearance where they used to sit together, scattering flowers among their people, we saw steps leading down. And suddenly we were children having an adventure . . . neither of us had ever had the chance to be really a child. We were natural as children ought to be . . . as every one ought to be. We started to throw aside the rubble which covered the steps. Karaden told me to be careful in case there were snakes, but on that night I knew even snakes would be friendly. We found wine-jars, each sealed with a cartouche in gold, which did not deign to give the year of Pharaoh's reign, or the name of the vineyard, but said only 'Beautiful! Beautiful! Beautiful!'

"Karaden cut off the seal very carefully because it was to become our amulet. We found a cup in one of the broken rooms of the Queen's palace, and into it we poured wine that had been pressed from a vineyard which they had forgotten to shield. Karaden became very protective; and I loved him even more because I knew he did so only because he wanted to be sure that if I cried it would be on his shoulder. He sniffed the wine, holding the cup between his hands, took a small mouthful and rolled it round his tongue. 'It is thin with age . . . but it still has the dignity of a great vintage.'

"We drank their wine and with it ate the bread we had brought with us. Then I said, because my sandal had rubbed my heel and it is difficult to live entirely in magic when you have a blister that suddenly demands to be noticed, 'If you ever want a secondary wife, or even a concubine, you must tell me at once . . . because if you want them I shall have betrayed you, so you ought to kill me instead of letting me become so disagreeable that I ought to have killed myself.'

"Karaden was shocked and said, quite primly, 'It is very wicked even to consider killing yourself; and it is also silly because you cannot kill more than your body. Suicide is a sign of ill-breeding, for no one else tries to escape from their responsibilities instead of being a good example.'

"I laughed——I think it was really more a giggle than a laugh because of the 'Beautiful! Beautiful! Beautiful!' and I said, 'Then so long as I give you everything I am, if you want any other woman I shall kill you. And you couldn't say that was wicked, for there are thousands of stelae recording how clever it is for Pharaoh to kill the enemies of Egypt—and what could be a more cruel enemy than someone who tried to pretend that we shall not love each other longer than any city, and probably longer than the stars?' "

XVI

VICTOR OF KARDESH

WHEN I went into the garden the following morning I saw that the curtains of the rooms Penpi shared with Karaden were still drawn. I strolled down to the swimming pool, which was sheltered from the estuary by a tamarisk hedge and lined with tiles, blue tiles with a design of water-plants and fish. Although it was so early some one had lit a brazier in the stone arbor at the far end: towels were warming beside it, and there was a plate of fruit on an ebony table.

I was eating a slice of melon and wondering whether the water was still too cold to be pleasant, when a man came through the opening in the hedge and dived into the pool. It was only when he stood up, shaking back his heavy black hair, that I recognized Ramoses.

"Even Pharaohs swim, Neb!" he shouted, and leaping up the steps flung his arm round my shoulders. "Neb, how good it is to see you again! I had told Karaden to bring you to the Palace as soon as you were awake, but I woke before dawn, impatient as a child on its birthday."

It seemed we had been away from each other only a few days. There were lines at the corners of his eyes, furrows from the curve of his proud nostrils to the firm mouth, but these were only a seal of maturity on the face of the boy I had known.

He punched me affectionately in the stomach. "Your belly is even flatter than mine, Neb, but we both do credit to our father. We shall go wild-fowling again. Are you still better than I with a throwing-stick?"

He toweled his hair vigorously and then took cushions from a chest and flung them down beside the brazier.

"Neb, do you know that giving you a cushion is the first time I have waited on anyone for more than twenty years—how magnificently refreshing! I have longed for your return. I cannot even be natural with Karaden, except when we are both in wine, for he has become more royal than I—and I am far too royal!"

"It must be difficult to be royal with Penpi."

"I was not thinking of women," he said quickly. "Let us not talk of women today, nor any other distasteful subject." There was a long pause. "Neb, I wanted to make you come back to me after Sensen died, but Nefertari persuaded me that I had no right to disturb your seclusion. In those days I still took advice from women."

"I should not have come even in obedience to a Royal Command; for I was a burden to myself and everyone else."

"A burden to yourself? Dear brother, thank all the Gods that you had not the chance of doing it on my scale! But today we shall speak only of happy things."

"Pharaoh has spoken!"

"Pharaoh is not present. He, poor fool, would feel a sharp twinge of annoyance that anyone presumed to mock him—though he is not such a fool as to be unaware they do so out of hearing of the Royal Ear. Neb, do you realize how lonely it is to be Pharaoh?"

"After Sensen I learned loneliness."

"I used to think of you both and try not to be jealous. No, that is untrue. At first I enjoyed power so much that I had the impertinence to pity you for having so easily relinquished the throne. Pitying others is sometimes the only way to defend oneself against self-pity. Neb, how is Iri? Is she happy?"

"She is contented—she asks no more."

"Has she children?"

"Three. Apu, the eldest son, is here with me."

"I must see him, later. Has he his mother's eyes?"

"No, they are dark, like his father's. Qen is a good man. I should have been glad had he married my daughter—if I had had a daughter."

"I have fifty-three daughters, and I love none of them except Bintanta, the eldest. It is a little ironical that she is the only one whose health causes me anxiety. But we will not discuss women—Pharaoh has spoken!"

"What subject would be congenial to Pharaoh?"

"Tell me what happened after we parted at the Well of the Three Sycamores."

"As we must not discuss women my story must wait, for Sensen would insist on playing her part."

"I dreamed of Sensen . . ." He broke off. "No, that we will speak of some other time."

"Perhaps Pharaoh will permit Ramoses to describe what happened to the younger of two brothers on a certain auspicious morning?"

He lay back with his hands clasped behind his head, and, parodying himself, declaimed, "Inspired by the Divine Fire,

133

given into my hands by my Immortal Father Seti the First, I, Ramoses, whose name belongs to the millennia, strode down from the Valley of the Dead, valiant in truth, lion-hearted for battle, magnificent in judgment. . . . How many times have I recounted that version of my return to Thebes! Neb, I have told it so often that sometimes I almost believe it—as you might had you not heard the truth from Iri. You must introduce me to the young Ramoses, for sometimes I fear we have grown out of recognition."

"I would like to hear of Ramoses the Warrior, who led the cohorts of Egypt to subdue the northern barbarians."

"He sent Egypt to war so as to escape from his mother, and to give his queens a chance to find his absence unpleasing. Even my first campaign was influenced by a woman, for I followed the plan designed by Hatshepsut and established a base on the sea coast, at the mouth of the Dog River to the North of Sidon. Unfortunately the Hittites realized that I intended this to be only a preliminary to a full-scale attack on Syria, and so Metalla drew on all his resources. Not content with inspiring our traditional enemies, he employed mercenaries—hordes of them, from Lycian sailors to Dardanians."

He pulled a vine-tendril from the fruit dish and began tying it into intricate knots. "My advisers must have found me most irritating, for I seldom took their advice. As you know, we had the Five Thousand of Amen, the men of Thebes; the Five Thousand of Ptah from Memphis; Heliopolis provided the Five Thousand of Ra; and our Eastern Allies, whose House of the Captains was here even before I rebuilt Tanis, followed the standard of Sutekh. I was always with the men of Amen in the forefront of battle, which disturbed Karaden who frequently implored me to remain with the priests and advisers. Poor Karaden, he found no pleasure in war and spent endless days harrying his fifty scribes who tried to keep accurate tallies to assess our gains in terms of future tribute against our expenditure.

"We had forded the Orontes at Shabtuna when I was told that two Bedouin who claimed to have deserted from the Hittite ranks had been brought into camp. I granted them audience, and they claimed that Ra had appeared to them in a vision and told them to go to Pharaoh, who would richly reward them for the information that Metalla had withdrawn from Kardesh and was to be found, still unready for battle, to the North of Tunia.

"I was about to reward them with two collars of gold, for a well-paid spy breeds others faster than a rotting hyena breeds maggots, when Karaden gestured to me not to be so hasty in my decision. I thought he was only trying to reduce the reward, but he affirmed that the men were lying. I was annoyed that he doubted my judgment, so I summoned an Amen priest to decide between us.

"The priests of Ptah had been so efficient in the care of our sick and wounded that I had begun to lose my distrust of the Amen priests . . . I knew Usermentu was evil but I had no reason to doubt that his followers would be men of power. To this day I am not sure whether the priest was a charlatan who hoped to gain my favor by siding with me against Karaden, or if the Gods of the enemy deluded him. On his advice I confidently went forward into the net prepared by Metalla as though I were witless as a driven quail."

"The Hero of Kardesh is over-modest."

"Hero: what else could I have done? Neb, the Gods must love the foolhardy, for by all the laws of men I should have been killed. To show my captains that they were over-cautious I deliberately drew ahead of the Five Thousand of Amen, with only a few chariots of my bodyguard. I had told the Commanders of Ptah, Ra, and Sutekh that their men could rest during the heat of the day and come up with us by an easy night march. How Metalla must have chuckled!

"I encamped with Amen in sight of Kardesh: I was going round the horse-lines when our scouts brought in two Hebrews. They also swore by the names of our Gods, not their own—this in itself should have made me certain they lied—that the Hittites were in full retreat. But something made me uneasy. Beating the soles of their feet served to open their mouths and they confessed they had been sent by Metalla who was poised to swoop down on us. Karaden poured reproaches on me and I regret to say I became most unjustly angry. He insisted that it was his duty to stay with me. I think he envisaged himself ransoming me from the Hittites! I used my well-tried 'Pharaoh has spoken' and dispatched him to summon the rest of the army to our aid. I shall never forget how fast his chariot took the road, the charioteer urging his horses while Karaden, blinded by dust, clung to the rail expecting to be flung out at the next bend. Amen protected him, for had he not insisted on taking a track which he was convinced was shorter than the one I had followed earlier in the day he would have met the Five Thousand of Ra, just in time to join their massacre by more of the Hittites."

"I have seen the battle recorded on several of your monuments," I said, not wishing to have to listen to a blow by blow description of the fighting. Even as a boy Ramoses had been apt to numb my interest in his exploits by reliving a day in the marshes bird by bird.

"It is recorded that I killed several hundred of the enemy practically single-handed," he said, throwing away the knotted vine-tendril and selecting a fig. "Neb, sometimes when I see myself through the eyes of my scribes and architects I suspect that I am either a God, who embarrasses himself and everyone else by his disguise of mortality, or else that I never led an army but instead hid in a cave wetting myself in terror. How relentlessly the kites of exaggeration disgorge on the boaster who hatched their eggs!"

"I have spoken with men who fought under you. I know that you earned their loyalty."

"We were surrounded. What else could I do but lead our chariots on an assault where their ranks were thinnest? It was again due to Amen that they had their backs to the river into which we drove them. Metalla's brother, and many men high in the king's favor, were drowned. The king of Allepo nearly suffered the same quenching—I always have him depicted held by the heels to let the water drain from his mouth which dared to challenge me."

"Did you really slay the enemy while driving in your chariot alone? It always struck me as an unlikely feat, even for you."

"I accounted for seventeen enemy chariots, and my charioteer was killed between the tenth and the twelfth—no doubt Karaden would have known the moment more exactly. I knotted the reins round my waist and left my mares to chose my next target. The mares were magnificent, worthy of their names 'Victories in Thebes.' At last I saw the spears of Ptah glinting through the dust of their march, and together we drove the Hittites to take refuge in Kardesh."

"Then you fell upon the Asiatics and their heads were like corn to the sickle of Pharaoh."

He laughed. "Our provision wagons conquered the Asiatics. During the battle they plundered our camp, gorging themselves until they were surfeited—Metalla never fed his troops adequately. Karaden, whose fortunate detour had kept him from the fate of the men of Ra, had also failed to make contact with Ptah, but he brought Sutekh up in time to prepare the Asiatics for the vultures. But old battles make dull hearing, as the scribes who taught me history knew only too well."

I followed his example and peeled a fig. "Karaden tells me that you intend to make an alliance with the new king of the Hittites."

136

"Karaden is never so happy as when he is making a treaty. This time I have to marry Khatusil's daughter, a child of nine. I am the Bee and the Reed, but I have not the sense to keep only one queen in my hive; nor a reed's resilience."

He frowned. "What use are treaties when Hebrews are more subtle than serpents! They have no lands I can conquer, no allegiance to Gods who can share honor with the Gods of Egypt. It is the Hebrews, the bastard spawn of Zuma which even Babylon spewed forth, who caused the Two Lands to be overthrown. Twice have their names been erased from the monuments—yet still they torment us as though they were ghosts who return to mock our unease."

"I noticed several of their villages on my way North. They appeared to be a mild people with more than usual skill in various crafts."

"Mild? And so is a sleeping snake. I dare not give them even the privileges due to prisoners taken in war. Should I let them go back after ten years, to plot against us? No, they remain here as a constant reminder that by their very existence they humble my pride, and woe to them who humble Pharaoh!"

In the late afternoon Ramoses drove me to the Palace in a chariot. His black mares were finer even than mine, and when I commented on them he said, "I must show you their granddams who saved my honor at Kardesh. That day I vowed that henceforward I would feed them with my own hand and that their drinking troughs should be of gold and their corn-bins of electrum. Their names are recorded in scarlet in the pedigrees of over a hundred direct descendants, but their sire is more fortunate than I for he is no longer expected to serve mares."

He glanced at me. "I see you think me cynical. You may feel more sympathetic when you have seen some of my problems."

He swung the horses away from the main gate and still at full gallop took a road outside the Palace wall until we reached the entrance to the stables—I hope Pasar was with us in spirit for the sight would have rejoiced his heart.

Each horse had its own box which opened to a paved yard —and the box could have enclosed a house for a large family. "I keep only a hundred here," he said, "the rest are near the soldiers' quarters."

A groom came forward and handed Ramoses a basket of carrots, each piece scrupulously clean and cut into slices.

In the center of the range of yards was one remarkable for its gilded rail, the elaborate frescoes of the "Victories in Thebes" at Kardesh which decorated the face of the building. Two mares, their noses gray with age, lifted their heads and whinnied as he approached. I wondered if Pharaoh's children had ever seen his eyes so gentle.

"It is not warm enough for the women to be in the swimming pool, but you will see some of them in the gardens," he said as we left the stables. •

I should have welcomed the opportunity to notice the trees and flowering bushes, for many were unfamiliar to me. But there were women in arbors, women being fanned by Nubian pages, women playing with children and women caressing monkeys. All of them tried to catch his eye, all of them were ignored as though they were the twittering birds of which their voices reminded me. The children were more fortunate, for he smiled at several and even patted on the head two or three who ran to greet him.

He went through a cedar-wood door which led to his private garden, and he slammed it behind him. "Now we are safe from them," he said with a sigh of relief. "No one comes into my part of the palace without an express invitation."

"Not even the queens?"

"Fortunately they prefer me to visit them—only concubines expect to be summoned to the presence."

Between hedges of rosemary we walked to the sea wall. "It is pleasant here in summer—I only stayed in Tanis so late in the year because I wished to show you what a fine city I have built."

A servant approached, an old man who went pale as he saw me. "This is the Lord Nebunefer," Ramoses said to him. "He is a kinsman of the Lady Penpi; I too was struck by the resemblance."

The man drew a long breath. "For a moment I thought I had seen a ghost—even the name is the same."

"Many were named after the prince, may his soul rejoice in heaven!" I said.

"Thenru has looked after me as faithfully as Hiboe served my father." There was a real affection in Ramoses' voice. "He is also a sphinx of discretion. If he once wondered why I did not grieve too much when my brother met such an untimely crocodile, he will now know that I am not lacking in fraternal feeling."

Thenru beamed. "It is a most fortunate resemblance," he said. "The Lord Nebunefer may rest assured that I shall protect his interests as though he were a Prince of the Royal Blood."

"Thank you, Thenru," I said. "The heart of the stranger warms to your welcome."

He smiled, then turned to Ramoses. "The Prince Merenptah asks that he may be permitted to enter the radiance of the Divine Presence."

"What does the boy want?"

"He has won a contest of arrows and is eager to recount his triumph."

"Tell him he may come to me—but I cannot spare him more than a few minutes. The Lord Nebunefer and I will eat alone together tonight, in the room of the flying swans."

When Thenru had gone, he said, "I think you will like Merenptah, he has inherited all the good qualities of his mother and few of my bad ones."

"In Thebes I heard rumors that you will soon declare him your Royal Heir."

"Nothing has been decided. When you know the boy it will be time enough to consider the matter further."

As Merenptah came running down the path towards us I was struck by his resemblance to his father: I might have again been seeing Ramoses at fourteen.

He greeted me casually, and then poured out the story of his success. "I split the reed five times at forty paces! Every one said I could lead a chariot charge. Will you have a war soon so that I can prove what I can do?"

I saw Ramoses was displeased that his son considered him too old to lead his army, but he smiled, though a trifle ruefully. "It seems unlikely that we shall have call upon you in the near future, for we are about to seal a treaty with Khatusil."

"Oh, don't listen to Karaden, Father! Everyone knows that the Hittites listen to the Hebrews and they hate us even more than they used to do. Please, Father, make me a Captain of Captains. Even Mother thinks I am old enough to fight."

"I am sure your mother continues to keep my well-being in the forefront of her mind. However, I am not yet senile."

"Of course you are not *senile*," said the boy, with the lack of tact which is so usual in the young when considering their middle-aged parents.

I expected Ramoses to be angry, but instead he dismissed the boy with a smile, saying he had important matters to discuss with me. Then he put his hand on my arm. "Neb, when I was fourteen did I show the same contempt for my elders?"

I thought it wise to treat the incident as humorous. "Almost exactly—though Tuaa did not allow you the same freedom of expression."

"Must every king give his son the right to conquer, hoping to relive his youth?"

"Do you not want a son who can repeat your triumphs?"

He paused, watching a pair of wild ducks skim low over the sea. "I thought I did," he said slowly. "Neb, I used to believe that nothing could be better for Egypt than a son who was a reflection of myself. Why did I have so many children? So that I could be sure of having a son like me . . . and Merenptah is very like me in so many ways."

"And still you are dissatisfied?"

He smiled though his eyes were sorrowful. "Instead of Merenptah being a mirror in which I see myself, valiant in youth yet salted with experience, he shows me myself in *his* mirror. Must I accept that my sun has passed its zenith, that my deeds are useful only for scribes to record on yet more unwieldy monuments?"

He walked to the parapet and stood drawing deep breaths into his lungs, flexing his muscles.

"I still look moderately young, when I am on guard against age. But a man is seen by the Gods when he is alone, when he cannot pretend to be more or less than he is."

The wild ducks circled overhead and a feather drifted down to settle on a rock-pool. He went slowly down the steps, picked up the feather and held it on the palm of his hand. Then he stared at his reflection in the water, and saw it distorted by the ripples, a man shorter, more thickset than he really was.

"A feather, so light that I cannot feel its weight against my skin, and yet so heavy. Truth is very heavy to bear, Neb: heavier even than the Double Crown."

"You must not allow yourself to be upset by Merenptah."

"Is the boy to be blamed because I am dissatisfied with a decision I made before I became mature?"

"He is your favorite son. Would it not be wise to declare him your heir? Karaden thinks so."

"Must I listen to Karaden, and be condemned on the stelae of the future because I created an heir before I knew what I wished to create? Merenptah is the son of my youth; must my spirit be barren? I have no son in Horus. I want a son who is wiser than I, a son whose heart I honor above my own." He became increasingly vehement. "I have been so besotted with pride that there is even a temple which depicts me worshiping myself—Ramoses the Man serving Ramoses the God. I ordered it to be made when I was in wine—and let it be fulfilled to remind me of my folly. And everyone thinks I did it in all seriousness!"

He beat his palm with a clenched fist. "Karaden can talk until his throat is dry as mummy-dust, but I will never take as my co-ruler a boy who is no more than I used to be!"

"Then marry one of your daughters to whomever you consider worthy to succeed you."

"I want a son; not a daughter who will serve only to remind me that the real strength, the real subtlety, is always in the power of women. A son who will fulfill my dreams and hide from me the harsh reality that I am growing old."

"It is said that the Captains speak of Merenptah as they spoke of you in your time."

"It is still my time!" he said passionately.

"How often must the Nile rise before even Ramoses is forgotten?"

"Ten years? Ten thousand? I cannot be judged by the female rhythm of the river, but only by the cycle of the stars." His voice faltered. "Neb, have I asked the Gods too much? Am I unworthy of their son?"

XVII

PHARAOH'S DAUGHTER

THE following evening I went with Penpi and Karaden to a banquet given by Ast-nefert in honor of Khatusil's vizier.

Penpi was looking remarkably beautiful in a dress of finely pleated mist-linen embroidered with gold wheat-ears. In addition to a wreath of gold and silver leaves she wore on her head a cone of jeweled mesh containing a ball of linen-fiber soaked in perfumed oil, an odd but enduringly fashionable conceit. Her sandals were gilded to match her toe-nails and she carried three blue water-lilies tied with a silver ribbon.

Karaden's cloak was dyed with Tyrian purple and clasped at the neck by winged lions in gold and amethyst. He was so splendid with ornaments that it was difficult to recognize him as the same man whom an hour earlier I had seen naked except for a towel round his loins, bitterly complaining that the rich food he would be expected to eat would give him indigestion as inevitably as the conversation would inflict him with a headache.

We proceeded to the Queen's Palace by carrying-litter, each with four Nubian bearers. The curtains, of yellow linen embroidered with Karaden's insignia in gold and scarlet, were drawn back so that we could be seen by the crowds who lined the wide streets with apparent enthusiasm. If some of them were poor or discontented, the Royal Bodyguard had seen that they were hidden from us by ranks of more fortunate spectators.

The palace forecourt was brilliantly lit by torches, each carried by one of the hundred Nubian pages whose oiled skins gleamed like black granite. The carrying-litters of lesser guests were ranged in double ranks before the steps leading to the entrance hall, waiting for the Keeper of the Queen's Household to summon them in order of precedence.

Penpi and Karaden entered with a fanfare from the eight trumpeters. I was amused to find that as Penpi's cousin I was allowed to enter before the wife of the Master of the Royal Barges, but ten paces later than the Great Royal Scribe. My earlier experience of Court etiquette had been less complicated: except in the presence of my father I had taken precedence of all men.

The audience room, its forty pillars garlanded with pink and white lotus, was already crowded when I made my unobtrusive entrance. Ast-nefert was seated beside Ramoses on a gold and ivory throne set on a dais approached by three steps of polished cedar-wood.

Only when I saw that each guest made the formal obeisance usually reserved only to Pharaoh when he wore the Double Crown, did I realize how difficult it must be to touch the Royal Foot with one's forehead without appearing ridiculous. This gesture had been made to me many times when I represented my father, but until now I had never been concerned with the difficulties of the technique.

"Penpi, you should have reminded me to practice my manners," I whispered.

"How could I instruct you, dear cousin? Had you forgotten that I never met Pharaoh until I could salute him with a sisterly kiss on the cheek?"

"Then if I overbalance, and clutch the Royal Foot to prevent myself falling backwards down the steps, you will have to blush for your uncouth relation."

"To those unfamiliar with Court, who have lived in the dusk beyond the circle of radiance shed by the Royal Countenance, all is forgiven."

One of the fanbearers had been eyeing me with concern. It was his duty to see that I took my exact place in the line of guests, but how could he interrupt the conversation of so illustrious a personage as the wife of the Vizier? Penpi pretended to adjust a petal of her bouquet and nudged me gently. "Take your place, Neb, or the keepers who control this circus will think the sky is about to fall."

As I moved slowly forward, the breath of the woman behind me warm on my shoulder-blades, I suddenly remembered that I had been inaccurate in claiming that I had never practiced a formal obeisance. A scene flashed vividly into my mind. Karaden, aged nine, sitting on an upturned onion-basket in the kitchen garden of the palace at Heliopolis, as Pharaoh in Audience. Beside him Sensen the Queen, determined to prove that she was old enough to play with us, draped in a net which had recently covered a fig tree to protect the ripe fruit from wasps. I, lavishly smeared with a mixture of soot and oil, was the Governor of Nubia, and with us was Ramoses, chubby and tearful because we had stolen him from afternoon sleep to become an Asiatic prisoner.

As tribute I carried five collars of gold, five slices of

melon, supported on strings round my neck, whose sticky juice made runnels down my chest before Pharaoh graciously accepted them. Sensen nearly disgraced herself by licking one, until, at a frown from Karaden, she hastily put it with the others on the offering table—a chopping-block borrowed from an unobservant kitchen-boy.

Having completed my role as the Governor of Nubia, I took up the ceremonial mace, a turnip on a stick, and became the Captain of the Royal Bodyguard. Ramoses, realizing at last that he had been greatly honored in being chosen to play with his betters, allowed me to tie his hands behind him with Sensen's hair-ribbon and was obediently crawling forward on his knees. I commanded the groveling prisoner to touch his forehead to the Royal Foot in abject humility. Suddenly he refused to believe in the game and with a squeal of rage cried out, "I am not an Asiatic!" and sank his teeth into Karaden's toe.

I found I had reached the second step. Laughter plucked at the muscles which fought to hold my face in a suitable solemnity. I allowed my mouth silently to form the words, "I am not an Asiatic."

Now the Royal Foot was before me. The face of its owner was benign and remote as a gold death mask. His lips hardly moved, but I heard him whisper, "Don't bite it, Neb, for your teeth are much sharper than mine were."

Ast-nefert offered me her hand to kiss, a mark of unusual favor to one so unexalted, but I realized she did so only as a compliment to Penpi. She knew Ramoses had spoken, but would have been even more puzzled had she heard what he said. Her small, pointed face looked pale under the heavy wig, each plait tipped with a gold lotus. She still had the figure of a girl although she had given her husband nine children, five of whom were still living.

Later, when she was moving among her guests after the banquet, I saw her eyes were anxious as she looked at Merenptah who was talking rather too loudly to a boy whose eyelids were painted with malachite.

"Poor Mother, she worries far too much about Merenptah," said a voice at my elbow.

I turned to see a girl who resembled Ast-nefert but who had a glowing humanity that the elder woman lacked. "I am Bintanta, the eldest of Pharaoh's innumerable daughters. I find the atmosphere somewhat oppressive in here so would you escort me to the garden?"

She led me to a secluded seat under an arbutus tree. "Now that no one can see us, I can take off my head-dress—Mother

144

makes me wear it because it is the fashion, but I find it ridiculously uncomfortable."

She leaned back, clasping her hands round a slender knee "Do you approve of your eldest niece, dear uncle?"

While I was wondering whether to pretend to misunderstand her, she kissed me lightly on the cheek. "Dear Neb, please do not deprive me of a rare opportunity of being honest. How do I know you are my uncle, do you really want to know?"

"Most fervently, O wise and beautiful niece! I presume I would be wrong if I thought you knew only because Ramoses told you."

"I expect Father knows I know, though he has not bothered to tell me so. Mother does not even suspect you are more than a relation of Penpi's, so be careful not to betray yourself. It hurts her to be reminded that there are so many things Father does not wish to share with her. She is a sweet and gentle person, but very easy to deceive for she seldom listens to any one except Merenptah, and he is only interested in himself."

A row of dancing-girls passed smoothly along the terrace and suddenly reminded me of a freize I had once seen on some temple wall.

"I was in a temple for five years," said Bintanta as though I had spoken my trivial thought aloud. "I became a priestess of Hathor, rather a competent one. At that time Father had decided that it was too optimistic to expect a Winged Pharaoh in one person, so I was to be the Winged part and he was going to select a husband for me who could be relied on to be a brilliant leader of armies."

"It still seems a most admirable solution to the future of Egypt," I said with very real enthusiasm.

"But quite impracticable, for a most mundane reason. I was supposed to be delicate, but I never thought anything was really wrong with me until I was sixteen. Then I fell down some steps and hurt my spine, not seriously for I could walk by the end of the year; but Ptahmas, Father's physician, discovered that for some odd reason the bones of my pelvis are set in a way that means if I have a child either it or I will almost certainly die. I minded a great deal at the time, but being surrounded by so many brothers and sisters makes it easier to become resigned to virginity."

The music of sweet singers drifted down to us through the night air which rustled the heavy leaves of the trees. "There is nothing really destructive about virginity unless one makes

145

a cult of it," she said. "But it is a little ironical to be a daughter of Hathor, the Great Mother Goddess, and yet barren."

"I also have nothing to offer Hathor."

She linked her fingers in mine. "I think you are too modest, dear uncle. Ramoses has quantities of children, but still there are more at the Living Water who think of you as their father."

"How do you come to know the number of people who live in my small oasis?"

"That is what I began to tell you before we wandered into such irrelevant byways as the shape of my pelvis—which, after all, decided my destiny no more surely than the shape of my mother's nose! Did Father ever tell you that he chose Mother for his queen because she was the only woman he knew whose nose turns up a little? He thought in his children it would modify his own, which is the only feature with which he is not perfectly satisfied."

"Your profile is an admirable demonstration of the effectiveness of intelligent co-operation. And if that statement is not pompous enough to remind you that I am consumed with curiosity to know why you recognized me as your uncle, I shall have to think of some even more verbose pattern of words."

"I learned about you through my grandmother, Tuaa, who I am sure you remember only too well."

"Tuaa! But she is the one person who could not have told you."

"If you are going to spoil my story by interrupting I shall take you back to watch the jugglers."

"Then I swear to be as silent as though I were in fact surrounded by the digestive juices of a certain crocodile."

"Hawks carved on the back of a seat look very nice, but they are uncomfortable to lean on when one is wearing as little as I am, so may I borrow your shoulder?"

"My shoulder is greatly honored," I said, putting my arm around her.

"You are a very companionable person, dear uncle. It is odd that no one wanted to be born to either of us, for I think we should have been understanding to children."

I felt a tear fall on my wrist, but knew she was shy of tears.

"Tell me about Tuaa," I said.

"I still believed in the crocodile legend even when I became quite an adequate priestess. One of the things I can do is to watch people's nightmares and see which bits are only terror patterns made from their own guilt, and which were sent by Set to torture them . . . sometimes, of course, the pictures are made by one of the kindly gods as a warning not to go on deliberately making themselves miserable by being unkind.

"The temple where I learned this was dedicated to Hathor: fortunately its traditions were very dissimilar to those followed by the Amen Ra faction. Ptahmas was trained there, which is why I know he is not mistaken about my need for virginity. Father did not let me stay there all the time because in an odd way he relies on me, and I happened to be at Thebes when Tuaa started to die. Mother said it was my duty to do what I could to prepare her for her journey through the Underworld. To be honest, I think Mother believed that I was the only person who might be able to prevent Tuaa coming back to haunt us."

"Tuaa alive was sufficiently unpleasant: as an ubiquitous ghost she would be insupportable!"

"I tried to love her, because unless I could make myself feel real affection I knew I would produce only clever little magics like the Amen priests, but I think that all I really achieved was to feel pity for her—a very poor substitute. Pity was easy enough, for she suffered extreme pain and became so emaciated that her fingers looked like a rat's claws. Her vitality was almost terrifying when one realized it was because she was too frightened to die. Even on the last morning she outlined her eyes with kohl and had her nails stained with henna."

"Where did she die?"

"At Thebes, in the room where Ramoses was born. The only things that had been changed were the god statues. At the foot of her bed she had a Sebek in black granite; but instead of a man with the head of a crocodile it was a crocodile with a human mask. The weather was hot, and the room became very unpleasant when she insisted that there should be rotten meat on the offering-table. When she became delirious she demanded human meat; to pacify her we produced goat's flesh and said it was pieces of foreign prisoners that had been cut into unrecognizable chunks to avoid gossip."

"I hope that 'gossip' is a deliberate understatement!"

"Tuaa requires no exaggeration. She accused Sebek of ingratitude for having forgotten that she had already sacrificed to him a prince of the Royal Blood. At first I thought it was only one of the concubine's babies—poor little things, they were often apt to die if Father showed too much interest in their mothers, but then I realized that she thought she had murdered you and Sensen."

"I hope you considered it naughty of her and uttered some suitable rebuke."

"It would have been redundant. She was convinced that you were waiting to testify against her before the Forty-two Assessors."

"She should have thought of that sooner—or at least had the wit to know that the Assessors do not require material witnesses to supply them with evidence."

"People who try not to believe in magic are usually very illogical, Neb. You ought to be flattered that she selected you as the only one of her victims who could prevent her meeting your father again."

"It would be worth being eaten by a crocodile to perform such a beneficent service to Seti!"

"And quite unnecessary. His heaven and her hell make the presence of each other impossible. The Ushapti figures she had chosen to be included in her mummy wrappings had been made in your father's image, but fortunately they were only glazed figurines instead of real amulets. She kept them in an ivory box beside her bed. Only when she knew she was dying did she tell me to open it and give her the picture I would find there.

"It seemed quite an ordinary picture; a young man holding a gazelle by the collar, drawn with red chalk on a piece of slate. 'He is your uncle,' she said. 'He would have been Pharaoh unless I had given Egypt to my son.' Her mouth began to twitch and I thought she was having another seizure. Then she sat upright and cried out, 'Bintanta, seek him on the other side of the River and implore his clemency!'

"She tried to crawl to the end of the bed, screaming to Sebek to protect her. I had to call one of the physicians to help me quieten her with poppy-juice.

"I took the picture to my room and stared at it for a long time before I went to sleep. Then I saw you, looking older by at least fifteen years than the artist had seen you, mending the axle of an ox-cart. It seemed an unlikely occupation for some one in heaven, so I woke myself and looked in a silver mirror which I use when I want to see something which is of Earth and is divided from me only by space which is measured in cubits and time which is measured in hours.

"You had finished the axle and were now sitting on a wall beside a lake. Several children were bathing in it and I remember seeing a woman plucking grapes in a small vineyard. I like being accurate about details, even when they are irrelevant, so I took the trouble to find out that you were living several days' journey South of Thebes, but North of the First Cataract. You find it surprising?"

"The only thing I find odd is how you managed to find me at the Living Water when the defenses were impregnable to Usermentu and the other Amen priests."

"Dear uncle, are you not being a trifle obtuse? Magical defenses are necessarily selective. The seal of the sanctuary was simple: 'No enemy may enter here.'"

I embraced her fondly. "Bintanta, you have lifted a burden from your aging uncle. Now that I have met you, I know there was no need for me to come here except as an inconspicuous guest. You know why I came?"

"Not officially, but I presume it has something to do with Father's latest experiment with paternity."

"Exactly. And you are far better equipped than I to tell him which child, if any, is the one acceptable to Horus."

"So now he expects to be sent a Son of Horus." She laughed ruefully. "In my day it was to be a Daughter of Hathor . . . or should I say a granddaughter? When one tries to assess human ancestry with godly lineage, precise relationships become a little confusing."

"I believe such a child will be born to him. Bintanta, you must help me: the future of Egypt rests in your hands!"

"Neb, dear, I am sorry to appear unhelpful but the responsibility is yours, not mine. Tomorrow I leave for Punt, where one of my sisters is married to the eldest son of the governor. I have promised to stay with her until after the birth of her first child . . . as an unembittered maiden aunt I am frequently in demand."

"But the Son of Horus is of far greater importance!"

"Not to me, at this juncture."

She waved to Penpi who had come on to the terrace with Karaden.

"You must go now, for my elder uncle does not like to be kept waiting. Sleep well tonight, dear Neb. We will meet in the spring, when we have both fulfilled our duties to Hathor, as midwives to the children we could not of ourselves bring forth."

XVIII

SHADOW OF AMEN

KARADEN refrained from asking my opinion of Merenptah until he had seen us together on several occasions. Then one evening, when Penpi had gone to bed and we were lingering over a particularly fine wine grown in his vineyard at Heliopolis, he said abruptly:

"Neb, you don't like the boy, so I must resign myself to the fact that you will not try to influence Ramoses to appoint him the Royal Heir."

I was feeling pleasantly tired and in no mood for serious discussion, but I could not avoid a direct challenge. I said without enthusiasm, "I like him well enough. It is not fair to blame him for being arrogant. How could he be anything else? His mother is almost slavishly devoted to him, his father prefers him to all the other sons, and most of his brothers and sisters toady for his favor. He has the makings of a good soldier, and no doubt he will find an excuse to prove it as soon as he comes to the throne."

"There is no need for a new war," said Karaden defensively.

"Merenptah will not agree with you. Only yesterday I heard him boast that treaties were for old men who dared not lead chariots against the foreigners. He said it in the hearing of one of Khatusil's emissaries, which I considered somewhat undiplomatic."

"You should have rebuked him severely, Neb!"

"I did so, to be told that though, as Penpi's cousin, I was tolerated at Court, I was in no position to criticize the behavior of princes. When I laughed at him, he flew into a rage and threatened to report my insolence to Pharaoh. So you see, dear brother, I do not share your glowing view of our nephew."

Karaden pulled the lobe of his ear, always a sign that he was perplexed. "He has never been uncivil to me, but I fear that Penpi shares your unfavorable view."

There was a hint of disapproval in his voice which nettled me. "No doubt Merenptah is fully aware that it is you who

150

decide how much he can spend on gifts for those he deigns to honor with his approval. He won the Contest of Arrows last month. Did you know that the man who allotted the prize now has a new chariot, with a pair of stallions descended from the Victories of Thebes?"

"He told me they were for his eldest brother, as a marriage gift!"

"And you believed him. Perhaps I have underrated his subtlety, for the Master of Expediency is not often gullible."

He refilled my goblet, and though some drops fell on the inlaid table he did not seem to notice it: few things could more graphically have demonstrated his agitation.

"This is all most distressing; I hardly know what to say. It seems I have been most remiss in not doing more to encourage the Gods to send us a true Son of Horus." He paused, then looked more cheerful. "However, it is not too late. There could be a promise of more temples, perhaps some trading-barges on the Nile, or the whole of the salt tax. It will require most careful consideration . . ."

I laughed derisively. "I fear that the Gods, unlike the majority of those who claim to serve them, cannot be bribed."

He was shocked by my levity. "Neb, I am surprised to find you so cynical. I can assure you, from my personal experience, that the murrain on cattle in the Nome of the Black Bull ceased immediately after Ramoses went there to sacrifice in person at their new temple. It occurred in a manner which cannot be explained except by divine intervention."

"No doubt the people decided that if Pharaoh prayed for them it would not be beneath their dignity to perform the same service for the well-being of their animals."

"This flippancy is most distasteful. Why should we build temples and maintain a rapacious priesthood if the Gods listen to the common people? I must beg of you to keep such dangerous heresies to yourself."

"I can assure you that I am neither flippant, nor cynical, about the efficacy of prayer. Real prayer, however, is far more rare than gold in Egypt, and infinitely more pleasing to the Gods."

Karaden was startled. "You think Ramoses should pray for a son?"

"Surely it would be no less than courteous to ask for what he hopes to receive?"

He became suddenly ebullient. "Splendid, Neb, splendid! The hypostyle hall of the temple at Karnak would be the place. At the Min festival, do you think? Or should one con-

151

centrate on pleasing Ptah? Horus of course must also be given special honors. . . ."

"Shall I summon a scribe so that you can calculate how much should be offered for a Son of Horus? A hundred times his birth-weight in gold, and ten times his weight at twenty to assure he reaches maturity? A thousand tusks of ivory, or shall we decide on a hundred tusks each time he cuts a tooth? Perhaps fifty ostrich feathers for each hair as it sprouts would be a pleasing addition."

"I presume you are jesting. I assure you this matter is of the utmost importance. There is need for haste, for as Penpi reminded me only this morning the first child is due to quicken within a few days. Once the soul is firmly established in the foetus we cannot expect it to be changed—though to the Gods nothing is impossible."

"Karaden, at forty-four you still have the pomposity I found so engaging when you taught me to make mud-pies. Do you remember how your nurse tried to uphold your royal dignity by telling the attendants of less illustrious children that you were already conscious of your duty to Egypt? The mud represented the fields, the water the river on which our welfare depends. In blending the two with such diligence you were assisting the Nile to rise."

"I used to be angry with you for laughing at me."

"And now you trust me because I still do. Poor Ramoses, he never enjoyed the advantage of being teased. Tuaa was always so conscious of her royalty that I often wondered how our father could endure her."

"Tuaa taught Ramoses to hate women. I shall never forgive her for it."

"Nor I. Tell me, does our brother share your view that the Gods can be beguiled into sending him the son he desires?"

"He intends to make the festivals more than usually elaborate this year, certainly at Heliopolis, Thebes, and Memphis —and here too of course."

"How tiresomely dramatic, and how futile! Surely he does not think that Horus can be influenced by the spectacle of Pharaoh officiating as Min, no doubt with an accompaniment of Sacred Bulls, their horns gilded, garlanded with poppies and wilting lotus. There are times when it is difficult to be patient with him."

"Ramoses takes himself a little too seriously." Karaden permitted himself a smile. "No doubt you have an alternative plan which will appeal to him."

"I shall tell him to pray in secret and without bombast for an heir who will cherish Egypt. I shall warn him that the

Gods will not send him a Son in Horus only to gild his vanity."

"Ramoses is not vain, Neb. Believe me, there are times when he is pitiful."

"I love him too. I pray that the Gods will pity his loneliness."

That night in sleep I was with Sensen. She led me to a pool of clear water and in it I saw the reflection of a scene which belonged to my side of the River, but I did not recall it until I was standing with Karaden beside his swimming pool.

He was talking about some trivial matter concerning the Royal Granaries, when I interrupted him. "Wait—I am trying to recapture a dream. . . . Yes, now I can see it again. There is a pavilion set among flowering papyrus reeds in a clearing near water. Above it is poised a great hawk—a hawk with feathers that shine brighter than gold. The hawk holds an open lotus in its beak."

Karaden usually had little interest in dreams, but he said cagerly, "Is there a pennant, a scarlet pennant, flying from a spear driven into the ground where the path enters the clearing?"

I hesitated. "I think so, but I am not sure. I was watching the hawk."

"A remarkable omen, most remarkable. Neb, we shall have to take very serious notice of this warning. You understand its significance?"

"Tell me your reading, then we shall know if we think the same."

"The pavilion in the marshes, it must be the place where the virgins were brought to Ramoses. Scarlet pennants are always put at the entrance to the game-tracks to warn bird-snarers that no nets may be spread while Pharaoh is wild-fowling."

He sat down on a stone bench whose carved lions were piercingly white against the tamarisk hedge, and touched the tips of his fingers together as I had often seen him do when pronouncing a verdict on some problem of administration.

"We have now established that you saw the hunting-pavilion of Ramoses, and that he was using it—otherwise there would have been no scarlet pennant. The hawk, the great hawk 'brighter than gold' can be none other than Horus. He carries the Open Lotus, symbol of the fully initiated priest. What could be more conclusive?"

"We are greatly honored, my dear brother, for it appears that we shall soon be 'Uncles in Horus.'"

"I wish I could treat the prospect as lightly as you do," he said severely. "This omen increases the apprehensions which tormented me during the night. No, I did not dream, I was sleepless as I too often am if I forget to eat sparingly. The prawns were excellent, but I fear I over-indulged."

"Karaden, I feel this is hardly the moment to discuss the inadequacies of your digestion."

"Forgive me, Neb. This is all so overwhelming."

"As the subject has been in the forefront of your mind for several months I am surprised you find it novel."

"But the implications! Neb, I frankly admit that until yesterday I never seriously considered any alternative to Merenptah. A Winged Pharaoh, the Priest King, the fulfillment of Seti's dream for Egypt!"

"Seti once thought that I would fulfill his dreams," I said nostalgically.

"You must not reproach yourself, Neb. You had the wisdom to recognize that the truths which our father wished you to uphold are not taught in the temples of Amen. What use was it for Seti to build a temple to Za Atet at Abydos, or for Ramoses to enlarge it, when the light flickers on our altars? There is power in Amen Ra, but which power? To destroy or to create, to bless or to curse?"

His pedantry was infectious: I heard myself saying sententiously, "The power of the Nile is not changed whether it revives the fields or floods the causeways."

"But we have built sluice-gates, aqueducts, water-channels to direct the force of the river. Ramoses has forgotten that priests must fill a similar beneficent office. He dedicates adjoining sanctuaries to Ptah and Sekmet, to Horus and Bast. Are we a generation of madmen that we worship the opposing factions of heaven and hell in the same breath?"

Remembering Ramoses' hatred of Usermentu this struck me as a somewhat shallow judgment. "It is to discriminate between good and evil that Ramoses wants a Son of Horus."

Karaden beat on the palm of one hand with his clenched fist. "Ramoses wants a son who can prove himself stronger than the priesthood; stronger, not wiser! His overweening ambition used to be held in check because he was wary of the priesthood, and they were wary of him."

"And what checks him now?"

"There is outward peace because temporal and magical powers are balanced against each other, like a drop-stone and its counterpoise, so ordinary men like myself can administer the country. But consider my position if Pharaoh was both warrior and high priest! Life would become intolerable for everyone."

"If we can believe the records, life was much happier in Za Atet's time. Even most ordinary people went to the temple when they were troubled—now they go in fear of the Gods and look for comfort only from their own kind, or in a jar of beer."

"It was safe to put magical power in the hands of men who believed that even when they had passed the Forty-two Assessors they must still be able to declare in truth, 'Thee have I conquered, for upon Earth there is no sinful one, no sorrowful one, no suffering one, through any act of mine.' Neb, until I loved Penpi I never believed such an ideal was possible. Yet as a child I said those words before sleep and at waking."

"As I did, Karaden," I reminded him.

"But Tuaa taught her son to pray for strength: 'Let me wake stronger than when I slept: let me not sleep until I am stronger than I awakened.' I used to shiver when I heard Ramoses say it, for his voice shook with longing for power."

"His prayer has been answered."

"Did the Gods hear our prayers? I think so, Neb, for they gave Sensen to you, and Penpi saved me from being only the Master of Expediency. Yet if they want Egypt to be again as it was in the time of the Priest Pharaohs, they would have sent us children. Why have neither of us conceived a child by a loved woman when Ramoses has so many that he hardly remembers their names?"

"The Gods may think that the time has again come to make the Son of Horus more than a royal title."

"But who thinks so, Neb? Which Gods, the Lords of the Bright Moon or of the Dark? I believe in your dream—may Horus protect me, I cannot disbelieve it! In Merenptah you have seen what happens to a prince brought up at Court, for I promise you that he used to be a boy whom I would have been proud to call my son. You must forgive me for allowing affection to blind me to his failings."

"Affection is not blind, dear Karaden. It has only given you an insight, which I lack, to see his real quality."

"You are generous, Neb, for in your place I should have judged him more harshly."

While talking we had left the bench by the pool and were now pacing between lines of fruit trees in his orchard. He pointed to a single stalk of wheat which was growing on a pile of rotted dung, half smothered by a tangle of dead cucumber-vines. "What harvest will grow from Pharaoh's seed?

155

The corn which grows seven cubits high, the corn of the Fields of Garnered Experience, cannot flourish among tares. If this child is sent to us. . . . No, I must rid myself of the cowardice of doubt, *when* this child is sent to us, we must protect him with all our strength. The pattern is becoming more clear. Why did you establish a sanctuary, which might be a little Nome of the older, wiser Egypt, at the Living Water? The boy must live there until his soul is so strongly rooted in truth that he will be able to resist even the most subtle temptations of the priesthood."

I felt it timely to show that he could not so easily make decisions which closely concerned me. "You think Ramoses will permit us to decide his son's future, or himself be content to live as I did in seclusion?"

"Somehow we must convince him! Neb, I know this to be vital to Egypt. You have dreamed of the hawk: it is you and you only who will recognize this child. Unless you are sure that Ramoses will allow us a share, a major share, in the child's upbringing, you must convince him that none of the new children is in any way remarkable. If we cannot persuade the mother either to relinquish the child or else to come with him to the Living Water then we must take him there by force."

"You seem to have planned a future for me which is less restful than a hornet's nest. First I must bring upon myself the wrath of Horus, who is unlikely to be tolerant of a dishonest messenger. I must destroy Ramoses' faith in the Gods' clemency. I am then to kidnap a princeling, in the hope that he will recognize my good intentions when he comes to power."

"It is for the welfare of Egypt," said Karaden pleadingly. "Personal considerations must not be allowed to influence your judgment. In any case you exaggerate the dangers. Horus would not have revealed himself to you unless he had some good reason. If he preferred the usual channels of communication, why did he not appear to some important member of his priesthood?"

"Or to Pharaoh himself."

"Exactly, Neb! Ramoses has proved to be most neglectful of his children, except when he is over-indulgent. It now becomes clear why neither of us has had children of our own. It is the will of Horus that we shall devote our considerable talents to the training of the future holder of the Crook and Flail." He beamed at me, his saturnine face looking almost rubicund. "I shall take Penpi into my confidence: it will be a great joy to her to know that our lack of children is neither her fault nor mine but fulfills the purpose of the Gods."

"I am always a little chary of claiming to understand the Gods' purpose, for they have a habit of proving that we saw from one eye instead of both."

"A man can do no more than act as seems best to him at the time. Naturally if our nephew, our Nephew in Horus—forgive me for thinking that you used the phrase facetiously, prefers to be known as the adopted son of the Vizier rather than remaining with you at the Living Water then we must make suitable arrangements. Consider the glorious fruits which will fall to us through a Pharaoh born of the Gods and trained by me in expediency. Even the Hebrews will not be able to negate our treaties . . . we should gain Babylon without loosing an arrow!"

"So, like Ramoses, you hate the Hebrews?"

"I fear them—for they possess many qualities which I dislike in myself: they are so clever at intrigue, so skillful in making one collar of gold serve where an honest man would offer two, so implacably determined to get the best of a bargain."

He paused to stare resentfully at a neat row of baskets purple with ripe mulberries. "Neb, even while I have been talking on a matter so vital to us all, a little scribe who never leaves a secret corner of my mind has counted those baskets and appraised their value. Sometimes I even find myself assessing the Son of Horus by terms of his future worth in *utens*. What trait of character could be more deplorable! At Kardesh—though I have never admitted this even to Penpi, when I saw corpses stacked like carcasses in a butcher's yard, to me they represented not warriors secure in heaven or the tears of women, but so many men expended, so many chariots useless, so many spears and arrows which also required replacement. Except for Pharaoh, I have more personal property than any man in Egypt, and yet I am constantly haunted by the fear of poverty."

"A fear so ephemeral is easy to dispel."

"Ephemeral? Dear brother, you have been well protected by the Living Water." He laughed sardonically. "Sometimes I think there must be Hebrew blood in my veins, for though I grudge every *uten* which is spent on needless extravagance, the lavishness of my household gives me a kind of hollow security. I am not alone in this folly, for though between Ramoses and Amen Ra the country is taxed so heavily that the people begin to mutter in the wine-shops, we are envied of the world."

"The world has good reason for envy." I said this only to console him, but my remark increased his unease.

"But where is the greater part of our gold, our ivory, our precious woods? In Pharaoh's treasure city? No, it is hidden in the temples and no tallies are available even to me. There are temples of Amen Ra in Punt, in Nubia, in every province and every subject country: if Ramoses challenged them, within a month Egyptian gold would topple Egypt's king from the throne of Egypt."

At last I realized why Karaden had suddenly become more eager for the birth of a Winged Pharaoh even than Ramoses, or I.

"But if Pharaoh were also High Priest of Amen Ra?"

"It would be the salvation of the Two Lands." His voice was almost shrill. "Neb, I dare not tell Ramoses that we cannot afford new cities, new roads, new monuments to his vanity. I have tried to do so, but always he says that Pharaoh will cure our poverty with a new war of conquest. He means it, Neb. He means it, although I have tried to prove to him by the records of many viziers that war is never expedient."

"You consider war imminent?"

"No, for there is sufficient in his treasure city to keep him amused for ten years, for fifteen years if we have good Niles. You understand me?"

"I think so." I said this guardedly.

"Then tell me: this matter is too urgent, too vital for misapprehensions."

"Your brought me to Tanis because you hoped that I could make Ramoses forget his dreams and declare Merenptah the Royal Heir. You hoped that Merenptah would become popular with the common people, so popular that you could have used him as a curb on his father's extravagance. When you came to the reluctant recognition that the boy would prove even more headstrong than Ramoses, you grasped a new opportunity. The twenty-eight virgins had seemed no more than another example of Pharaoh's difficult vanity, but now you believe that the outcome may fulfill your purpose beyond your most optimistic expectations. If this child is born, and we for the first ten years can train him in secret to become a master of integrity, then he can be produced at the precise moment when you have to inform Pharaoh that he will have drastically to reduce his scale of expenditure. Ramoses, instead of attempting to prove that the thunder of Pharaoh's chariot can shake the world from Sardinia to the Euphrates, will become content to rest in the reflected glory of his Son in Horus. Have I read your mind correctly, Karaden?"

There were tears in his eyes as he turned to face me.

"As usual you over-simplify, my dear brother, and put words into my mouth which were as yet only half-formed thoughts at the back of my mind, but the broad outline is correct. On this child the future of Egypt depends: may our prayers be answered, or it were better that Ramoses had never been born."

XIX

PAVILION IN THE REEDS

THOUGH, my dear Nephew, I have already tried to give you an account of certain earlier incidents in the life of Ramoses to which I was not an eyewitness, you may think that the Pharaoh he had become would never have revealed sufficient of his heart for me to attempt to describe experiences so intimate as those when he received the virgins in his hunting-pavilion. In fact, had I not spent several days alone with him wild-fowling in the marshes, it is unlikely that I should have been able to recapture that sense of shared experience through which, less by direct statement than the inflection of the voice or a fleeting expression, understanding beyond logic can be created between one man and another.

He had decided to return to Tanis the following morning, so before dawn we were in a hide by one of the patches of open water, waiting for the flight of the wild geese to their feeding grounds. Skein after skein passed overhead, their wings creaking like the oars of a thousand rowers. He killed three and I another, but by noon their feathers were almost hidden by the brighter plumage of mallard and teal which were heaped in the prow of the boat.

Ramoses was more proud of this boat than of the Royal Barge, for he had made it himself, cutting the reeds and binding them with three-fold cords spaced an exact handsbreadth apart. It drew less than a cubit, but often we had to carry it through shallows until another water-lane threaded its way between papyrus which at this season stood nearly twice a man's height.

One of us poled while the other stood ready with a throwing-stick. His twin hunting-cats crouched between us and when we had to wade they rode on his shoulders, rubbing their heads against his and purring loudly, as though to urge him to bring them good hunting.

A mallard flew overhead, swift but not swift enough to escape the whirling death which seemed to leap from the hand of Ramoses as though it too were winged. The bird faltered, then fell with a broken neck to lodge in a tuft of flowering

160

papyrus. The cats leapt forward; one tried to avoid a patch of open water and so lost the race to his sister who clambered up the reed like a boy up a date palm. It bent, and she dug her claws into the smooth stem until she was sure the bird was not going to fall into the water. Then she crept slowly higher, until she could pat it with her paw to make sure it was dead. I watched her seize it by the neck, bracing herself to take the sudden weight. She slid down, then leapt from tussock to tussock, holding her head high, as she had been taught, so that the bright feathers would not be draggled in the mud.

She crouched at her master's feet, purring while he examined her offering; then sleek with praise she joined her brother, who pretended to be too occupied with his toilet to notice her triumph.

"If only women really resembled cats how simple our lives would be," said Ramoses. Having had some small experience of the life of the Palace I most fervently agreed with him.

The reeds seemed like pillars that supported the canopy of sky; which began to turn pink with sunset before he suggested it was time to return to the hunting-pavilion.

I was hot and more tired than I would have liked to admit. The mud was pleasantly cool to my bare feet as I thrust the pole firmly into the ooze and secured the boat to it. Ramoses unwound a cord from his waist and tied the birds by their feet so that they would be easier to carry. Although the game-track was dry enough to hold the imprint of small animals, the cats pretended that they were too fastidious to trust it and insisted on being carried.

The reeds opened to a clearing walled with reeds. Yesterday we had returned to a different clearing, but a similar platform of split palm-logs raised the pavilion above the soggy ground.

Thenru, who still delighted to pretend that my likeness to Pharaoh's brother was no more than a chance resemblance, had hot water ready to sluice over us with a copper dipper, saying that we should be more than usually pleased with the way the wild duck was cooked for he had personally supervised its preparation. He had set the table and two folding chairs beside a brazier that gave off clouds of aromatic smoke to discourage the mosquitoes. Then, after serving the meal, he withdrew to his tent, set discreetly beyond a barrier of reeds.

A small wind stirred the scarlet pennant which hung from a fish-spear at the opening of the path to the river. It seemed vaguely familiar, even before I remembered that I had seen another like it in a dream.

Ramoses extinguished a fly which had evaded the smoke; then flung another handful of incense on the brazier. "Neb," he said, "this is where I thought my Son of Horus was conceived."

It was the first time he had spoken of his hopes directly, so I was uncertain how much I should know.

He smiled. "Neb, there is no need to pretend that you have not discussed the matter exhaustively with Karaden, for I know that it has profoundly disturbed him. Perhaps I should not have foisted so much responsibility on him. Poor Karaden, I have never seen him so dismayed as when I commanded him to choose the twenty-eight virgins."

"A curious command, even for Pharaoh. Why did you find it necessary to pretend that you could not be bothered to express a preference between one girl and another?"

"To all women I am Pharaoh, so Pharaoh sees them all as Woman, a force relentless as the Inundation, and as unpredictable. You have been to the Palace; do you still find it odd that my nostrils no longer twitch at perfumes from Punt or Syrian unguents, that I am bored by dresses embroidered in Tyrian purple and indifferent to Sidonian sandals? Hennaed nails echo the color of old blood, and green eyelids are no more attractive than a fading bruise."

"If you dislike women, why have so many of them?"

"Because fear, like most things, stales with repetition. There is privacy in numbers, for each thinks I am with another and so I can sleep alone without being thought inadequate. Even the king of Aleppo, who has five hundred concubines, thinks me the better stallion. I found his chagrin, though so ill-founded, most gratifying to my vanity." He shuddered. "I can assure you that the Virgins' Moon was an ordeal, not a self-indulgence. It is proper for concubines to be well versed in the arts by which some men are pleased, but a virgin determined to bear a royal child can be more rapacious than a starving hyena. I tried to feel sorry for them, for they were only behaving as they had been sedulously instructed, but I will frankly confess that some of them were more difficult than I have always found the Ceremony of Osiris, when in his name I have to bless the corn for the sowing in such a peculiarly intimate manner."

"Karaden should have let Penpi choose them," I said sympathetically.

"I think she must have chosen the last girl, though at the time I thought Karaden had remembered Iri and found some

162

one who resembled her. I loved her, Neb, although she was one of the common people—how glibly that phrase comes off my Vizier's tongue, as though they were a different breed from nobles. Neb, do you remember saying, long ago at the Well of the Three Sycamores, that one day a woman would really love me. It is odd how a chance phrase can survive so many disappointments."

A vagrant breeze caused the brazier to glow more brightly. His face looked very young, as though the lines on his forehead were only a boy's transient furrows of perplexity. I obeyed an impulse to make him speak the thoughts which I knew were lively in his memory . . .

The flowering reeds were precise as the carving of a pediment against the rising moon, but the clearing where Ramoses waited alone was a dark pool of shadow.

A night-bird cried, and his hunting-cat leaped on the knee of the lonely man who raised his head at the sound of a boat grounding against the bank where open water led to the river.

Unless he had been watching he would not have seen the girl who moved so quietly down the path, and stood looking towards the gauze curtains which gleamed like river mist in the light of the lamp in the outer room of the pavilion.

He saw that she was young, perhaps fifteen, and very slender. Her breasts under the white tunic were firm and pointed as pomegranates, and something in the way she stood, proud and yet timid like a gazelle, reminded him of Iri. The others had all been over-richly dressed, but this girl had for ornament only a wreath of moon-daisies and a string of faience beads.

For a moment he was amused that Karaden's insistence on ancestry had given place to a secret conviction that a strain of peasant blood would improve his over-bred family. Then he was annoyed, for if to the others he had been too royal this child would be numbed with awe even by the name of Ramoses.

At least she would not be another Duat, the fifth girl who had been unable to conceal her disappointment that he did not receive her wearing the Double Crown. It was partly because of Duat that he had not troubled to change from the hunting-kilt that he had worn during the day, though it was stained green with water-weeds. Thenru had been a little shocked and said that even a fisherman would wear better sandals.

He began to envy the imaginary fisherman, who could have waited for a girl with excitement instead of this odious sense of duty. Suddenly his pulse quickened. Why not pretend to be an ordinary man? A servant, no, better a soldier, a mercenary such as a man unaccustomed to the marshes might hire as a protection against fugitives who were said to hide there from Pharaoh's justice.

He spoke to his cat, and the girl swung round, startled to see him. He gestured her to keep silent, as though afraid of her being overheard by some one inside the pavilion. He beckoned and she came slowly towards him across the clearing. He saw that her eyes were the color of dark silver and innocent of kohl, and in them there was no sign that she found his face familiar.

He realized that he should not have found this surprising for even some of his children had not recognized his portrait statues until they could read the flamboyant inscriptions. Merenptah, for instance, had once asked him why such a large man had to have a doll with him—it almost caused him to discard the convention of having his queens shown only the height of his knee.

Waiting for him to speak, she bent to stroke the cat who had left him to weave round her slender ankles.

"My master is in the pavilion," he said. "I saw him go into the inner room and draw the curtains, so I expect he is already asleep."

He took her hand, which felt cool as Nile water. "My master has been wild-fowling since dawn and was so tired by evening that I almost had to carry him back; so if you are cold we could go into the pavilion without fear of waking him."

"I am not cold, but I am shivering because I am frightened," she said. "Did you know I was coming here tonight?"

"One of his servants prepared food for a guest, but I did not know who was expected. I am only a soldier he hired in Tanis—he is a man of small importance or he would have brought his own men with him."

"I am very glad you are here," she said, "for if I know about him it will be easier not to be frightened; nothing is quite so frightening if you know what to expect."

"Did your mother not instruct you?" he asked quickly. Until that moment it had not occurred to him that any of the girls chosen by Karaden might be unwilling.

"I have no mother, only an aunt who has let me live with her since my mother died."

"And your father?"

"I cannot remember him; but I know that his eyes were gray like mine and that he was a soldier and very brave."

It amused him to think that tomorrow a soldier might

boast in a wine-shop of the warriors' heaven that his daughter had pleased the Hero of Kardesh.

"You think your father would be glad you are here?"

"I think he would say I must obey my aunt: soldiers are taught to be obedient."

"You still have not told me why she sent you here."

He listened anxiously for her reply. Obviously Karaden had not told her to expect Pharaoh or she would not have spoken so frankly.

"I was washing clothes in the canal—it is not easy to do for the water is dirty and it is difficult to find a clear patch among the scum of rotting vegetables. I was beating the last of them with a flat stone when the old man's servant saw me. I knew the old man must be rich for otherwise his servant would not have worn two gold armlets and such a fine cloak. He sat on the water-steps and watched me for a long time and then he asked where I lived. At first I would not tell him, and then I thought he had been told that through me he could find the way to the house of my aunt."

"Why should he wish to meet your aunt?"

"My aunt is a midwife, and sometimes people pay her many *utens* for potions that she makes in a caldron at the full moon. I knew my aunt would be angry if I lost her a good customer, so I took him home and they talked together for a long time—I was told to wait outside so I do not know exactly what they said."

"Was your aunt pleased or angry?"

"Oh, she was very pleased. I thought he had paid her more than she expected so I was glad. I did not know then that she had sold me instead of a brew of dog's liver and crocodile's heart—she says there is lion-fat in the brew, but this is not true for it is far too costly."

"You should be worth more than a thousand lions."

"No, but in my aunt's estimation I am far more valuable than she ever expected. In one night I can earn for her three large and five small cattle: two cows and a bull, and five milch goats. She will sell the bull to the slaughterers so as to buy fodder for the rest. We shall be very rich."

"Are you glad to be rich?"

"No, I am not at all glad, which everyone says is a proof that I am ungrateful and wicked. I even threatened to run away, but at last my relations were so angry that they made me understand that to rob my aunt of three large and five small cattle would be worse than an honest thief who steals only from strangers."

"Are your relations violent with thieves?"

"A thief is beaten on the soles of his feet and sometimes he limps for the rest of his life." She pulled aside the shoulder-piece of her tunic, to show a jagged scar. "I have never stolen anything, except a melon that was already over-ripe, but the last time I was disobedient my aunt used a broken water-pot and it took a long time to heal."

He thought how pleasant it would be to see the old woman cringing in the dust under the thongs of whip-men. "What must you do to please your aunt?" As he asked the question he decided that the whip-man would be merciless if the girl had been taught to offer some curious complexity.

She glanced apprehensively towards the pavilion. "You are quite sure he cannot hear us?"

"He will sleep soundly for hours. He drank far too much wine tonight so even if we spoke in loud voices he would not wake."

"Then perhaps I shall not be able to obey my aunt, for the man who brought me here said the boat will be waiting for me an hour after sunrise. She will be very angry, but I am used to her anger and I am glad the old man sleeps. Tell me about the old man. Is he very fat, or hairy like an ape?"

Ramoses glanced down at the taut muscles of his belly, seeking for reassurance. "Being an Egyptian he tries not to be fat, and I think he has succeeded better than one might expect considering that his cooks are highly skilled."

"Then he is bald like an Amen priest?" She sounded appalled.

"He has plenty of hair, in the proper place, so he need not wear a wig except on formal occasions."

"Then he must be horrid instead of just very ugly as I expected. Oh, I hope he doesn't wake up!"

"Why should he be horrid?"

She looked at him in astonishment. "Don't you know why I came here? I thought men knew all the things my aunt tried to tell me."

"You must enlighten the ignorance of a soldier who has no aunt," he said gravely. "But it is cold out here, so we will go into the pavilion and together enjoy the supper that was prepared for you."

In the eyes of Pharaoh the pavilion was furnished with stark simplicity. A leopard skin on the floor, a mattress, a traveling-chest, a table, and two folding stools, but she looked at them with awe. Running a slender forefinger along the fillets of ivory which patterned the ebony table, she said, "I am glad your master is so rich, for we can eat his supper without feeling guilty. Can old men really eat so much food? Quails, and prawns, and stuffed vine-leaves; fruit as well . . . it is enough to feed a village!"

She took a prawn in her fingers and carefully pinched off the shell. "After I have eaten another of these I will tell you why I came here, for friends should be honest with each other." She sat on the mattress beside him and took off her sandals. "They are rather too large and have made a blister on my heel. My aunt borrowed them for me, and this tunic: I usually prefer walking with bare feet."

He took her foot in his hand and was pleased to see that water could have flowed under the arch of the instep. "You have very beautiful feet. I should like to give you sandals of gilded leather or would you prefer scarlet studded with turquoise?"

"Soldiers cannot afford to give presents like that, for I know that sometimes they cannot pay for their beer. Colored sandals are worth perhaps a hundred *utens,* much more than a donkey and nearly as much as a cow, but I should be pleased if you would let me have one of those quails."

She crunched the bones delicately as a cat then wiped her fingers on the fringed napkin. "I should like another quail later, but first I must tell you why I came here, for there are many wicked people in Egypt and one should be warned against them."

She smiled at him, trying to look very grown-up. "Some men are afraid to grow old because they have cruel gods who will punish them, when they are dead, for all the sins they have done since they were born. Their gods are more dishonest even than tax-gatherers, for they accept bribes yet keep a tally of every big and little sin and still demand full payment. Old men want to feel young so that they can stop thinking about what is going to happen after they die. People will give gold or ivory for lion-fat to make them strong, and if an old man buys a girl's virginity he becomes young for a little while."

Ramoses wondered if he had unwittingly suffered from the same unpleasing delusion. She saw he was momentarily abstracted, so took up another quail and then smiled at him reassuringly. "You must not think my aunt is a silly woman. She does not believe this really happens, but she believes very firmly in large and small cattle."

"A woman to rejoice my brother's heart; he too is very interested in the value of things."

"But not in the value of people? It must be nice to have a brother even if he is dull." She stroked the cat which was rubbing its head against her. "This is a very friendly cat, so I

167

know she belongs to you and not to the old man, for cats are wise about people. I am very fortunate that you are so different to his other servant, the one who wore the gold armlets, for I can see that you are sorry for me; and he would have offered only two large cattle unless my aunt had been shrewd at bargaining. He seemed to think I should be honored!" she added indignantly. "Do I look so young and silly that I could never hope for a husband who would love me more than three large cattle?"

To his astonishment Ramoses heard himself say in sincerity, "You look young enough to believe in dreams and make them come true; and wise enough to restore men's faith in beauty."

"I know you say that only to make me feel braver, but I am very grateful. The soldiers I have seen do not talk like you. They drink much beer, and then grumble that it is not worth even a *uten*."

She sighed. "I can see the moon through the curtains and it is much lower in the sky than when I came here. I am afraid I was boasting when I said that I hoped the old man would sleep until more than an hour after dawn. My aunt says it is dangerous to offend nobles, especially when they are old and unloved and greedy. I do not wish to make things more difficult for my aunt. To be really honest, I do not wish to make things more difficult for myself: for when she is cross, I am hungry, and I do not find it comfortable to sleep on the floor when I have many bruises. It is odd how one's body asks for things that one would be too proud to ask for oneself. My aunt says it would be very cowardly if I were to disobey the old man and leave her to bear the wrath of Whoever-he-is."

"Do you not know the name of Whoever-he-is?"

"No, and please do not tell me, for it will be easier not to hate him if I do not know his name. I shall shut my eyes while it is happening so that I do not know his face either. It is not pleasant to hate anyone, and if I do not know his face or his name I shall not hate him enough to have to hate myself too. Why is it so difficult to believe something your mind says is true? I expect you try to believe that you are doing a good thing in serving Whoever-he-is, but the real part of you is unhappy because it wants to work for someone it can honor. I think you are like me, the real part of us is the only light we believe in; we try to carry it like a torch, but our head is not strong enough, and when the torch flickers in a high wind we are afraid. But a lamp, even a small lamp of tallow when you cannot afford oil, is better than the dark.

168

But I am talking too much." She glanced towards the curtains. "Will I have to wait until dawn before I am hurt by the old man?"

"The old man will not hurt you," said Ramoses gently.

Before he could stop her, she bit her forearm until the blood ran between her small, white teeth. "I am not a coward! You will not hear me cry out when he makes me bleed."

Remembering how he too used to bite his arm to punish it for letting him be afraid, he could have wept for her.

She saw he was distressed and kissed him on the cheek. "Please do not be sad because of me," she said. "Your eyes tell me that you also dream dreams which are too splendid for little people like us. You are a soldier, guarding an old man who cannot command your real loyalty. But I expect you used to think of yourself as a captain protecting thousands from oppression."

"That is true enough, but what are your dreams of the future?"

"They may seem silly to you, because they are so ordinary. I want to have a child, by some one who loves me as though I were as beautiful as the women I see smiling from their carrying-litters in the city streets. I want to be able to give that child everything I have ever wanted, because I love him so much that the meadows beyond the evening clouds will be as familiar to him as the pot of moon-daisies on my window-sill."

Ramoses put out his arms and drew her back to lean against his shoulder. "You and I are caught between our splendid dreams and the pitiful world we live in, yet this hour belongs to us. The weary old man is asleep. His dreams will be fuzzy with wine, so in the morning he will believe anything I tell him. You will not leave my arms, but I will swear that he received youth from you."

She clapped her hands like a happy child, then hesitated and slowly shook her head. "You are very kind and very clever but your beautiful plan cannot come true. You had forgotten that my aunt is a midwife. She is not guillible like Whoever-he-is, and she will insist on making sure that I have done what is expected of me."

Very gently he kissed her on the mouth and said humbly, "Would you share your virginity with me, a soldier who cannot even buy you a pair of sandals?"

Joyfully she smiled up at him. "My aunt will be pleased and I shall be pleased too. The Gods are very kind to us. You are quite sure Whoever-he-is will not wake and find us cheating him?"

He went to the curtains which closed off the inner room and pretended to peer through them. "The old man is so fast asleep that even a colossus of Ramoses toppling on a limestone pavement could not wake him."

She was sitting with her feet curled under her, trying to pretend that she was flushed because the pavilion was warm and not through his kisses.

"There is a statue of Ramoses near our village. I hope it does not fall over yet, for sometimes I sleep in its shadow when I have been to the market at Tanis with the knives that my cousin makes. You will please not tell anyone that I go to the city market, but it is sometimes necessary. I quite often feel sorry for Pharaoh: it cannot be pleasant to tread on the necks of prisoners who even in pictures are dangerous unless they are bound. But we must not think of Ramoses, or Whoever-he-is, or any other sad things."

She stood up, curling her toes in the deep pelt of the leopard skin. "I did not listen carefully to my aunt, but I know she told me to take off my tunic in case it got torn. I will pretend I am going to swim in the canal and then I shall not be shy of being naked."

She pulled the tunic over her head and he decided that all his statues of her should be carved in ivory. The wreath of moon-daisies slid from the dark cloud of her hair which fell below her shoulders. Why did women wear wigs, when hair should be soft and alive and free?

"Shall I lie on the mattress?" She stood on tiptoe to kiss him on the mouth. "I know you are shy too, for you do not resemble the statue of Min which I once saw carried through the streets of Tanis."

He was shy, but with the innocence of those who receive the joy which Ptah conceived for his children when Earth was young. Her skin was smooth as silver, and her bones felt light as the wings of a singing-bird.

"You arms are stronger than the branches of a tree," she said. "Even if there was a great storm I know you would not let me fall."

He set her very gently on the mattress, glad that the flower-blue of the coverlet was so exact a foil for the shadows in the curves of her body.

He laughed, the laughter of a boy who discovers he is no longer afraid of being young. "Perhaps if I take off my kilt and we lie naked in each other's arms I shall be strong enough to protect you from the anger of your aunt."

She thought he could do no more than protect her from the cupidity of an old woman, the lust of an aging man. But the Gods had given him a new Iri, an Iri he could cherish above Egypt for into her hands he would put the power of Pharaoh.

"It is very odd," she said in a small voice, "that although I am trembling I am not at all afraid. It is an odd feeling, as though I were quivering and yet still, like the wings of a hawk when it rests on the air."

Then Ramoses forgot all he had learned of the art of love-making, which he had so often exercised with the skill of a gymnast or the deliberate patience of one trained in ordeals. His body and hers obeyed a rhythm which the trees know when they bud in the young year, which a bird obeys when it sings with the morning.

Towards dawn they slept, she with her head on his shoulder. And Horus came to Ramoses in a dream.

In the dream Horus told many things to Pharaoh that were both terrible and splendid. But when Ramoses woke he knew only that he had seen a great hawk, with feathers of gold, circle three times above the pavilion in which he slept with a girl whom he loved in his arms. And the hawk carried in its beak an open lotus.

And Ramoses rejoiced with the joy that only the young in heart dare remember.

For three days Pharaoh remained in the marshes, for he was reluctant to return to the Palace where he would have to pretend to be the same man who had left there so recently and yet who had been so utterly changed.

He had told his love that when he was no longer bound in service to the old man he would meet her in the shadow of the colossus of Ramoses, where she would wait for him at noon and at sunset.

When he returned to the Palace he summoned the Maker of the Royal Sandals, and ordered him to create a pair of scarlet leather with ribbons of turquoise tipped with gold lotus buds. And these were made before evening. Pharaoh knew they would fit, for her feet were the length of his hand and the breadth of four fingers. Before sending for Karaden he wrapped the sandals in fine linen and packed them in an ivory box.

He showed the box to Karaden and said, "It contains my first gift to the mother of my Son in Horus."

Karaden looked at him with the patience they both found so exceedingly irksome and said, "I am gratified to hear that the Gods have indicated their choice so expeditiously."

Ramoses laughed. "They have been more than gracious.

They allowed me to choose, and then informed me of their approval. Do not look so dubious, Karaden, for when the Gods and Pharaoh agree men must join in their thanksgiving."

"I join most heartily. Now there will be no need for the elaborate preparations I have made on behalf of Pharaoh." He tried to sound enthusiastic. "Twenty-seven girls can return to their homes, with such emoluments as I have already arranged."

"And one remains here, to rejoice the heart of your brother. I shall make her a secondary wife without delay. When my son is born she will become my queen. Karaden, do you realize what it means to me, to find all that I hoped for in Iri and Nefertari has become true in one woman?"

"It all sounds most encouraging, if a little premature," said Karaden cautiously. "It would have been easier if the Gods had sent you a more timely dream—I presume you have had a dream?" Ramoses nodded and he went on. "However, one must not expect the Gods to be expedient as Pharaoh's Vizier. Tell me, which of the chosen is chosen in fact? She had better occupy the house which used to belong to my Chief Scribe. It is comfortable and secluded, and will be convenient for your discreet visits."

"I am flattered by your concern for my welfare, dear brother. In the meanwhile you will continue to guard my real identity with the same admirable discretion you have already shown. I have somewhat improved on the role you selected for me: I am no longer an aging nonentity, with a pathetic faith in the theft of virginity as a specific against impotence, but a mercenary soldier who was freely given the joys which his master missed through a surfeit of wine."

Karaden stared at his brother in horror. "Surely you are not telling me that the last girl, the one who came to you on the twenty-eighth night of the moon, is the one you mean?"

Ramoses smiled and said in a voice laced with patronage, "Your choice of one whose ancestry will not please your more pedantic scribes was pleasing to Horus, and more than pleasing to Pharaoh. Karaden, I beg of you to conceal your dismay, for to invent a suitable genealogy should be well within your powers."

"Ramoses, this is terrible news!" He clutched the arms of his chair as though he clung to an overturned boat in a river of crocodiles.

Suddenly Pharaoh was afraid. "Karaden, what are you trying to tell me? Karaden, speak!"

"This is impossible! The Gods cannot be so heedless of my

172

intentions, so cruel as to make a mockery of all I have done!"

"Is she dead, Karaden?" said Ramoses.

Karaden stared at him, then bent his head. "Pharaoh, she is dead."

Words fell from the mouth of Ramoses harsh as chips of stone from a tomb-worker's hammer. "So even Horus cannot protect Egypt from the ineptitude of her Vizier."

"Forgive me, Ramoses," he whispered abjectly. "The guilt is mine, all mine."

"How did she die? Speak Karaden!"

He hesitated so long that it was almost a relief from the anguish of apprehension, when he said, "She was killed by a chariot. The street was narrow: no one saw who drove the horses. She suffered no pain, she was killed instantly. She is dead, Ramoses. You must not think of her anymore. She is dead."

XX

THE OLD PALACE

I ARGUED with Ramoses until dawn before he showed any sign of believing that although the girl was dead his dream of the hawk with a lotus was a true dream. Over and over again he accused me of trying to bring him false comfort.

"It is not false, I swear it by Horus himself," I repeated with increasing vehemence.

At last he said grudgingly, "Dreams are notoriously difficult to interpret, but how could I, Pharaoh, be mistaken?"

"Because you are fallible as any other man, though too arrogant to stomach the fact! If Horus shared your opinion of yourself, would he have bothered to send the same dream to me?"

"He did not send it to you! Sensen showed the vision to you, in a pool of clear water, you never claimed anything more!"

"And why did she show it to me? Because she knew you had misunderstood the meaning. Ramoses, you are behaving like a spoiled child, who refuses to unwrap a present for fear of disappointment! Your prayers have been answered, yet you deny the Gods because the answer does not entirely please you. A Son of Horus will be born to you; who are you to question the Gods' choice of his mother?"

"Then why did I have to love a girl who was not acceptable to the Gods? Why, Neb, what have I done that the Gods give me everything except the thing I want—to be loved for myself? Is it too much to ask?"

"Can love be measured in hours? Do I love Sensen less because I have had to live without her for so many years?"

"You dream of her, it is better than nothing."

I began to lose patience. "Self-pity is unbecoming even to Pharaoh."

His nostrils flared like a stallion flicked with a whip. "So you also find the heart of Ramoses contemptible!"

I took him by the shoulders and swung him round to face me. "Ramoses, listen to me! Your dream, and mine, were sent by Horus. It came to you on the last night of the moon.

The true meaning is that during those twenty-eight nights a child was conceived whose name will be remembered even when your greatest monuments are dust."

"And it was no more than an odd coincidence that she was with me that night—or was I too preoccupied to notice the visitation of Horus when he approached me on the relevant occasion?"

"You asked for the truth: you may find it unpalatable. You have always depised women and therefore you have been divided against yourself. If I shout to a man whose eardrums are broken, can he justly revile me for keeping silent? The Gods are not heard by half-men or by half-women, but you loved a girl and so were healed of your separation. She, and she alone, made it possible for the soul of your son to enter the vehicle prepared of your seed."

"So you believe she is the mother of my son, even though he is born of another womb?" There was a new note in his voice, which seemed to echo the dawn wind that was stirring the listening reeds.

"I believe it as I believe in my love for Sensen."

He sprang to his feet, suddenly alert, vigorous, exalted. He shouted for Thenru to bring wine, to tell the Master of his Barge that we were returning to Tanis within the hour. Reluctantly I put away my desire for sleep, for I knew his moods of consuming energy could not be curbed until they had run their course.

"The Court will move to Memphis at once," he declared, then paused. "No, the Court can go to Heliopolis, and Karaden to Memphis so that you can be at hand for the birth of the first child. Messengers must be dispatched immediately to bring the women to the Old Palace. You can be in attendance on them until Sensen tells you which is to bear my son."

"Why Memphis?" I asked, with what seemed to me a most natural curiosity.

"Neb, don't try to make difficulties! Karaden suggested, and for once I agreed with him, that they should be born at his estate near Amu, but I have now decided that Memphis would be far better. The Old Palace has not been used since our grandfather's time, but it is built on one of the most honored sites in Egypt—the birthplace of Za Atet, what could be more suitable? Later it can be rebuilt. I may even make Memphis my capital, though I prefer the Delta."

"Without wishing to appear needlessly obtuse, why is my presence there necessary?"

"There was a portent at the conception, therefore we may expect a portent at the birth—such things are by no means

175

unknown in the records of our ancestors. As I was fallible in the interpretation of my vision of Horus there is no one I can trust save you, my dear brother. Ptahmas will attend all the women, for this birth is too important to be left to midwives. I shall tell him who you are—he has probably guessed already, and say that you are to be present when each child is born. Each child, that is, until Horus declares himself—the others will be Karaden's concern, and doubtless he will make suitable arrangements."

"Then I must hope that he is the first born," I said with feeling. "For though I have acted as midwife to several mares, and been not unhelpful in the matter of litters of greyhounds, I have not yet performed a similar service for a woman."

"It is a simple process," he said, with the easy conviction of one who has no intention of sharing an experience. "None of the secondary wives are with child so we can take the Royal Birth Stool from the Queen's Treasure House without arousing unwelcome curiosity."

While we were talking, Thenru and the other servants had dismantled the pavilion and we were pacing up and down the wooden landing stage waiting to embark for Tanis.

The sail creaked up the mast. I hoped Ramoses would take the steering-oar and leave me in peace, but his voice kept steadily on, and as the wind freshened and we drew into the river-mouth my drowsy comments seemed irrelevant as the sound of water slapping against the side of the boat.

Karaden was annoyed that he was expected to reside at Memphis, for it would mean his having to travel frequently to Heliopolis on matters of state. I also was annoyed, for I had begun to enjoy the entertainments which I used to find so tedious when I was the central figure instead of a minor guest.

After interminable discussion, it was decided that Penpi and I should go to Memphis to supervise the preparation of the Old Palace, leaving Karaden to join us there when he had first attended to the more urgent of the affairs which awaited him at Heliopolis.

I began to sympathize with pregnant women, for every morning until our departure Karaden at the first meal questioned me in the hope that I had had another dream which would simplify his plans. He sounded so much like an anxious husband trying to find out if his wife had developed a significant symptom that I felt inclined to announce a sudden craving for pomegranates or prawns, or some more rare food preferably out of season. I tried to hide my secret fear that I might fail to recognize the child, or worse, misinterpret a dream and so unwittingly burden Egypt with someone even more unsuitable than Merenptah. I even fasted in the hope of breaking a long sequence of dreamless nights, but this exercise, made difficult by the excellence of Karaden's cooks, produced only a vague dream that the mother chosen by Horus had a scar shaped like a sickle moon over her right eyebrow. I kept this news to myself, for it was not clear enough to be relied on.

Penpi and I had a pleasant journey by one of Karaden's smaller sailing-barges, but on reaching Memphis we found that the Old Palace presented unforeseen problems.

In the time of the first Ramoses it could have housed six hundred people, but now only the state rooms, which had ceilings and pillars of limestone, were habitable, for the wooden roof-beams of the smaller apartments and the servants' quarters had been riddled by white ants and had either fallen or else were palpably unsafe.

"We shall have to turn the audience halls into dormitories —curtains can be hung between the pillars if they want privacy," I said to Penpi, who was standing on one leg shaking pieces of rubble out of her sandal.

"Neb, neither you nor Karaden have any conception of the quarrels that will go on here! The Court is bad enough, but at least each newcomer knows that she will be only one among many. Didn't Karaden tell you that each of these girls thought she was the only one?"

"No, he didn't," I said with mounting dismay. "Penpi, do you mean that I will be the only male, except Ptahmas, among twenty-three ravening women each of whom thought she was going to be the only fish in the pool?"

She laughed. "Fish is a simile which does great credit to your essential optimism; wildcats would be more apposite! Some of them may be friendly to each other—they can use the main gardens and take their meals together, but most of them are sure to sulk, so the poor creatures must be provided with lairs to hide in!"

"When I have to eat here I shall bring my own food. Even a field-worker's bread and radishes would be preferable to a dish prepared for a rival."

"I don't expect they will try to poison each other," said Penpi consolingly. "They are all under twenty, and poison is more usual in women of middle-age. But it is a thought all the same. I shall arrange for all the meals to be prepared in the main kitchen, and served to each girl by her personal servant."

"That should remove at least one of the dangers attendant on this project, for presumably each personal servant will zealously guard her charge—like grooms their horses before a chariot race."

"Neb, how clever of you! We will use the stables. There are boxes for fifty horses, and I noticed this morning that they are still in good repair. We will have doors cut to join them into pairs. One box can be made into a living room, and the other divided into a sleeping apartment, looking out to a small private garden, a small toilet room and a place for the servant."

"Aren't private gardens a needless complication?"

"Even the sulkiest ones must have sunlight or they will become pallid as slugs."

She walked briskly to the blank outer wall of the stable buildings. The ground had been neglected for years. Thistles had burst their way between cracked paving-stones, lizards basked on piles of potshards, a few straggling currant bushes still grew among matted stalks of long-decayed melons and cucumbers.

"I told Karaden we should need two hundred workmen. He must give us four hundred or we shall never have it ready in time," she said cheerfully. "Find me a flat piece of stone and I'll draw the plans."

During the following month I found how easily Penpi would have fitted into the pattern of life at the Living Water. I was glad that Karaden remained at Heliopolis for he might not have approved of his wife wielding a broom to clear moldy straw from a stable, mixing color-wash in a tub to make sure the walls were the exact shade of pink she desired, driving pegs into the newly cleaned ground to mark where walls of reed matting should divide each garden from the next.

In the main gardens the same ceaseless activity prevailed. Water-courses were cleared, pools freshly tiled, hedges clipped and flowering shrubs set in yet more cart-loads of rich river-mud. Her scheme to provide a private shade tree for each girl was not very successful and in place of those which did not survive transplanting she had a thatched shelter built, its palm-wood supports enlivened with flowering vines in pottery jars.

The central courtyard in spite of gaily colored plants in the water-troughs was still strongly reminiscent of a stud-farm, and I often wished that our preparations were being undertaken for occupants so uncomplicated as royal mares.

Two days before the women were due to arrive, Ramoses

sent a messenger to say that he wished me to join him at Heliopolis.

"You deserve a rest," said Penpi. "And there is nothing else to do here until the first of the babies is due. Tell Karaden that I am being exceedingly efficient and that if he doesn't come back to me soon I shall leave him in charge of everything."

So reluctantly I went to Heliopolis and to be honest greatly enjoyed myself. My affection for Ramoses constantly strengthened, though at times I found it difficult not to become irritated by the excessive pomp with which he surrounded himself. He never managed to be natural except when we were alone together and on all other occasions expected his most trivial or inaccurate remarks to be accepted as though they had the weight of a divine utterance.

He seldom mentioned the matter which so deeply concerned us and I might have thought he had lost interest had I not seen an ivory tablet that he kept in a box by his bed on which the days of gestation of each of the twenty-two girls were carefully tabulated. The first day on which, according to the calculations of Ptahmas, a live birth could take place was circled in scarlet. The seven days of the completed cycle were underlined in gold. So that he would not think me dilatory in my duties I returned to Memphis five days before the first red circle.

Penpi welcomed my return with enthusiasm. "I have done my best with them, Neb, but in future I will find an easier occupation, such as trapping giraffes or the large apes for Pharaoh's zoo."

"She has enjoyed every moment of it," said Karaden. "Women contrive to find amusement in the most unlikely occupations."

"Such as soothing their boorish husbands." She ran her fingers through his graying hair. "But now they are Neb's responsibility . . . or will be tomorrow morning when I introduce him to his curious harem."

Later in the evening I told her that I had a half-formulated idea that the girl chosen by Horus would have a sickle-shaped scar above her right eyebrow.

"How very tiresome of Horus," she said. "The only one with a scar on her forehead is Duat, the daughter of the Captain of the Ships of the Narrow Sea. He lost his right arm in a skirmish with the Lycinian pirates, and until I met his daughter I thought he must have permanently lost his temper at the same time. But she has inherited his ill-humor and has already proved more troublesome than all the rest put together." She sighed. "I have tried very hard to like her, but have managed only to be just. Justice is such a poor substitute for affection, whatever Karaden may say—it is like giving a bowl of millet porridge, luke-warm and lumpy, when one wishes to offer a banquet."

Penpi preferred chariots to carrying-litters, and as the morning was pleasantly cool we decided to take a longer way to the Old Palace so that she should try the paces of a pair of black stallions which were a recent gift to me from Ramoses.

When we came to a long stretch of paved road I let her take the reins. She leaned back, her feet braced against the gilded footboards, her hair flying like a black pennant in the wind. On our right, a rutted track led to a village enclosed by a high wall. She pointed towards it with her whip.

"Apu has been there several times. It is very broad-minded of you to let him talk with Hebrews, but I have had to warn him to be discreet."

I was annoyed that Apu had not taken me into his confidence, though I realized it was my own fault for being so unresponsive when he tried to discuss Hebrews when we were in Goshen.

"I shall forbid him to go there again. It is discourteous of him to have done so while we are your guests."

"Don't bother to do that, Neb, but warn him to say nothing that might remind Karaden of Hebrews—the subject always irritates him, especially recently, though he won't tell me why."

The road entered a wood, mostly acacia and sycamore, which surrounded a small lake where Sensen and I had sailed toy boats when we were children. It looked much smaller than I remembered it and the water was shallow and muddy. Penpi took a corner too sharply and the chariot tilted on one wheel, frightening the horses which broke into full gallop. I seized the reins and we approached the entrance pylon of the Old Palace at a more sober pace. Apu was waiting to take the horses, having gone ahead of us by the direct route, and he smiled at me with frank sympathy. Ruefully I recognized how much I needed it.

I followed Penpi through the entrance hall, whose walls had been newly frescoed with a design in which hawks and lotus predominated, into the main garden. In the shade of ancient fig trees, couches had been placed at a discreet distance from each other. On them reclined what seemed to be an inordinate number of young women, though a further glance assured me that they were in fact only seventeen pairs of eyes staring at us with piercing curiosity.

"Duat is not here," said Penpi in a low voice. "I expect she is sulking again so I will take you to see her after you have met the others."

Some of them were languidly toying with a piece of embroidery, others pretended to sleep, one was teasing a small monkey which I hoped would soon bite her. To each of them I made polite conversation, it being increasingly difficult to conceal how alarming I found this plethora of fecundity. They showed a tendency to describe their symptoms, not unnaturally as they had been told that I was a famous physician from the South who had come to assist Ptahmas. Jealousy was tangible as biting-flies before a thunderstorm, and I had a lively sympathy with Karaden's refusal to come near the place.

Penpi spoke to one of the servants who was carrying a pitcher of fruit-juice and then drew me aside. "It is as I thought, Duat has shut herself in her room again, but I expect she will agree to see me. She usually does, for I pretend to sympathize with her endless grumbles."

To my surprise, she set off briskly along the path to the kitchen garden. "Oh, I forgot to tell you I had to house her away from the others for she said they deliberately kept her awake by banging on the partition wall. She is living in the storehouse where they used to keep onions, not very comfortable but quite good enough. Even her personal servant dislikes her, though she's been with her since she was a child."

I felt mounting unease as Penpi knocked on the outer door of the mud-brick shed. Was I to be the cause of giving Egypt a Royal Mother who seemed likely to be another Tuaa? The door opened grudgingly and through the narrow crack peered an old woman, her face deeply scarred with a skin disease. When she recognized Penpi she flung the door wide, exclaiming, "How I rejoice to see the Princess Penpi! Grumble, grumble, grumble, is all I hear except when you take pity on me!" She came out into the sunlight pulling the door shut behind her. "Has the Princess Penpi spoken with Ptahmas the Physician today?"

"Not yet: should I see him before going to your mistress?"

The old woman shrugged her narrow shoulders. "I can tell you myself, for bad news is bad whoever tells it." She glanced at me suspiciously. "Have I the Princess Penpi's permission to speak in front of the lord her companion?"

"This is Nebunefer, famed in the South for his skill in the bringing forth of children. He is, of course, in my confidence

181

and shall be given the same obedience and respect as are due to Ptahmas."

The woman muttered something under her breath, of which I caught only enough to know that she disapproved of male midwives and that she had recently been eating too much garlic.

"We await your news with all eagerness," I said genially, hoping to make her less hostile.

"Ptahmas the physician has decided my mistress is to have twins. As though one child wouldn't be enough for me to look after, and too much."

"Is he sure?" said Penpi, glancing at me to see if I was startled by the news.

The old woman sniffed and rubbed the end of her long nose with the back of a none too clean hand. "He is sure enough. I could have told him myself, two months ago, if he had not been too grand to listen to someone so unimportant as me."

A voice, shrill as an ungreased axle, pierced through the cracks of the door. "Who is there? Or are you talking to yourself again, you horrid old hag?"

"Now you see what I have to put up with," said the woman, throwing open the door with a clatter.

"It is I," said Penpi, beckoning me to follow her, which I did with extreme reluctance.

The shutters were closed, and at first I could see no more than a tangle of dark hair and a shapeless mound under the crumpled bed-cover.

"It is naughty of you to lie here in the dark," said Penpi firmly. "I told you, three days ago, that I should be most displeased if on my next visit I did not find you in the garden."

The mound resolved itself into a girl whose eyes reminded me of an angry leopard's. I turned away for fear that I should see a sickle-shaped scar above her lowering eyebrows.

"Why should I be driven into the garden? Why should I let myself be tormented by the . . . the . . . Oh, I cannot soil my mouth with words to describe them!"

"Duat, you are being hysterical and ridiculous." Penpi's voice was brisk as cold water but it produced no beneficial effect.

"So now they have turned you against me! Mine are the only royal children! The others are trying to foist bastards on Pharaoh, the spawn of field-workers, soldiers, grooms—any low-born filth they could entice into this dreadful deception."

"Duat, I have told you, over and over again, that there is no possibility that any child born here will have a different father to your own. If you continue to talk like this, the physician Nebunefer, whose presence you have not had the courtesy to acknowledge, will think that your tirade hides a secret guilt of your own."

"You are as cruel and wicked as all the others! I shall punish you too when my son is declared the Royal Heir. I shall make every one sorry . . . no one will ever dare to be cruel to me again."

"Which son, if you carry sons and not daughters, will you choose as the instrument of your vengeance?" I said caustically, for in that moment I decided that if Horus had chosen this woman, then we might expect Gods to be born from crocodiles' eggs.

Penpi ignored her passionate tears and threw open the shutters. Seldom had I found a movement more difficult than turning my head towards the bedplace. Relief was brilliant as the sunlight which flooded the frowzy room. Duat had a scar on her forehead; to be exact five scars, but they were only the relics of old boils.

XXI

BIRTH DAYS

THE room where each birth would take place had originally been one of the private apartments of Ramoses the First. Here was placed the Royal Birth Stool and the Royal Birth Robe, a circular cloak of white linen embroidered with the Goddesses who protect women in labor, which the Queen traditionally wore when receiving the officials who were supposed to be present at the birth of an heir to the throne. It was clasped at the neck by interlaced gold cobras and hung to the ground, covering the birth stool itself.

"Pharaoh insisted on sending the Birth Robe here," said Ptahmas regarding it dubiously. "But I have no intention of letting it be used. The Royal Birth Stool may be an object of veneration but it is somewhat fragile, so I have provided another which will be more serviceable."

"Must I actually be in the room?" I inquired, trying to look unconcerned.

"That is for you to decide. I, being only a priest physician, am not sure at what precise moment you expect Horus to inform you of his intentions. When the child gives its first cry, or when the cord is severed?"

"I have no idea," I said frankly. "I am still hoping for a dream which will put an end to this embarrassing indecision."

He smiled and patted me on the shoulder. "We must take heart, for I feel sure that there will be some clear portent which will set our doubts at rest. I shall treat them all as though there was no particular significance about their children, and you will find that one woman in childbirth is remarkably like another. As Pharaoh insists that no one but ourselves is to be present, a wise decision for the personal attendants would be overawed should a God manifest himself at such a homely ceremony, you may have to help me if any complications arise."

"What kind of complications?" I said warily.

"If instead of the head presenting itself we are offered a buttock, or even a leg. Fortunately neither position is unduly difficult, and I am glad to say that I had considerable experience before I was raised to my present illustrious status.

"They all look remarkably healthy," I said hopefully.

"They are healthy; but we must not underrate the influence of the mind on the body. It has been my experience that women who bear a child to a man they deeply love often find the experience as pleasurable as its conception. Expediency, however, is a harsh midwife. It would be foolish of us not to expect some difficulties in labor, for several of them have already produced symptoms which show that ambition is a poor substitute for affection."

He led me into the adjoining room and took a papyrus from one of the chests. "Here I have a complete record of all the births I have attended since I became the Royal Physician: it is a most illuminating document. A queen on an average is five hours longer in labor than a secondary wife, being so determined not to let a gasp or a cry escape her that she holds her breath instead of assisting the muscles of her belly to expel the child. The only exception to this rule was Nefertari, at the birth of her second child. Pharaoh, displaying more than his usual grasp of the humanities, ordered Tuaa to leave the birth-room, took off the Birth Robe and assisted his wife to the bed; where he held her hand, displayed considerable agitation, and in similar ways shared her travail as though he were the husband of a field-worker. It was most interesting: she expelled the child with the ease of a field-worker's woman."

"Obviously we can expect an easy birth to the mother of the Son of Horus," I suggested with determined optimism.

"My dear colleague, in this matter I am no better informed than yourself. I have seen one hundred and thirty-three of Pharaoh's children born from a diversity of women, but I have yet to witness the birth of the son of a God."

Duat, though she was the fifth of the expected sequence, was the first to enter the birth-room. As she walked ponderously across the garden, she looked at the other girls in a manner which must have caused them to pray that she would never earn the title of Royal Mother.

She insisted on wearing the Royal Birth Robe and sitting on the Royal Birth Stool. Later, she allowed Ptahmas to persuade her to lie on the high and solidly built bed he had provided. The birth was prolonged and difficult. During the final stages Ptahmas sent me to wait in the adjoining room, where the old woman I had met when I first saw Duat guarded a pair of basket-work cradles like a ruffled goose defending her nest.

Ptahmas pushed open the door with his foot and put into my arms a naked, slippery baby. "It is a girl," he said, "may the Gods be praised. But you had better get used to handling them so as to be ready for the real one."

The baby screamed lustily. It had an unpleasing resemblance to its paternal grandmother. I caught myself considering how much happier many people would have been if the midwife who first held Tuaa had been even less dexterous than myself. I handed it hastily to the old woman. Oddly enough she seemed to find its appearance gratifying.

I drank some wine: I read more of the papyrus which Ptahmas had suggested might be apposite to the hours of indecision; I stared out of the window and was surprised that the shadow of an acacia moved so slowly across a plot of hyacinths.

Ptahmas came into the room carrying the second child. "It is another girl," he said, giving it to the old woman who seemed as eager for it as she had been to take its sister.

He mopped his forehead. "I have not yet told Duat that she has two daughters, so prepare yourself for tantrums."

Tantrums proved a most inadequate description. She accused us of substituting foundlings of our own; of casting spells to emasculate the children in her womb; even of cutting off the male attributes of the rightful heirs of Egypt.

I had to hold down her hands to prevent her clawing Ptahmas, while he performed some intimate service from which I averted my eyes. Eventually, with the aid of a strong brew of poppy-juice, she subsided into a morass of bitter dreams.

Apu, who was waiting with my chariot to drive me home, was too tactful to inquire why my forearms were furrowed as a field for the sowing. I decided that in future part of the birth ritual should be the cutting of women's nails.

Three days later I was again summoned to the Old Palace. The girl was only fourteen, with a wide forehead and small delicate bones.

When Ptahmas told her she had a daughter, instead of being angry she wept with joy. "Now I can go home and marry my cousin," she said. "He told me that if I prayed very hard to Hathor she would let me have a daughter instead of a son."

"Why didn't you tell your parents that you did not wish to bear Pharaoh's child? He was most insistent that no one should come to him against her will."

She smiled up to me. "It is clear that you have never met my parents. They could not believe that I wanted to be happy instead of being made royal. But now I am happy, for the boy who is going to marry me will love the baby because she is mine and never remind me that she is Pharaoh's child."

I looked at Ptahmas, and knew that he also was thinking that her remark would have been most salutary hearing for Ramoses.

Until then I had presumed, as had Penpi, that all the women hoped to bear the chosen son, but now I realized that should another one display this pleasing lack of ambition I should encourage it by pointing out the advantages she might expect to enjoy. So when I got home that evening I asked Karaden to tell me more explicitly than before what arrangements had been made.

I had waited until the servants had cleared away the last dish of the evening meal: he leaned back in his chair, his face displaying pleasurable anticipation at the prospect of a meticulous discourse.

"The girls who did not conceive no longer concern us. However, as you are interested, for the loss of their virginity which, regrettably, is not considered a matter of great importance in these modern days, they received gifts of personal ornaments and household furniture, including ten rolls of fine linen and five rolls of woolen stuffs from Syria. It is understood that the value of these gifts will be returned to the Keeper of the Royal Treasure if at any time there is reason to believe that anyone except the girl and her parents or guardian knows that she has even made the acquaintance of Ramoses. I insisted on this clause in the agreement, for if it became known that she had not conceived then rumors that Ramoses' powers had begun to fail might cause unruly ambitions among the subject countries."

"Surely even Ramoses cannot be expected to display infallible fertility."

"Pharaoh is expected to be infallible," said Karaden severely. "Especially by the common people and by foreigners."

"What will Duat get, and the others who do not please Horus?"

"I made no provisions for twins, which is most remiss of me. I have not yet decided whether Duat should have a double portion, or only an additional two-thirds of the agreed property. Do you think she ought to have a double portion?" he added anxiously.

I tried not to smile. "Am I correct in thinking that usually the mother will retain a third for life, but that two-thirds become the property of the son or daughter on his or her fourteenth birthday?"

"That is correct. Except if she divulges the name of the

187

child's, or in this case the children's, father to anyone except the man she marries. If he dies and she takes a second husband the child will be presumed to be the child of the first husband. I make myself clear?"

"Clear as spring water, Karaden. But are you not expecting too much of any young woman's discretion? A sister, or even a friend, might surely inquire the name of a bastard's father without displaying unnatural curiosity."

"Neb, I keep on forgetting how long you have been shut away from the world. I find it most refreshing. In spite of the curious times we live in, it still remains a woman's prerogative to name, or not to name, the father of her child. In some things we may be impractical, but not so impractical as the foreigners who accept inheritance through the male line. Such credulity amazes me; however, at times it is to our advantage."

He paused and carefully selected a grape from the bunch on the gold dish beside him. "It has always been my policy to stir the pack-donkey to further efforts by the use of a piece of honey-comb dangled in front of its nose rather than to belabor it with a stick. Therefore I added a clause which states that if after ten years the father of the child is unknown by any third party, except those expressly described in the agreement, then it may expect official recognition, thereafter enjoying the same status as the children of Royal Concubines. I hinted, though I did not put this in writing, that if the child showed outstanding merit it might look forward with some confidence to the advancement usual to the children of Secondary Wives."

"You have done admirably, my dear Karaden. I only wish you could relieve me of my present duties—I fear they will become increasingly arduous."

He pushed back his wig and scratched his head with his little finger, then seeing me watching him, hastily set his wig straight again. "Neb, you are not getting worried, are you? Three girls . . . well, that makes it easier, but will you be sure of the boys?"

"I had another dream last night . . . rather vague I regret to say, but Sensen was exceedingly real."

"Tell me," he said eagerly. "You ought to have told me this morning."

"It was only symbolic. For some reason I do not understand, the room where the child was born was dark—there was a feeling that it was below ground level, and no larger than an unimportant rock tomb."

"Interesting, very interesting, Neb. No doubt it represented the grave from which the spirit rises to rebirth; or do you think it might be a representation of the Caverns of the Underworld? You did not see a jackal, suggesting Anubis, by any chance?"

"No, but I saw a cobra—a gold cobra."

"Excellent, Neb! The uraeus which the child will wear on his forehead. What I cannot understand is why Sensen will not be more explicit. It seems to amuse the Gods to set us conundrums, but Sensen ought to sympathize with our difficulties."

"I am relieved that you feel, as I do on more mature consideration, that the cobra is the uraeus: I confess that on waking I looked under the bed in case it was real."

Karaden made a sudden movement of alarm which knocked over his wine-cup. "Neb, what a shocking idea! Could it be a warning? I must send snake-charmers to the Old Palace immediately—cobras sometimes infest disused buildings." Then he sat back, sighing with relief. "Neb, for a moment I was seriously alarmed. Of course no cobras are there, for I made special provision for fifty mongooses to be let loose in the Old Palace some months ago. Their keeper informs me that they found only five harmless snakes, and two asps. But my foresight was well justified for they have killed over five hundred rats, large rats such as cost more to the granaries than a low Nile."

"I agree that our fears are groundless, but I suggest you mention my dream to no one, not even Penpi. If it became known that I had even the most ephemeral cobra at the back of my mind they would be smuggled in baskets to the birth-room—and though I already bear the scars of Duat's nails a cobra's fangs are far more conclusive!"

In spite of having treated my dream as trivial to Karaden, I was disappointed when my most fervent prayers let me see nothing but a most ordinary baby when late the following night Ptahmas put a male child in my arms. His face was dusky as a blue grape, but this, so Ptahmas assured me, was a condition due to a slow birth and did not indicate that a Nubian page had been more alert than Karaden's precautions.

Another boy, and yet another, were born on succeeding days; so very ordinary, so small, so helpless, and yet so powerful in their dependence that when one of them bubbled mucous when he tried to draw air into his lungs, Ptahmas and I went without sleep for two days until he could suck strongly at the nipple of his wet-nurse.

I learned a new kind of weariness, the weariness of giving every iota of vitality to a stranger who demands everything because it never occurs to him that one is not overflowing with abundance.

I went home to sleep. The unborn seemed to feel the urgency of horses in a chariot race, for the first cry of one seemed to challenge another to strain for freedom from the womb as though they were greyhounds on the scent of gazelles.

I became so used to letting Apu drive me home because I was too tired to take the reins, to letting Penpi bring me a tray of food in bed before I fell into sleep, that I was still able to feel surprise when Karaden said:

"Tomorrow we will know, Neb . . . if it be tomorrow. There is only one child still unborn to Pharaoh."

I slept until noon and woke strong with joy, for I had been with Sensen and she had told me that within three days I would hold in my arms the promised son.

Without bothering to do more than put on a loin-cloth I ran to seek Penpi and Karaden in the garden. I was so excited that my words tumbled over each other like puppies playing in the sun.

"Everything will be all right. . . . Sensen told me he will be born within three days. I have never seen her more vividly. He will have a small birthmark shaped like a leaf on his right ankle. . . . We must send a messenger to summon Ramoses immediately."

Karaden, who had been pruning a rose bush, straightened his back as though he suddenly felt a heavy burden lifted from his shoulders. Penpi dropped her flower-basket and flung her arms round my neck. For a moment the three of us were caught between laughter and tears.

"It is easy to be wise after the event," said Karaden, "but of course we should all have known that Ramoses saw Horus after the last child was conceived because the chosen son is the last to be born. How stupid of me not to have realized the import sooner, for it would have saved you much needless effort—and myself much needless anxiety."

"And Mara is the nicest of them," said Penpi. "I ought to have guessed Horus would choose her. I hope the baby inherits her coloring, for her hair is the exact shade of new copper and her eyes are almost a true green."

"Red-haired women are inclined to be temperamental," said Karaden.

"Well, she isn't! The only reason I haven't spoken about her more is that she is such a gentle, unobtrusive little person that she never caused any trouble."

"I will now go to compose a suitable letter to Ramoses," said Karaden, "informing him that we have every reason to expect splendid news for him in the near future. It will be a pleasant change, I assure you, from sending him disappointing news in a sufficiently tactful manner."

"Oh dear, did I forget to tell you?" Penpi put her hand to her forehead. "Yes, I did forget. I was worried this morning, for Neb looked so tired yesterday that I couldn't bear to think he might have to face another disappointment."

"Forget what?" said Karaden patiently.

"That Thenru came here last night to say that Ramoses will reach Memphis this afternoon. Apparently he has been feeling the suspense as much as we have and wants to be at hand so that he can hear the news without any needless delay."

"Then may the Gods be praised for Neb's dream! Breaking bad news to Ramoses in person would be even worse than trying to write it in suitable words."

In the distance I heard Apu calling my name and knew he would have waited to find me unless the matter were exceedingly urgent. I shouted, and he came running through an opening in the hedge of roses.

"Ptahmas has sent for you to come immediately," he panted. "I've told one of the grooms to harness the red mares. . . ."

"Shall I come with you?" said Penpi.

"No. . . . Yes. . . , No, you had better stay in case Ramoses comes straight here instead of waiting at the Royal Residence. You can cope with him better than anyone else."

"At all costs he must be prevented from going to the Old Palace," exclaimed Karaden. "No one will continue to believe my carefully nurtured story that the place is only being used for Ptahmas to do some research into modern methods of midwifery if Pharaoh arrives there, especially in a state of extreme agitation."

"Neb, don't worry about Ramoses. I will look after him. But you had better hurry."

"And put on some clothes first!" shouted Karaden as I ran toward the house.

Apu had had the same thought, for he met me on the terrace carrying a kilt and a pair of sandals. "I'll drive and you can dress on the way," he said breathlessly.

Only someone who has tried to arrange the pleats of a kilt in a chariot at full gallop knows how difficult so familiar a gesture can be to perform.

As I ran down the passage leading to the birth-room I saw Ptahmas coming towards me.

"Why such haste, Neb?"

"Is he born yet?"

"No, and unlikely to be for several hours."

His mild amusement made me conscious of my disheveled appearance. "Apu said I was needed urgently—the message must have grown in transit."

"Or did Horus send you a message?" he said shrewdly.

"How did you know?"

He laughed and led me to his room. "Now sit down and get your breath back—your heart is beating faster than the hooves of your horses when they galloped into the courtyard. So this is the child we have been waiting for? I am glad Horus did not tell you sooner or I should not have had the pleasure of your company during our earlier efforts. I will now go to see how the future Royal Mother is progressing."

The hours passed slowly. Ptahmas remained calm but I gradually began to see that he was growing anxious. Mara was pathetically grateful for the little we could do for her. Sometimes she gripped my hand so tightly that she whispered an apology. I told her that she was bearing the child who would rule Egypt, and she said that she would try to show courage worthy of him.

XXII

DAWN HOUR

IF Apu had not been waiting to drive me home I think I should never have found my way. Karaden heard the horses and came out to meet me. When he saw my face he put his arm round me, led me to his day-room and made me lie on the couch.

"Don't try to talk yet, Neb. I will fetch Penpi . . ."

"Then you know?"

"I have seen your eyes. You are sure you are not mistaken? A girl could be a Winged Pharaoh. Za Atet himself had such a daughter."

"Don't try to comfort me, Karaden. Save your comfort for Ramoses: I deserve nothing. I have betrayed you all. I have betrayed Sensen. For sixteen years I have believed in my dreams, and now because I have proved them false I do not even believe in the Gods!"

"Hush, Neb! No one dare utter such blasphemies."

"No one except Nebunefer! The boy who had not the courage to become a priest: the husband who let his wife die because he was too proud to have a physician at the Living Water: the renegade prince who crept back from his hiding-place to break the faith of a great Pharaoh!"

I swept a statuette of Horus from the table with my outflung arm. "My faith is broken, so let the Gods destroy me as I destroy their image—and if they let me continue to live I shall know they have not the wit to design a deeper hell."

"Neb, what's happened?" Penpi carrying a lamp stood in the doorway.

"He doesn't know what he's saying." Karaden stood between us, trying to save me from the humiliation of letting her see my tears.

I pushed him roughly aside. "Behold a fool bemused by dreams who now has awakened to harsh reality! At noon I left you to welcome the Son of Horus. I return like some hideous grub from a rotting corpse with news of the dead. The child is dead, a male child whose skull was crushed like an overripe fruit squeezed by an ape because the doorway into life was too narrow for so great a man to enter."

"Mara . . . what happened to Mara?"

"She had courage which would have made Captains humble. She died like Sensen: in a torrent of blood. There is blood on my hands—blood everywhere—blood—blood!"

In the distance I heard Penpi's voice. "Bring wine and covers from my bed." The floor was no longer hard and cold under my cheek-bone. My head was in Penpi's lap and she was stroking my forehead.

Then I heard Sensen speak to me. "Neb, have you so little faith in me? I said, 'In three days.' "

I put out my hand and clutched the broken pieces of faience that had been a statue of Horus.

"Horus has betrayed me, or else I should not have betrayed you."

"The Gods cannot betray any one or they would still be mortal. . . . Listen, my dear and foolish love, and hear the truth."

"Penpi, are you sure he has only fainted?"

Why must Karaden speak when I was trying so desperately to hear Sensen?

Then it was Penpi's voice that I heard. "Karaden, hand me some wine—no, not too full or I'll spill it."

I tried to let the wine slide down my throat, but the cup clattered against my teeth.

"Penpi, try to make him understand that there is still another chance!" Surely that voice quavering with emotion could not belong to Karaden? "Penpi, tell him that it is I who nearly betrayed us all. The girl Ramoses loved is not dead—she is a Hebrew, but who are we to question if Horus prefers Hebrews? Penpi, make him understand, for Ramoses will be with us within the hour—Thenru was waiting here to fetch him as soon as Neb's chariot was sighted."

I think the anguish of Karaden's appeal would have raised a mummy from its tomb. It certainly raised me from a pit of despair, exhaustion, and horrid self-pity that I had thought eternal as the Underworld.

Before the Royal Chariot entered the courtyard, Apu had taken me to my room and poured several jars of alternately hot and cold water over me, dressed me in a clean kilt and made me swallow four raw eggs. Penpi had painted her face and combed her hair. Karaden had carefully collected the pieces of faience, wrapped them in linen and secreted them in the box where he kept the Royal Seal.

Only when Ramoses entered the room did any of us realize that we had not had time to decide which of the three should break the news to him—news which to us was infinitely better than total despair but might not be acceptable to Pharaoh.

Ramoses had the advantage of careful preparation. He wore, in addition to the garments of ceremony, the Warrior Head-dress: the Pectoral of Horus: the Golden Sandals of a High Priest of Amen Ra—none of which, except for the head-dress, he could claim except by virtue of title. He was obviously surprised to be received in such an inconspicuous room, and I could see him being rather self-consciously understanding that we had been too occupied with urgent matters to prepare the Audience Room with appropriate decorations, to summon trumpeters, to unseal wine-jars suitable for a toast to the future.

His opening remark showed he was at his most Pharaonic.

"My son will claim also the title of the Son of the Morning, for his arrival has brought forth Pharaoh even before Ra's chariot has left the stables of the sky."

I glanced towards the window and realized that in fact it was still the dawn hour, when servants stir on their pallets and those whom they serve sink into deeper sleep.

"Ramoses, dear," said Penpi, "you know how impulsive I am? Well, for some odd reason I suddenly realized we must all be here together at the dawn hour . . . between the sun at noon-day and another sun at noon-day . . . symbolic for you and the next Pharaoh. Forgive me if I sound illogical, but after all I am only a woman and we do the best we can."

There was a protracted and ominous pause. "Do you mean that you have got me out of bed in the middle of the night for no good reason?" said Pharaoh.

"But it is a very good reason, what could be better? We all thought that the four of us should be together to drink to the Gods who are so much wiser than we are."

Karaden, who was pale with desperation, took his cue and hastily gave Ramoses a brimming goblet.

"I can drink to the Gods at more convenient hours, and sacrifice to them, if need be, at any time," said Ramoses coldly.

Karaden leaned forward in his chair and I knew that at any moment he was going to leap to his feet and make a full and improvident confession.

Penpi motioned him to keep silent and, smiling at Ramoses, said, "If you let Karaden tell you about it he will go on for hours and hours using beautifully balanced words. So, Ramoses dear, wouldn't you rather I told you?"

Before he could answer, Penpi went towards him, saying, "That head-dress is terribly heavy, so let me take it off. Why should any of us suffer needless discomfort when we are just the family?"

To my relief he even allowed her to remove the Golden Sandals, and flexed his toes which were marked with the hard metal.

"Penpi, I am grateful for your sisterly attentions but I am also aware that none of you would expect me to come here in the middle of the night, or even in the fourth quarter if you wish me to be exact, unless I thought to hear news of the most vital importance. Has my Son of Horus been born?"

Karaden and I both started to speak at once, but Penpi interrupted us. "Not yet . . . but I will explain."

"Then why is Neb not at the Old Palace? It never occurred to me that he could be so remiss in his duties!" Ramoses rose to his feet. "I will go to Ptahmas immediately and apologize to him for my brother's indifference."

"Neb would not be here if he was needed at the Old Palace."

"His presence proves that you lie . . . no doubt with the most generous motives."

"I have never lied to you, Ramoses. Why should I, when you would know the words false before they came from my mouth?"

He smiled at her, the first smile which had moved the Royal Lips since he entered the room. "There shall be silence until Penpi has spoken."

Drops of sweat were slowly rolling down Karaden's forehead: my nails had already scored deep into the palms of my hands. Penpi managed to look as though she was doing no more than entertaining a rather difficult guest on a sultry afternoon.

"Do you remember when we were children our nurse used to tell us stories? No, of course, you had a different nurse, but they are all much the same. The Hero goes out to slay the Monster, the starving man seeks the pot of gold . . . but always the treasure is found only in the last cave, beyond the farthest desert."

"My nurses also were not lacking in imagination," said Ramoses.

"They gave us much more than we realized: the wish to believe in the impossible and make it come true. But it is very difficult to believe in the magical truth when you have been trained in logic and expediency. You knew in your

196

heart that Seti chose you in place of Neb because he believed that you might make his dream for Egypt flower into reality. Why did you have so many children?"

"That is a question which no one has had the courage to ask me, and I have seldom dared ask myself. It is the considered opinion of Ptahmas that my initiation into sexual experience at Tuaa's instruction, together with a pitiable belief that the rites of Osiris had to be factual rather than symbolic, caused in me such a deeply ingrained fear of impotence that I have to demonstrate that I am more than capable of inspiring fecundity."

"How shallow of Ptahmas! You knew that the child you wanted could be born only to a woman you really love. Because you are too humble to believe that anyone could love you as an ordinary man, you let Karaden choose the twenty-eight virgins."

"I have doubtless been accused of many things, but not, so far as I know, of being the victim of false humility."

"Then beware of the Thirty-Seventh Assessor: 'Hast thou a vision of thyself in thy heart in honor?' If you knew how lovable you are, Ramoses, you would not have to be so arrogant."

Ramoses frowned in a manner which would have stricken the governors of provinces to their knees.

"I did not come here to be rebuked, even by you, Penpi."

"I do not rebuke you. I only want to tell you that the girl you love, the girl who will be the mother of your Son of Horus, is alive."

I saw Pharaoh's hands clench until it seemed as though the knuckles must split the skin.

"Karaden swore she was dead!" he thundered.

"And Karaden lied. You know him far too well to suspect him of a base motive—but he lied."

"Why should my brother lie to me? Why did he try to deprive me of the only thing I wanted? Can I command no loyalty!"

"Karaden had to choose between two loyalties: he chose the lesser because it was more difficult. He tried to protect me, his wife, against your just and terrible anger."

"I have never given you cause to fear me, nor will I ever do so," said Ramoses, but I saw that he was flattered by thinking she was afraid of him.

"Then let me confess my sin."

She looked so contrite that I was not surprised when he said more quietly, "Speak, and be assured of my clemency."

She knelt before him as though she were in fact a supplicant for mercy.

"It was I who suggested to Karaden that among the virgins there should be one who was born of the common people. If Horus came down among mortals, then Pharaoh also could raise the lesser to his stature."

"I have never shared Karaden's view that the common people are necessarily different to ourselves. Continue with your story, my sister."

"The girl he originally selected was the daughter of the overseer of our vineyards at Heliopolis. She was to come to you on the twenty-eighth night, being the last in order of precedence. Karaden, though he tries to conceal it lest it cause you anxiety, is subject to sudden and violent bouts of fever. One such afflicted him on the twenty-sixth day. Lest he should endanger his life by leaving his bed, I withheld from him the news that the girl had been killed by a chariot. He had impressed to me the need for the utmost discretion, so, determined to find another to take her place, I sent my charioteer to seek a girl who was younger and more beautiful than myself."

"Your charioteer must have thought it an odd request: it is unusual for a wife to choose concubines for her husband."

"I told him that the girl was for an illustrious guest whom my husband wished to please. I told him to walk with her along a certain road where I waited in my carrying-litter, peering between the drawn curtains to assure myself that he had chosen well. As you love her, Ramoses, you cannot blame me for thinking my charioteer is an even better judge of women than he is of mares."

"I have not blamed you, Penpi. It appears increasingly clear that the guilt is entirely with Karaden . . . a guilt so profound that it still remains inexplicable."

"But you have not yet heard all that I have to say. When Karaden recovered from his fever I told him what I had done. He sent for my charioteer and questioned him. Can you conceive of his horror, and my own, when he discovered that the girl came from one of the Hebrew villages! I was tormented with such anguish that Karaden, to protect me from your wrath, said that the girl was dead."

She sat back on her heels, her hands folded in her lap, defenseless before Pharaoh.

"She is alive," said Ramoses. "Penpi, of your charity, do not lie to me however much I deserve it. She is alive?"

She glanced over her shoulder and signed to Karaden and me to leave them together. We did so with alacrity.

"Is any of it true?" I asked Karaden as we paced backwards and forwards in Penpi's bedroom.

"It is a fabric so brilliantly woven of truth and falsehood that even I am bewildered to see where the weft joins the warp. No one was killed by a chariot . . . the daughter of the Nomarch of the Sistrum came out in a rash which I thought might be the symptom of an infectious disease. How could I know it was only due to eating stale prawns? It was too late to find a suitable substitute, so I told my Captain of the Guard that I wanted to entertain an envoy from Syria. It is true that I was temporarily confined to bed with fever or I should have been more explicit in my instructions. It was only after she had been to Ramoses that I discovered she was a Hebrew. I was disturbed, but not utterly dismayed: I thought if I told Ramoses she was among those who did not conceive he would never want to see her again—he always dislikes to be reminded of his failures. How could I expect him to fall in love with the only one who was entirely unsuitable? With a Hebrew—it seemed preposterous!"

"Why did you invent the chariot incident?"

"Considering I was caught off my guard I thought I lied with extreme efficiency. I am not used to lying, Neb, except in matters of diplomacy, and then one has ample time to do so with conviction."

"You took Penpi into your confidence; why did you not allow me the same courtesy?"

"I told Penpi nothing about it. All I had time to do, just before Ramoses arrived, was to say that I had had the girl and her aunt sent to the Hebrew village near here. It seemed wiser to do that than to leave them at Tanis. How could I know that Ramoses would suddenly change all my plans and decide that the children were to be born at the Old Palace?"

Angry as I was, I almost pitied him for sounding so petulant.

Nearly three hours passed before Penpi came to us. Karaden looked like a child who expects to be slapped. "Has he forgiven me?"

There were shadows of exhaustion under her eyes. "Not yet, but he will. You will be severely reprimanded for trying to undermine my faith in his understanding . . . that is the best I could do for you." She took off her gold fillet and dropped it on the floor. "Ramoses will let us know when he has made up his mind what to do."

"But the child may already have been born!" I exclaimed.

She ran her hand wearily through her hair. "Sensen said

'Within three days.' I heard her say it, while you were lying with your head in my lap. But just to make certain, I sent Apu to find out if the girl had been seen yesterday. Apparently she was washing clothes in the canal at sunset."

"But how did Apu know where she lives?" said Karaden.

"Oh, do stop being so guileless! Your Captain of the Guard never believed the story about her being wanted for a guest . . . how could he when there was no one staying with us at the time?"

"Then what did he think?"

"That my charms were beginning to pall. When you went so discreetly to the Living Water he thought it was only an excuse to be with your concubine. None of the servants were particularly surprised at your choosing a Hebrew. They are supposed to be more amusing, in some ways, than Egyptian women."

"Why did you never tell me of this monstrous suspicion!"

"Because at the time I believed it." She sat at the toilet-table, and began to smooth oil on her face.

"I am horrified, Penpi. How could you be so cruel, so wicked, as to think me capable of infidelity!"

She wiped the kohl carefully from her eyelids with a piece of linen. "Dear husband, whom I love most dearly even when he seems to think I do not love him at all, I have been exceedingly patient this morning but do not try me too high! You decided not to trust me with a secret so important that it affects the future of Egypt, yet you expect *me* to apologize for believing that you would never lie to me about anything less trivial than a physical infidelity."

"I have never been unfaithful to you!"

"We are all too tired to be troubled by exactitudes, Karaden. You lied to Ramoses because you thought he was not strong enough for the truth. You had no reason to suspect the same failing in either Neb or myself."

"Penpi, I was only trying to spare you anxiety! Can you blame me for trying to conceal how unforgivably careless I have been? I will go immediately to Ramoses and tell him that I, and I alone, am guilty."

"And spoil all I have done?"

He looked so abject that she suddenly relented. "Forgive me for being unkind. I should not have spoken so bitterly unless I had been very tired."

He fell on his knees and pressed his head against her like a child in search of comfort. "You lied for me, my beloved. You thought I had betrayed you with another woman but you still lied for me."

As I edged quietly from the room I heard her say, "Dear husband, when will you realize that if lies are necessary to the truth a woman in love will lie better than any man can imagine?"

XXIII

THE SON OF HORUS

A LION and a lioness lay in the shade of a thicket of stunted acacia on the edge of the cultivation. Between them sat Ramoses, staring towards the mud-brick wall of the Hebrews' village which shimmered in the noon heat. The man was afraid, as he had not been afraid since he left the Well of the Three Sycamores to become Pharaoh. But this fear had a new and more terrible quality, for the boy had feared his mother, but the man feared himself.

He tried to find comfort in the reflection that at least he had been able to conceal his fear from his brothers, perhaps even from Penpi: had he succeeded well enough for them to believe that he had trembled not with fear but with anger? He could lie, he must lie, to defend himself against their insight, but he could no longer afford to lie to himself.

He found that examining his heart was more subtly painful than it had been to pull away the crusted bandage from the arrow wound he had received in his first campaign. Did he really love the girl whom he had known for only one night in the pavilion among the reeds? Was it she whom he loved; or only his memory of Iri, who with the passing years had become his secret excuse for his failure to love women? Karaden had pretended she was dead, but was this only a proof that Karaden knew him to be incapable of real affection?

He tore his thumb-nail to the quick but hardly noticed the sharp flick of pain. He was Pharaoh, the greatest of all men —except in the eyes of his family. Was it to hide from their pity that he pretended he could demand love as well as worship? If they knew that he fled from love as lesser men fled from arrows he would no longer be able to believe in his own majesty.

He had dreamed of the hawk; but was it the Hawk of Horus or only a symbol of his belief in his own omnipotence, another facet of the arrogance which had caused him to allow his architects to show him as Ramoses the Pharaoh offering to Ramoses the God?

A still more fearful doubt assailed him. Had Horus caused him to love a Hebrew girl so as to humble his pride?

No, this was blasphemy! The pride of Pharaoh was the pride of Egypt, and the Two Lands were beloved of Horus. Why did he, Ramoses, fear Hebrews? Because Yahveh was so powerful that he could protect them even against the gods of Egypt whom they steadfastly refused to acknowledge. Even Neb or Karaden could not understand the power of Yahveh; but if, through the mother of his magical son, he could learn the secret by which Yahveh received such implacable fealty, he might be able to cause the Hebrews to work for instead of against Egypt.

He began to smile. By a bold stroke, so bold that it would be remembered even after Kardesh was forgotten, he would set a Hebrew queen beside him on the throne of Egypt! The whole of Syria would be confounded by such a spectacular gesture. Without an arrow being loosed the treasure-rooms of all the Northern Princes would be put at the disposal of the Two Lands. And the beauty of the plan lay in its subtlety: none of the Northern Princes would realize that the idea, the Hebrew idea, was diminishing them as once it diminished their natural master, the land of the Nile.

Even in the moment when he envisaged his triumph, doubt and suspicion returned to torment him. Dared he trust love? He had loved Iri, and in a lesser degree he had loved Nefertari, and through both women he had deeply suffered. Could love, the love for which he had always longed, come to him through a Hebrew?

If only Iri were here she would tell him the truth. "Iri," he said aloud, "have you forgotten the boy whom I used to be?"

The lion raised his head, a growl rumbling in his throat, and bounded away towards a boy approaching by the narrow path through the bean-field. The lioness blinked lazily for she had recognized the boy.

It was Apu. "Apu," thought Ramoses, "Apu, the son of Iri. So perhaps Iri has not forgotten me."

He waited anxiously for the boy to speak. Had he come only to bring a message from Neb?

Instead of making a formal obeisance, Apu sat cross-legged on the ground beside Pharaoh, his arm round the neck of the lion.

"He appears to know you—my lions are not usually so friendly with strangers."

"I have not met him before, but I thought that if he let me approach you I would know that it is right for me to say what is in my heart."

"Speak freely, Apu." Ramoses smiled. "You have his full attention, and mine. If you wish it, I will tell his mate to rouse herself."

"I should not have dared to follow you here unless my mother had said to me, the night before I left the Living Water, that if I should ever feel that I had something very important to say to Pharaoh I must speak to him as though he were only the younger brother of Nebunefer." He hesitated, "She said . . . she said that I should speak as though you were my father."

"I wish that she had allowed you to be my son," said Ramoses gently.

"Qen is my father, yet several times I have been taken for one of your concubine's children—not a Royal concubine, of course. I think it is because she has always loved you. If I ask something which sounds very impertinent will you be angry?"

"In Iri's name I promise not to be angry. If you doubt my word consider your profile, for until this moment I thought that only I could sire that nose."

"Do you really want a son who is greater than yourself? Perhaps it is different for a Pharaoh, but I think very few men want such a son."

"When they are old they do, Apu."

"How do you know what you will feel when you are old? I was standing near you when Prince Merenptah won the chariot race. Why did you challenge the Holder of the Gold Whip to the same course and win by three lengths, unless you wanted to prove to everyone that you are still a better charioteer than your son?"

"A shrewd question," said Ramoses ruefully. "Merenptah boasts even louder than I did at his age; I try to prove to him that he has less reason."

"Will it not be very difficult to honor the Son of Horus when you see him in the body of a baby? His spirit may be greater even than your own, but he will still look, and sound, and smell like a baby!"

The boy spoke so earnestly that Ramoses laughed. "Horus bringing up wind in a milky gurgle! I confess that I had never considered how difficult it may be to feel humble before one who is so effectively disguised. Having taken so much thought for my welfare have you a plan to protect me?"

"I will tell you what Neb has planned—but I hope you will not agree with it. He intends to take Ptahmas to the Hebrews' village and bribe the aunt to allow them to be present at the birth of your child. At first Neb wanted her to be taken to

204

the Old Palace, but Karaden persuaded him not to do so in case the child should be only an ordinary one, like the others. Penpi agreed with her husband, so that if they have to disappoint you again nothing more need be said about his having chosen a Hebrew for you by mistake."

So Penpi had lied to protect Karaden, thought Ramoses; and wished that he could inspire the loyalty which would make women lie for him—they tried to lie *to* him often enough!

"Even if the child is an ordinary child, the mother is not an ordinary mother," said Ramoses.

"That is why I think they are both so important to you. Neb tells the people who come to the Living Water that they will never be happy until they learn to be ordinary. It is ordinary to be a man or a woman, to be old or young, to be healthy or crippled: ordinary to be born and to die and to be born again. Neb says, and I know it is important because I have seen what happens to people after they have understood what he means, that once a man realizes that his particular burden is shared by thousands and thousands of other people he can also begin to share the joy of those who are happy."

"Happiness is not ordinary, Apu."

"It can come from very ordinary things. Sleep, and food, a fire when the night is cold and dark, or a cool wind from the river in the hot weather. And loving and being loved . . . loving is very ordinary."

"It is not ordinary for Pharaoh to be loved."

"I thought we were talking about Ramoses." The boy's hands held more firmly to the mane of the lion as though seeking courage from it.

"I think Horus prefers ordinary people, and would like his son to be born in an ordinary way. Surely if he had wanted anything else he could have asked Ptah to make a grown-up body for his son . . . it would be a very easy magic for a God."

"Such a thought had never entered my mind," said Ramoses slowly. "Apu, how can I learn to be ordinary?"

"What would an ordinary man do, after he had discovered that the girl he loved was alive?"

"He would go to her at once, in case she was as unhappy without him as he had been without her."

"Of course. You see how easy it is?"

"What else would he do?"

"He would invent an ordinary story, if the truth was too extraordinary for her to accept all at once. He could say that he had been suddenly ordered to the South, so suddenly that

205

he had no chance of telling her that he would come back the first moment he could. When he came back he found she had left her village and he has been searching for her in other villages till at last he has found her again."

"Does he find her before the child is born?"

"He must: that is very important. You have agreed that Horus wants this birth to be ordinary, and it is ordinary for the mother and father both to be there when a child is born."

"I have fathered a large number of children but I was present at the birth only on one occasion. No doubt your experience is wider than mine."

"Not much wider," said Apu. "I was with a herdsman's wife when she had her first daughter rather unexpectedly in the hill pastures. It seemed quite easy. She squatted with her back against her husband's knees and I took the baby's head in my hands when it came out of her. She made much less fuss than one of the Royal Mares. Neb has seen twenty-three children, no twenty-four counting Duat's twins, born during the last month, so with us to help you there will be no need to be frightened."

"And where am I supposed to prove my courage?"

"At the house of her aunt."

"You think, that I, Pharaoh, should go to the Hebrews' village? Apu, the idea is preposterous!"

"It might be preposterous for Pharaoh, but not for Neb's brother. Do you think Neb would let his child be born without his being there to help?"

"I have not said I will refuse to be present. Karaden must make some suitable arrangements—she can be taken to his house."

"Ptahmas says that women only have their babies easily if their minds are at peace. How could she be peaceful if she is suddenly taken to a very magnificent house among strangers? How would she believe that an ordinary soldier could take his woman to the Vizier's Palace? Oh, Ramoses, don't you understand *anything* of what ordinary people feel?"

A slow tear trickled down Apu's cheek and fell on the ear of the lion.

"I thought you loved Habaka. . . ."

"Habaka? Apu, do you know that this is the first time I have heard her name. She said to me, for reasons which are no longer important, that you could not really hate someone unless you knew his name. Perhaps I had to know her name before I could be sure that I love her."

"Then you do love her? You will come with us to the Village?"

206

Ramoses looked towards the drab walls which had been built to enclose the enemies of Egypt.

"Yes, Apu. I love her; and I find that I long to be ordinary."

I must have been more exhausted than I realized, for I slept until dawn the following morning. Apu then presented me with the surprising news which I have just attempted to describe, adding that, disguised as mercenaries, we were to meet Ramoses at a door in the boundary wall of the Royal Residence an hour before sunset.

I will not trouble to tell you of the interminable discussion which took place between Karaden, Penpi, and me during the day. Undoubtedly Ramoses was behaving in a manner which seemed entirely out of character, but when Pharaoh had spoken it was useless to do anything save obey.

We were early at the rendezvous, but Ramoses was already waiting for us. Apu had warned me that my brother was trying to learn to be ordinary, but I was still amazed when the boy addressed him as Ramoses and offered him a handful of melon-seeds, which he not only chewed with apparent enjoyment but laughed when Apu spat husks at a chariot which passed too close and bespattered us with mud.

Earlier in the day there had been heavy rain and the scent of bean-fields was strong in the air. Water still lay in the ruts of the track we followed and the thongs of the shabby sandals which Apu had obtained for me from one of the gardeners began to chafe my toes.

We came to the road which led only to the Hebrew village and in the rising wind the leaves of a solitary palm tree rattled like arrows in a half-empty quiver. A span of oxen plodded toward us, the cart shrill with ungreased axles.

"It is the seventh day, when food is given to the Hebrews," said Apu. "I was there when they began the distribution this afternoon. Habaka's aunt received five handfuls of millet and a fish—the fish had been too long from the water."

A gong boomed through the dusk and Ramoses quickened his pace. "We need not hurry," said Apu, "for though that is the signal for the gates to be closed, we, being Egyptian, shall not have to pay the fine of five *utens* to enter."

"Fine? What fine?" said Ramoses.

"Five *utens*, or five lashes, to any Hebrew who is not inside the village before the sunset gong. Foreigners have to bribe the guards with ten *utens* or more."

"Who but Hebrews and their guards enter the village?"

"Anyone who prefers to buy many hours' work by a

skilled craftsman for a few eggs or a piece of goat's flesh rather than pay a fair price in the marketplace."

"But it is the law, *my* law, that Egyptians shall not mix with Hebrews!"

Apu remained unabashed. "Then Pharaoh is well served by disobedience, or we should have had to darken our faces with soot and hope to be mistaken for Nubians."

If Ramoses had any doubts as to the efficacy of our disguise, they must have been dispelled by the ease with which we were allowed to pass the gate. The three guards were cooking their evening meal over a brazier and gave us no more than a cursory glance before signaling us on with a jerk of the thumb.

"The lack of discipline is disgraceful," muttered Ramoses, but fortunately too low to be overheard.

Inside the gate there was an open space where a stall under a tattered awning still displayed a few wilting vegetables. In the light of a pottery lamp which burned with the acrid smell of rancid fat, cabbage had the harsh green of verdigris and flies crawled in the yellow slime of a broken pumpkin.

An old man, his beard white as bone against the dark draggle of his robe, held out a bunch of carrots, then turned to spit in the dust, seeing we were Egyptian. We entered a narrow alley, a cleft between the hovels which seemed to press toward each other as though gasping for air. Where other, even narrower, alleys intersected the one we followed, tall jars of glazed pottery added their stench to the pervading decay.

"Are they too idle even to dig cess pits?" said Ramoses angrily.

"Not too idle but too poor," said Apu. "Urine is valuable: it is used to clean grease from clothes and also in dyeing wool."

"They have not even the decency of swine—and yet I treat them as though they were honorable prisoners taken in war! Karaden should come here and then he would cease to plague me for greater clemency to Hebrews!"

The sound of hammer on metal bored into hearing like an arrowhead grating on bone. We paused outside a small yard where a man whose greasy hair hung in ringlets to his shoulders was beating the blade of a dagger on a stone anvil. Beside him a boy was blowing a brazier to fierce heat through a hollow reed.

"They are fine copper-smiths," said Apu. "Several of the Royal Bodyguard carry Hebrew daggers."

208

"And if it were not for Pharaoh they would wear Hebrew daggers between their ribs."

The Hebrew boy thrust the blade into the glowing heat with a pair of tongs, then into a jar of water where it hissed like an angry cobra.

Ramoses grasped my arm and hurried me on. "Neb, will Horus understand that it was only through ignorance that I allowed his son to endure such squalor?"

"Even the souls of Pharaohs have to visit the Underworld for instruction by Anubis."

"Thank you for reminding me of that, Neb." He squared his shoulders. "My son will confound the priesthood of Amen Ra because he will find it so easy to pass the Seven Great Ordeals, having already conquered this hell while still unborn."

He paused to stare into a room that was below the level of the street which had risen through generations of dust and refuse. "Neb, hell must be very similar to this village: dark and full of hatred, crowded with Egypt's enemies."

His remark seemed inappropriate, for the sole occupant of the room was a girl who was rubbing oil into her hands which were swollen and radish-red.

"What is wrong with her hands, Neb?" I thought he was moved by pity until he betrayed his personal anxiety by exclaiming, "Is there a pestilence here?"

"She is only a linen-weaver," I said. "Fine linen is woven under water for the thread is brittle. The skin soon becomes affected, but the finer the linen the higher the price."

"The greed of Hebrews passes belief! The disease is not infectious?"

"You need have no need to distress yourself, dear brother. The ladies of the court can continue to wear mist-linen without anxiety as to its origin."

Three steps led down to the open door of a wine-shop. "You must wait for me here," said Apu. "It will be better if you do not see Habaka until I have spoken with her aunt."

As we entered, two old men who had been sitting at a gaming-board, stared at us and then carefully put away the pieces in a cloth bag. Three soldiers, more than a little drunk, were sprawling on a bench against the wall. They looked at us with suspicion, then satisfied that we were also Egyptians, called for more beer.

A crone shuffled forward, her eyes bright with cupidity. She led us to an alcove and wiped the greasy table with a dirty cloth. I told her to bring the best wine, and she hobbled away to return with a stone jug and two cups.

When she had left us Ramoses whispered, "Surely we need only pretend to drink here? The place is filthy and we might catch some disgusting foreign disease."

An argument began between the old woman and the three men in the outer room. She returned holding a gold pin in her clawed hand.

"It looks like one of my soldiers' cloak-pins," said Ramoses. "Did she steal it?"

"Only through barter in which, as you know, these people are highly skilled."

"Penpi told me they were starving . . . I almost believed her!" His forehead glistened with sweat. Suddenly he said hoarsely. "Neb, I have changed my mind. I cannot see my son born in such squalor. I will send Ptahmas to you, but I must leave this accursed village."

"You cannot run away. Apu has told Habaka that you hope to be with her before the child is born. If she is disappointed the child may be born dead."

"The other children lived . . ."

"None of their mothers loved you. Ramoses, at the Well of the Three Sycamores I said that one day a woman would love you. Are you afraid of love?"

"Yes, Neb. But I was afraid then too."

Apu stood beckoning in the doorway. I threw ten *utens* on the table and the soldiers stared at us without a glimmer of recognition as we passed.

The aunt was waiting for us in the street. Although no one could have mistaken her for an Egyptian her eyes had a horrid likeness to Tuaa's. In her gnarled hand she clutched a gold armlet. "So the father of my niece's shame returns to pay gold for his bastard." She gave an obscene chuckle. "If she dies you must give me more gold, twice as much gold . . . but you can fling your spawn alive on a dunghill."

Ramoses pulled the latch-string, and the door to which Apu had led us swung slowly open. Steps led down to a room where a small lamp flickered against the shadows. A girl was sitting on a bed in the far corner. When she saw Ramoses she covered her eyes with her hand and said, "Don't let me wake up. Oh please, my love, keep me asleep with you."

"I am real, Habaka," said Ramoses.

She let her hands fall to her side, but still dared not look at him.

"I can hear you . . . I have never been able to hear you before in my dreams," she whispered.

"I am not a dream." His voice was low and caressing as

210

though he were soothing a shy gazelle. He put his hand very gently on her bowed head.

She looked up at him and suddenly her eyes were luminous with incredulous joy.

"Oh my love . . . oh my dear, dear love."

I think neither of them heard the door close behind me.

"There is a sickle-shaped scar above her right eyebrow," said Apu, "so I am sure the baby will have the leaf-mark on his ankle."

"Now that I have seen them together I know that our prayers will be answered."

"We will know long before sunrise, or so the aunt told me," said Apu. "I have put water to heat on the brazier. The bed-covers are clean."

"Why did she think Ramoses was only a dream?"

Apu looked a little embarrassed. "Because I forbade the aunt to let her know he was coming. You see I was afraid that he might run away when he saw where she lived." He hesitated, "Neb, will you promise never to let him know I thought he might be too frightened to stay?"

"I shall never tell him."

"None of us must ever show that we realize how difficult it is for him to be ordinary. Was it difficult for you, Neb?"

I smiled. "So difficult that I nearly died in the process."

"I thought it must have been, or you would not be so patient with the people who seem so slow to learn." He pointed to a pile of rotting melon rinds that scurried with rats. "I should not find it easy to be patient with Hebrews. Are all foreigners so dirty?"

"Some of them are, and so are some Egyptians."

"If you had been Pharaoh all Egypt would be like the Living Water," he said loyally.

"No, Apu: had I been Pharaoh a Hittite might now rule Egyptians."

"Neb, I suddenly understand why Ramoses is so different from all of us, why he has to pretend he is almost a God. I think that if you believe in something enough it must always come true. Ramoses believes he is unconquerable and so the Two Lands are safe with him."

"And what do Hebrews believe?"

"I don't know, do you? Perhaps they will live in villages like this until they forget they are Hebrews and remember they are only people like everyone else."

I heard Ramoses call my name and his voice was urgent.

He was sitting on the low bed with his back against the

211

wall. Between his knees sat Habaka, leaning against him and supported by his arms.

"I think he will be born very soon," she said. She turned her head to kiss Ramoses. "You are quite sure, my love, that you do not mind seeing him born?"

"Of course I am not afraid." His voice reminded me of the boy who thought he spoke to the ghost of his father in the Royal Tomb. He glanced at me and then said rather too loudly, "How could we be afraid of seeing a child born in love?"

She pointed to a rush basket, lined with pieces of clean woolen cloth and carefully patched linen, that was raised from the floor on four glazed bricks.

"I made his cradle myself, from reeds cut in the marshes. My people are forbidden to cut reeds, but I thought they would remind him of the happy place where his body began."

She gasped and leaned forward clutching Ramoses' arm. I hastily sat cross-legged on the floor in front of her, thanking all the Gods that I had learned at least a little from Ptahmas.

"The bricks . . . the bricks which raise the cradle out of reach of rats and beetles . . . were given to me by the potter's wife . . . she is not a very nice woman for I had to wash clothes for her . . . for much longer than she said I need do . . . in payment."

"Don't try to talk, my love," said Ramoses, who looked as though he were riven by a sharper pain even than she suffered.

"I like talking . . . because . . . I am not very comfortable . . . and don't want to think about it."

A damp stain slowly widened across the blue coverlet and clear fluid dripped to the floor.

"The Nile is rising," she said and managed to smile.

Silence was urgent as drums on the horizon. "I think . . . he is . . . being born now. Now!"

Into my hands came the warm, moist head of the child. She gave a cry sharp as a copper blade as I drew him forth from her body.

"It is a son," I said.

She leaned back in the arms of Ramoses. "Since he began I knew he was a son," she said.

As I severed the cord, which gleamed like silver in the lamplight, he cried lustily, thrusting strongly with his legs. On the right ankle there was a red mark shaped like a leaf.

"Thank you, Sensen," I whispered. "Thank you, my dear love."

I put the Son of Horus in his cradle, while I attended to

his mother with gratitude to Ptahmas for having shown me exactly what I must do.

Suddenly I heard Ramoses whisper, "Don't move, Neb. Don't move!"

His eyes, wide with terror, stared over my shoulder at something behind me. Very slowly I turned my head.

Above the cradle a cobra swayed, its hood glinting red-gold in the glow from the brazier. Its head waved majestically from side to side like the feathers of the fanbearers of Pharaoh. Had it come to strike or to shield: to honor or to destroy?

The child waved his small fists in the air. The royal snake seemed to bow its head, then slid to the floor and glided into the shadows.

XXIV

THE HEART OF RAMOSES

YOU will by now have realized, my dear Moses, if you have not done so much earlier in my narrative, that it was your birth which I attended in the Hebrews' village.

I confess that I was in a state of considerable emotion, and after the cobra withdrew from your presence I found myself pressing the sole of your foot to my forehead as though prostrating myself before majesty.

I was in two minds, in fact I still am, as to whether the cobra was an actual snake directed by Horus, or a divine messenger who, though plainly visible to our mortal sight, had no physical reality. Lest the first be the correct interpretation, I wiped the joyful tears from my eyes and seizing a blanket stuffed it hastily into the hole through which the cobra seemed to have departed. I felt strongly that a second visitation would be alarming and redundant.

It was obvious that both you and your mother must immediately be taken from such unsuitable surroundings, so I went to consult Apu, who was waiting outside the door, as to how this could best be achieved. He was in no wise disconcerted by the difficulties I had envisaged, and said that as the rest of us had been fully occupied he had taken on himself the responsibility of arranging our discreet withdrawal.

As soon as he heard the child cry, he had opened the door and assured himself that the joy so freely expressed by myself and Ramoses was a proof that our prayers had been answered.

He then went to the wine-shop, where Habaka's aunt had reached a stage of pliant intoxication. Feigning a degree of alarm, he informed her that both mother and child were dead. He stemmed her lamentations by saying that to prevent her being adversely criticized for leaving her niece in the care of strangers, we would arrange for her dead to be buried with decency and dispatch.

Her wish to enjoy the prestige of chief mourner was less than her desire for gold, and another of my armlets, which Apu had brought with him in case of need, was all that was needed to persuade her to drown her doubts in a further quantity of wine, which rapidly reduced her to a stuporous inattention.

Apu had already noticed a small yard in which several coffins were stacked against the wall. It was in one of these that you and your mother left the place where you were born. An incident which, though trivial in itself, I commend to your memory if at any time you should feel yourself becoming unpleasingly arrogant.

The situation would have been easier in every way if Ramoses, during a hasty conference which took place in the squalid, and fortunately deserted, street, had not vehemently insisted that at all costs Habaka must continue to remain ignorant of his real identity. I confess that at the time I was angry with him, thinking that he was still unconvinced as to your divine origin; but I soon understood that he was fearful lest your mother should cease to love him if she knew too soon that he was the focus of her people's hatred.

Again Apu displayed an outstanding grasp of essentials and a most praiseworthy power of rapid decision. He reminded me that the house which Karaden had built for his favorite scribe had been unoccupied since the man's death. It was small, having only two rooms, but the garden was enclosed by a thick hedge of tamarisk, further strengthened by prickly pear which had been planted to keep cattle from straying in from the adjoining pastures.

The coffin was of thin boards, and the lid fitted so ineffectively that there was no danger of either your mother or yourself suffering from lack of air. We lined it with blankets and straw from the mattress, but it must still have been very uncomfortable. Our anxiety that the wails of a newly born child from a coffin might cause interference even from a race so unlikely to question the actions of Egyptians as are Hebrews, was stilled when you displayed an unusually prompt interest in your mother. I am glad that at the time I did not realize that the scarcity of timber made it unlikely that you were the first occupants of this macabre carrying-litter . . . the usual custom among your mother's people being to remove the corpse and bury it wrapped only in a shroud, thriftily retaining the more valuable funerary trappings for further use.

Carrying a coffin any distance is far more difficult than carrying a much heavier litter that has been properly constructed . . . or so I hope, though I have never been a litter-bearer. We avoided the tracks and set off across the cultivation, reaching the Scribe's House when dawn had begun to color the sky. So absorbed had I been in immediate problems that only when I went to collect a bed and other necessaries and saw a light in Karaden's window did I realize that he and Penpi were still waiting for news in which by now must have been a torment of anxiety. As I came up the path I whistled the song of victory which was composed by the Master of the Royal Music in honor of the Hero of Kardesh . . . it seemed a suitable tune, especially as Apu had informed me that Habaka's mother had been taken with other prisoners during an earlier phase of that campaign.

Had it not been for Apu, who took food to the Scribe's House twice a day, we would have had no news of Ramoses for nearly a month. He had given orders that no one else was to approach within a thousand paces and that even for Karaden or me to do so would arouse his extreme displeasure.

"And he means it," said Apu cheerfully. "He told me to say that if any one except me intrudes on his privacy he'll strangle them with their own entrails and feed the corpse to vultures."

"A most unnecessary addition to his instructions," said Karaden severely, "and one which in ordinary courtesy you need not have transmitted."

"Pharaoh's orders. And he says that he wants prawns every third day because she liked them when they were at the hunting-pavilion."

"Prawns, at this season! But I shall have to send to Tanis."

"Then send, dear," said Penpi. "It would be silly to annoy him. Apu, does she know who he is yet?"

"No, he is still a soldier who was lucky enough to save the man who hired him from being killed by a leopard. I heard them laughing about it, an old man they call Whoever-he-is, who was so scared that he gave Ramoses a collar of gold before he had recaptured his wits."

"Is the collar of gold supposed to have purchased the house?"

"Oh no, it is only hired until they decide whether to take a half share in the trading-barge which belongs to his cousin or a third share in a farm somewhere near Thebes. They ask my advice about it while I'm washing the dishes . . . sometimes I think that he almost believes in his stories."

"I only hope that the people will continue to believe in mine," said Karaden. "How much longer am I supposed to invent excuses for his absence? Memphis thinks Pharaoh is in Heliopolis, Helipolis thinks he has gone to Thebes. Ast-nefert

216

keeps on writing letters to him that I cannot deliver—for all I know they may be important."

"They are not," said Penpi. "I read them and, as Ramoses, sent a charming reply saying that he has had several most successful lion-hunts and will return to her as soon as you set him free from interminable wrangling with Khatusil's vizier."

"You should have told me, Penpi."

"But you might have told me not to read her letters," she said reasonably, "and a good wife prefers not to disobey her husband."

Like leaves in a slow but persistent current we often tended to drift towards a straw stack from which vantage point we could see the gate in the hedge which hid Ramoses from us.

"What I can't understand," said Apu, "is why you are all so impatient for him to come back. He was happy with Mother, and now he is happy again . . . it seems all very natural and ordinary."

"Apu is right," said Penpi. "It is we who have forgotten how natural it is to be ordinary."

"Ramoses is *not* ordinary," said Karaden impatiently. "He is Pharaoh and has no right to behave like a moonstruck boy. Pharaoh is not someone inconspicuous for whom it is easy to provide suitable alibis. How much longer will even our own servants believe that the Scribe's House is occupied by a distinguished foreigner and his wife who are suffering from a disfiguring skin disease which is being cured by a secret treatment invented by Ptahmas? I have decided that it may be infectious—though why Apu should be chosen to be exposed to infection I cannot imagine."

"My love, you did imagine it. Don't you remember? Apu had the same disease when he was a child and so is invulnerable."

I threw away the clover stalk I had been chewing. "Do you think Ramoses will see Bintanta? Thenru says she will reach Memphis sometime today."

"Why should he when he won't see any of us?" said Karaden gloomily. "In any case I think there is little point in taking her into our confidence unless we feel she can do something constructive."

"Persuading him to let Neb take Habaka and the baby to the Living Water would be constructive," said Penpi.

"No one will be able to do that," said Apu. "I am the only one who has seen them together so I know he will never let her be sent so far away."

"But he is fond of the child?"

"Of course he is, why shouldn't he be?"

"Then I shall point out to him, most forcibly, that to indulge his paternal instincts at this juncture will be to imperil our hopes for the future. A child known to be Pharaoh's chosen son would have a very poor chance of survival if brought up at Court."

"Surely there are honest cooks in Egypt," said Apu scornfully. "None of the girls at the Old Palace tried to poison each other, or at least they didn't succeed."

"My dear boy, you have no proper grasp of the situation. Except for Bintanta, and to a lesser extent Merenptah, Ramoses has never displayed more than a fleeting interest in any of his children . . . yet five of them to my knowledge have died in most suspicious circumstance. If my word is insufficient you have my permission to ask the opinion of Ptahmas."

"If Pharaoh can protect Egypt from the barbarians surely he can protect a girl and a baby!"

"But not against the Amen priests," Karaden hesitated and glanced anxiously at me, "Does he know about his mother?"

"No, but tell him if you think it necessary."

"What about my mother?"

"Well, it is a little difficult to explain, but she would never have gone to the Living Water had Ramoses been able to protect her from the curse of the High Priest of Thebes . . . Usermentu, a most unpleasant man, who fortunately is dead."

"Why did he want to curse her?"

"Because she interfered with his desire to dominate Ramoses . . . you must remember he was only fifteen when he came to the throne. This child is potentially a much greater threat to the power of Amen Ra, or to be more accurate, to the dark faction of the Amen Ra priesthood, than your mother could ever have been. Even if Ramoses is sufficiently discreet not to marry Habaka . . ."

"Oh, they are going to marry . . . they often talk about it."

"I repeat, even if he did not marry her, his surprising devotion will rapidly become the subject of profound and widespread speculation. The jealousy of the Queen's Women caused your mother extreme unhappiness, but what she suffered will be mild beside what Habaka could expect. The rival women will use the more ordinary weapons, spite, slights, covert hostility, and when these fail to dislodge the invader it is probable they will resort to more subtle means. They will consult the priests, and say that should a certain prayer be answered their gratitude to Amen Ra will be expressed in gold or ivory or cattle." Karaden shivered though the evening was warm. "No child, no adult for that matter, could hope to withstand the concerted onslaughts of a dark priesthood."

While he was talking I happened to be looking towards the tamarisk hedge whose flowering plumes swayed in the wind like pink ostrich feathers in the hands of indolent fanbearers. I saw the gate in the hedge suddenly flung open and Ramoses came striding towards us across the field.

Hastily we slid down from the stack so that he would not think we had come there to spy on him, and by the time he saw us we had reached the edge of the vineyard, where Karaden was pretending to instruct us in a new method of pruning grape-vines.

Karaden's recent description of Ramoses as a moonstruck boy seemed particularly inapt, for he was obviously in the grip of some violent and unpleasing emotion.

"She won't marry me!" he said. "And for what reason? Because I am Pharaoh!"

"Very sensible of her not to insist on marriage," said Karaden.

"But I, Pharaoh, insist on it! How dare she refuse to become my wife merely because I am not the soldier I pretended to be."

He stalked off towards the straw stack. "I will talk to you here. I wish to keep the gate in sight in case she tries to run away or something equally ridiculous."

I caught Penpi's eye and found it difficult not to smile as she said, "Ramoses, dear, what excuse does she give for such an improbable reluctance?"

"That is entirely a personal matter between myself and Habaka. For reasons which appear adequate to her, and which are entirely nonsensical, she wishes my son, *my* son, to be brought up as though his father were a farmer or a fisherman. She has been gracious enough to admit that she does not wish him to live in one of the Hebrew villages— she pointed out that as her father was also Egyptian she did not want him to suffer the same slights for mixed blood as she suffered herself. My son, ashamed of his Egyptian blood!"

Karaden gasped as though he had swallowed a fly. "Ashamed of being *Egyptian*!"

"Yes, odd, isn't it?"

"Let me take them both to the Living Water," I suggested, hoping I did not sound too eager.

"Neb, don't be a fool! For the first time," he glanced at Apu, "no, for the second time in my life I have found someone with whom I am happy, and nothing is going to take her

219

away from me—not even her own stupid pride. But what am I going to do? I have implored her to marry me, I have argued and shouted and cajoled but it seems she is determined to make me see her only furtively—as though I were a timid man whose wife has forbidden him to visit his concubine."

"Instead of a most ferocious man whose wives' jealousy in no wise disturbs him."

He glanced at Penpi and then permitted himself to smile. "Penpi, couldn't you talk to her?"

"With the greatest pleasure, dear Ramoses, though I doubt if my eloquence would prevail when yours has been unsuccessful."

"I may have broken the news a little abruptly—about my being Pharaoh, I mean. In much the same situation Iri remained perfectly calm, but Habaka was extremely upset. At first she thought I was joking and then she began to cry. Then the boy cried too . . . it's difficult to remember he is almost a God when he bawls like a calf with a bellyful of wind!"

He looked at us morosely as though daring us to smile. Then he stood up, shaking wisps of straw from his kilt. "Penpi had better come and see her tomorrow. I shall go back to her now—the boy likes me to be there when she gives him his bath."

It was Bintanta instead of Penpi who went to visit Habaka the following morning. Karaden, Penpi, and I engaged in endless and futile speculation as to how best we could protect the Son of Horus from the dangers which the stubborn refusal of his parents to agree seemed likely to bring upon him.

"Ramoses will never be able to visit her discreetly. He doesn't know the meaning of the word!" said Karaden. "Almost I am persuaded that he had better take desperate measures, and declare Habaka the Great Royal Wife. Bintanta may be able to convince her mother that it is a decision of the Gods—Ast-nefert has always had an almost excessive awe of Horus. None of the secondary wives would be sufficiently presumptuous to be openly jealous of a woman who holds a title that he gave only to Nefertari."

"If she won't become a secondary wife she certainly will refuse to be a queen," said Penpi. "How could she be a queen, poor child! A Hebrew of fifteen . . . the world would laugh at Egypt."

"Only half Hebrew!" Karaden reminded her. "It is a trag-

220

edy that the half is not paternal for then we could pretend that it did not exist."

"Iri would have refused to be a queen," I said. "She always knew that Ramoses wanted to be loved as a man, not as Pharaoh. I am glad that no one has suggested that I kidnap Habaka and the boy. The Living Water has certain magical defenses but they would be unlikely to withstand the armies of Egypt led by Pharaoh in person." My comment was received in gloomy silence.

"The horses of Ra's chariot appear to be lame," said Penpi, "for never has the sun traveled so slowly across the sky."

We were all too agitated to sleep during the noon hours and found ourselves drifting disconsolately towards the straw-stack. It was there that Apu came to announce that we were summoned to the Royal Presence.

Ramoses, looking benign if a trifle self-conscious, was sitting with Habaka on his knee under a flowering acacia. His son slept placidly on Bintanta's lap. For the first time I knew why Apu found it so odd that none of us could visualize them as an ordinary family.

Until then I had not realized that Habaka was exceedingly beautiful. Karaden adopted towards her a somewhat uneasy compromise between the deference due to a queen, the informality suitable between close relations, and the rather formal graciousnss expected of a distinguished guest when visiting his social inferiors.

Penpi took the easier course of admiring the baby, substituting bird-like noises for the more masculine words of praise which I employed. I must admit, my dear Nephew, that you were a remarkably handsome child even when only a month old, though I may have been prejudiced.

"I think you will all be glad to hear," said Ramoses, "that when it seemed that false pride and false humility were going to triumph over the happiness of Habaka and myself," he paused to smile fondly at his love who kissed him with the spontaneity of a child, "Hathor, through her emissary Bintanta, came to our rescue."

I looked at Bintanta, but she carefully averted her eyes.

"For a moment I must confess that I thought the solution to our apparently insoluble problem was inspired only by feminine subtlety, but Bintanta rapidly convinced me that it was only natural that in the birth of a divine child both a God and a Goddess would mutually be concerned."

He waited for his statement to be absorbed by his audience and then continued. "At first, as you may remember, I did not take into consideration the dangers to which my son—

221

our son—would be exposed if it were known that at birth he had already been chosen as my Royal Heir. But even these dangers, terrible as they might be, were not sufficient to allow me even to contemplate being separated from the woman on whom, although she has refused to wear the White Crown, I have conferred in perpetuity the title of the Keeper of the King's Heart.

"The interpretation of dreams, difficult as this may be on certain occasions, seemed relatively easy when set beside this problem. I think I may say without self-flattery that had it been humanly possible to guess the answer to this riddle I should have done so myself."

Karaden began to look less anxious. This Ramoses was one he knew and could understand.

"It is curious," said Ramoses, "how one is constantly surprised by the wisdom of the Gods, so all-embracing and yet apparently so simple. As all of you know, Bintanta is my eldest and beloved daughter. I hoped to see her son succeed me. That hope is now fulfilled; her son will succeed me, her son and mine."

I could see that Karaden and Penpi shared my sudden alarm. Ramoses was certainly not intoxicated with wine but was he with vain-glory? Surely he knew that even if he married Bintanta she could not give him a son, or had he ruthlessly decided that she must make the attempt even if she died in the process?

Ramoses laughed, the clear entirely sane laugh of a man who is delighted because his audience has reacted in exactly the way he intended.

"Hathor, the Great Mother, has no intention of inflicting upon Bintanta a dangerous and perhaps fatal ordeal; her plan is much more pleasing." He turned to his daughter and said fondly, "Perhaps you would prefer to tell them yourself, my dear child."

The baby squirmed, and Bintanta put him over her shoulder, patting his back until he brought up his wind.

"It is really very simple, once it has been made clear by a Goddess so wise as Hathor," she said. "Father wants to be able to see Habaka and my little brother as often as they wish . . . without anyone being jealous. No one bothers to be jealous of me . . . few women are jealous of another who has neither a lover, a husband, nor a child. So instead of his being Prince Ramoses, the son of Pharaoh and the son of Habaka, he will be my son, named after his illustrious grandfather—and Habaka's nursling."

"Hathor shows a remarkable disdain of the conventions,"

222

said Karaden. "Pharaoh's eldest daughter, the Princess Bintanta, priestess of Hathor, suddenly announcing that she has a son though no husband."

Bintanta laughed. "Hathor can also at times be expedient as a Vizier, dear Uncle. I have often been pitied for my barrenness: what is more likely than that I should adopt a baby —especially a baby given into my arms by Isis?"

"More Goddesses!" said Karaden fretfully. "Why Isis?"

"As Vizier you should be well acquainted with the custom by which women who have been too lavishly provided with children set an unwanted baby adrift on the river, as an offering to Isis."

"A disgraceful custom!" said Karaden. "I have done my best to prevent its continuance but I fear without signal success."

"Your failure is provident, for my father will cut some reeds and fashion them into a small but reliable boat to accommodate Moses. He will be set adrift," she smiled reassuringly at Habaka, "in very shallow water and well guarded by Apu. I, with court ladies in attendance, whom I shall select for their indiscretion and propensities for gossip, will discover Moses and declare my intention to adopt him. By a fortunate coincidence, Habaka, my devoted handmaid whom I brought back with me from Punt, has just suffered the loss of her baby. She will be wet nurse to the son whom Isis has sent to comfort me."

"It might be believed," said Karaden slowly. "By all the Gods I begin to believe it myself!"

"So do we all," said Ramoses.

The baby opened his mouth and made a cheerful though incomprehensible noise.

"I think he is trying to say, 'Pharaoh has Spoken,'" said Karaden.

XXV

A CHARIOT AND A JOURNEY

I RETURNED alone to the Living Water, for Apu remained with Bintanta as steward of her household. From him, my dear Nephew, I hear frequent reports of your progress. I know that you cut your first tooth on the day of the Min Festival; that you showed no alarm when Pharaoh's lioness, accepting you as one of her cubs, carried you in her mouth, refusing to allow any one to approach until she had given you to her master; that you appear equally fond of Bintanta and of your devoted parents.

Here everything continues in the placid rhythm which I confess at times to finding a little dull. I feel that I should provide you with suitable aphorisms which in case of need will remind you of the great destiny to which you are heir. But why should I consider myself more suited to the task than those you know so much more intimately than you will ever know me?

Tomorrow there will be no more to write, so the day without Sensen will seem even longer than usual. This morning Iri reminded me that the dates are ready for harvesting.

It is a very gentle evening. Two flamingos are circling over the lake, and the sky seems to reflect the rose-red of their feathers. The smoke of cooking-fires grows quietly in the cool air, the pillars of a temple dedicated to the joys of ordinary men and women—ordinary as Nebunefer.

Qen has just come to tell me that a chariot, a very magnificent chariot with a pair of black and white stallions, has arrived as a gift from my brother Ramoses.

I have told him that I will gallop them towards the hills tomorrow at noon. He is a little surprised that I am not more impatient to see them: but I have seen them before.

Tomorrow I shall describe them to Sensen.